STUDIES IN
COMPARATIVE
CRIMINAL LAW

CRIMINAL LAW EDUCATION
AND
RESEARCH CENTER

Publications of the Criminal Law
Education and Research Center

Volume 11

New York University
School of Law

STUDIES IN COMPARATIVE CRIMINAL LAW

Edited By

EDWARD M. WISE

Professor of Law
Wayne State University

and

GERHARD O. W. MUELLER

Professor of Law
Director
Criminal Law Education and Research Center
New York University

CHARLES C THOMAS · PUBLISHER
Springfield · Illinois · U.S.A.

Published and Distributed Throughout the World by

CHARLES C THOMAS • PUBLISHER

Bannerstone House

301-327 East Lawrence Avenue, Springfield, Illinois, U.S.A.

© *1975, by* CHARLES C THOMAS • PUBLISHER

ISBN 0-398-03168-1

Library of Congress Catalog Card Number: 74-7129

*With THOMAS BOOKS careful attention is given to all details of
manufacturing and design. It is the Publisher's desire to present books that
are satisfactory as to their physical qualities and artistic possibilities and
appropriate for their particular use. THOMAS BOOKS will be true to those
laws of quality that assure a good name and good will.*

Printed in the United States of America

C-1

Library of Congress Cataloging in Publication Data

Wise, Edward M.
    Studies in comparative criminal law.

    (New York University. Publications of the Criminal
Law Education and Research Center, v. 11) .
    "A bibliography of the writings of Jerome Hall": p.
    1. Criminal law—Addresses, essays, lectures.
    2. Hall, Jerome, 1901- —Addresses, essays, lectures.
    I. Mueller, Gerhard O. W., joint author.   II. Title.
    III. Series: New York University. Criminal Law
Education and Research Center. Publications, v. 9
    Law   345   74-7129
    ISBN 0-398-03168-1

Portrait painted by George Sheppard, 1971

Jerome Hall

FOREWORD

IF IN RECENT YEARS American criminal law has acquired its own culture, worthy of respect on the part of scholars all over the world, the credit is due largely to Jerome Hall. It is probably unique in the annals of criminal law that one scholar should have such an enormous impact on his subject matter, in every sphere: the historical, the philosophical, the sociological and behavioristic, but above all, the analytical and synthetic, and always in comparative perspective.

All of us who have contributed to this volume have had numerous occasions to express to Jerome Hall our admiration, respect and friendship. We want to reiterate these sentiments with this publication. *Ad multos annos.*

CONTENTS

PART IV—DEALING WITH DEVIANCE OUTSIDE THE CRIMINAL LAW SYSTEM

STUDIES IN
COMPARATIVE
CRIMINAL LAW

CHAPTER 1

SOME REFLECTIONS ON THE VALUE AND SCOPE OF STUDIES IN COMPARATIVE CRIMINAL LAW*

MARC ANCEL

Member of the Institute de France, Président de Chambre in the Court of Cassation, Président of the Centre Français de Droit Comparé.

JEROME HALL has made significant contributions at one and the same time to criminal law, to the sociology of law and to comparative law. His *General Principles of Criminal Law, Studies in Jurisprudence and Criminal Theory* and his valuable volume entitled *Comparative Law and Social Theory,* are all books which we have studied with care and which we have often had occasion to refer to in our own work. We are, therefore, particularly pleased to join in paying tribute to this great scholar and, in line with the general theme of his writings, we propose to offer some observations on the use, value and scope of comparative criminal law.

There is no need to insist at length on the utility of the comparative method in criminal law. However much its usefulness may at one time have been questioned, it is nowadays largely admitted, and the proof of this is to be found, albeit indirectly, in works as different from Jerome Hall's previously mentioned *General Principles*—at the opposite extreme, one might say—as the *Tratado de Derecho Penal*[1] of the lamented Jimenez de Asua. Nonetheless, it should not be forgotten that the comparative

---

* Translated by E. M. Wise.

1. 1st edition, Buenos Aires, 1949, uncompleted; the first volumes have been brought out in three subsequent editions.

study of criminal law does continue to face two obstacles—obstacles which are not negligible and which should be kept in mind.

The first of these obstacles is the particularism of criminal law. Each penal system is, above all, influenced and shaped by the social setting and the sociopolitical regime for which it is constructed. Criminal lawyers of different countries have always tended to explain and, consequently, apply rules of penal legislation according to the tradition and technique of their own system. From this tendency stems the resistance which specialists frequently offer to proposals for the adoption of foreign ideas and institutions. This has especially been the case in France and on the European continent—the "civil law" countries—with respect to importations derived from the "common law" system such as jury trial, probation, juvenile courts or, coming more specifically from America, the indeterminate sentence. If one puts this in terms of the distinction nicely drawn by Jerome Hall between "principles," "doctrines" and "rules,"[2] one will observe that the "rules" and "doctrines" of each system are largely national or at least particularistic and furthermore that many writers tend to discuss "principles" only to the extent that they are clearly those of their own system of law.

There are others, however, who have made an effort to get beyond so limited a view, especially at the level of broad principles. They speak of a general science of criminal law transcending national frontiers. But it is here that one encounters the second obstacle to the development of comparative study in matters of criminal law. The second obstacle is a certain legalistic dogmatism which claims to be derived from pure reason, standing above and beyond positive criminal law. The dogmatic tendency is old and dates back to Antiquity but it received new stimulus, although perhaps indirectly, after the Renaissance with the emergence of theories of natural law. The school of natural law[3] was properly universalistic, but it was not comparative. It

---

2. This distinction is sharply drawn in his *Cases and Readings in Criminal Law and Procedure* (1st ed. 1949) .

3. Cf. J. Hall, *Comparative Law and Social Theory* 70 et seq. (1963) .

looked to an ideal law, above and apart from positive law: "human reason insofar as it governs all the peoples of the world" said Montesquieu[4] (who is nonetheless considered to be the first comparatist); like Pallas Athene sprung fully armed from the brow of Zeus, it owes nothing to human endeavor. Beccaria himself is not far from this point of view, and it is significant, moreover, that unlike his master Montesquieu he hardly ever calls for the comparison of laws, even when he finds fault with them. Likewise, although Bentham's utilitarianism[5] tries to keep in touch with human reality, he too—like the legislators of the French Revolution who owe so much to him—does not disassociate the principles of his codification from a critical attack on the particular legal rules of his own time. The legalistic dogmatism that followed, from Feuerbach in Germany to Carrara in Italy, came to concern itself with constructing a science of criminal law on the basis of pure legal logic; and thus Carrara explictly proclaimed that one must ignore actual human codes, which are variable and uncertain, in order to reach in criminal matters to the immutable Code of Reason.[6]

These obstacles have been surmounted. They are still occasionally invoked by those who would put a tight rein on comparative inquiries or question their necessity. However, the extraordinary development which the study of comparative law has undergone in the last century has clearly demonstrated both the value and the utility of using comparative method in criminal law. It seems to us that this result is largely due to the operation of three principal causes, the direct relevance of which we believe is not usually stressed. Let us try to state them specifically.

In the first place, since about 1850 working experts have been trying to arrange among themselves joint meetings and conferences. It was not common for jurists to get together this way in other fields. But, from the middle of the century, specialists on penitentiary questions (who were not yet called penologists)

---

4. *L'Esprit des Lois,* I, 3.

5. Cf. Marc Ancel, *Social Defense—A Modern Approach to Criminal Problems* 93-94 (London, 1965).

6. *Programma del corso di diritto criminale* (1859). Cf. our *Introduction comparative aux Codes pénaux européens* 26 et seq. (Paris, 1956).

sought to compare their methods, study their common problems and assess their results. Several successful congresses, including the Penitentiary Congress of 1878 in Stockholm, mark the beginning in this matter of systematic comparison. This was one of the first conferences organized by the International Penal and Penitentiary Commission, founded at Berne in 1874, which came to have such a great and happy influence on the development of international legal cooperation. Through its meetings, its studies, its publications and its congresses, the Commission was, for three-quarters of a century, a preeminent body for comparative confrontation.[7] One should not be surprised at finding, moreover, that in the second half of the nineteenth century, penologists along with the commercial lawyers, at first were practically unique in getting together at such conferences. They were not concerned with general legal theory or with legalistic dogma but rather with looking for practical means of resolving concrete problems and with meeting immediate social needs. These were, for the one group, new forms of criminality, the problem of persistent offenders, the prison system and what later came to be called the treatment of delinquents; for the other group, the main problems arose, with the coming of a liberal Europe, from new facilities for the carriage of persons and goods, the age of industry, the appearance of great corporate entities, the development of the law of negotiable instruments and the desire to channel and to harmonize the institutions of international commerce. In both cases it was the pressure of practical necessities, travel by individuals and a new and widespread desire to become better acquainted with foreign countries that led quite naturally and necessarily to use of the comparative method.[8]

A second element favoring this new direction in criminal law was the development of the criminological sciences. The scientific or, at least, the extra-legal study of the phenomenon of crime was naturally favourable to comparative research. As soon as one no longer thinks about crime simply as a construct of pure law,

7. See Negley K. Teeters, *Deliberations of the International Penal and Penitentiary Congresses* (Philadelphia, 1949).

8. Cf. Marc Ancel, *Utilité et méthodes du droit comparé—Eléments d'introduction générale à l'étude comparative des droits* 12 et seq. (Neuchâtel, 1971).

a "legal entity," as Carrara said, defined by the terms of a specific statute or by those of an abstract dogmatism, one inevitably sees crime in its human reality, independent of particular national categorizations. Earlier in the nineteenth century, Quételet in Belgium and Bonneville de Marsangy in France,[9] as well as the Franco-Belgian Penitentiary School of 1840, had already turned their attention to the great range of sociohuman reality. Ever since Cuvier, in the first years of the century, comparison had become one of the essential techniques of the sciences of observation. As a newly constituted criminal science sought to take its place among other scientific disciplines, it naturally sought also to make use of the comparative method. There is little need to recall that the "positivist revolution" of Lombroso, Ferri and Garofalo, with its links to anthropology, sociology of crime and finally to criminology,[10] was not merely a feature of the controversy which preceded the Italian Code of 1889 or its subsequent interpretation and exposition. The new criminal science had an international vocation.

A third element stems directly from the preceding: the International Union of Criminal Law, founded in 1889 by von Liszt, van Hamel and Adolphe Prins, largely aimed at tacking on to the frame of traditional "criminal science," that is to say, to the general theory of criminal law, the teachings of a nascent criminology. It did this through means of a new or rather refurbished discipline, criminal policy (*Kriminalpolitik,* to which the Germans, from Liszt to Mezger,[11] gave so much attention), directed at studying how the system of social reaction against crime can be improved and, in particular, be adapted to take account of scientifically established facts regarding criminality and the personality of the delinquent. Here again, one sees a movement of natural internationalization. One might assert, as a general principle, that the moment a criminal problem is no longer viewed solely from the angle of pure legal technique, it is immediately inter-

---

9. Quételet, *Physique sociale* (1st ed. 1835) ; Bonneville de Marsangy, *L'amélioration de la loi criminelle* (1855).

10. Cf. H. Mannheim, Introduction to *Pioneers in Criminology* (1960) ; O. Kinberg. *Problèmes fondamentaux de la criminologie* 41 and 70 et seq. (Paris, 1960).

11. Ed. Mezger, *Kriminalpolitik auf kriminologisches Grundlage* (1st ed. 1934).

nationalized. This is precisely what has happened since the end
of the last century with the transition from recidivism as a legal
concept to recidivism as a criminological problem (and a problem of criminal policy), from the criminal responsibility of children to juvenile delinquency, from application of Article 64 of
Napoleon's Criminal Code (on insanity and compulsion) and the
English M'Naghten Rules of 1843 to consideration of mentally
abnormal or defective offenders, from a legal system of punishment, in the old sense of the term, to the treatment of delinquents and the reintegration of convicted persons into society. In
all these cases, the shift in point of view or the enlargement of
perspective has been very much dependent on the invocation of
foreign experience and on a systematic process of comparison.

We have to concede then that use of the comparative method
is rendered necessary nowadays by the new dimensions of modern criminal science. But to what methodological implications
does this lead us? We should not end without discussing this
question. Two main observations will bring us close to some of
the basic ideas of Jerome Hall.

As we have already indicated in speaking of criminal policy,
the sort of comparative research which we have in mind in criminal matters is not limited to analysis of, or to the drawing of
parallels between the legal rules and institutions of the countries
under consideration. It seeks instead to take hold, define and understand those phenomena, more sociological than legal, which
constitute the formal reaction of each system, at every phase of
its evolution, to manifestations of criminality. Comparative
study must, in this conception, concern itself with the organization of society's reaction against crime by considering the solutions adopted, on the whole or on particular points,[12] in the law
of those cultures which have arrived at comparable stages in their

---

12. One may especially refer here to Jerome Hall's significant work on *Theft,
Law and Society* (2d ed. 1952), which provides a striking illustration of this
method: concentrating on a particular offense and beginning with an historical
analysis of a particular case (Carrier's Case, 1473), it traces the development and
extension of the concept of larceny, the interpretation of substantive law and the
different technical issues involved and, later, the connection in the 18th century
between the problem of harm to private property and the state of public opinion,
the administration of criminal justice and the relevant socio-cultural context.

development. The connecting thread should not be some technical aspect of legal rules or institutions but rather the criminal policy which animates, shapes and transforms the system.

It follows that the study, so conceived, of systems of criminal law will have two aims: first, to trace and to explain the historical origin and evolution of positive institutions; then to inquire which directions ought best be taken in the domain of legislation as well as in that of judicial or administrative action. Surely it is clear that on these two points comparative law or, if one prefers, utilization of the comparative method can be of particular use. The comparative method has the great merit of pointing up the relativity of basic legal data. The fixity of law, which is praised so often by jurists, actually conceals a continual and fruitful effort to adapt old rules to new situations, and similarly at times an inner transformation of rules which externally appear unchanged. Further, the comparison of one system's institutions with those of another is nowadays more and more a matter of examining different technical devices for the solution of concrete legal problems; it is this that comparatists call the *functional* method. This method allows one to see that under different names—and even in spite of opposed ideological positions—the same needs or the same dangers tend to produce fairly comparable reactions.[13] To give a single and somewhat extreme example, there is a sense in which one can equate or at any rate compare the American "white collar crime" with the "official crime" of Soviet law. On a vertical rather than a horizontal plane, this same method will often show how the *lex lata* is not always completely separable from the *lex ferenda;* for the law of tomorrow is often largely contained, and its contours may be frequently discerned in the formulations, applications and hesitations of the law of today.

These methodological considerations could be developed at length. Without doing so, let us simply observe that we are at this point in agreement with one of Jerome Hall's basic tenets. "Instead of studying rules and doctrines in isolation, one must study

---

13. K. Zweigert, "Des solutions identiques par des voies différentes," 1966 *Revue internationale de droit comparé* 5 et seq.; cf. "Neue Systeme und Lehrmittel der Rechtsvergleichung," 1952 *Rabelszeitschrift* 557.

them in the context of the legal system," he has said, and he immediately adds that "the historical development of the law and the cultural factors which enter into the process of decision must also be carefully investigated."[14] Comparative law, above all in criminal matters, can ignore neither sociocultural context nor the socioeconomic context and the political setting which control the legal system under consideration. Jerome Hall even went so far as to maintain that comparative law ought ultimately to be termed "humanistic sociology of law."[15] In any case, to learn from him and to profit from his significant teachings is to adopt this sociological approach and to add a dimension of social science to comparative legal science.

---

14. *Studies in Jurisprudence and Criminal Theory* 117 (1958).
15. *Comparative Law and Social Theory* 42 and 117-123 (1963).

PART I

VALUES WITHIN
AND ABOVE THE
CRIMINAL LAW SYSTEM

CHAPTER 2

THE CONSCIENCE OF THE JUDGE: ITS ROLE IN THE ADMINISTRATION OF CRIMINAL JUSTICE

SHIGEMITSU DANDO

Justice of the Supreme Court of Japan
Professor Emeritus, University of Tokyo

"It is present action—not an impersonal and depersonalized process—that is significant."

Jerome Hall[1]

THE 1946 CONSTITUTION OF JAPAN, in addition to a provision which guarantees freedom of thought and conscience as a fundamental right (Art. 19), also contains a provision concerning the independence of the judiciary in which is included a conscience clause (Art. 76, para. 3). It reads as follows: "All judges shall be *independent in the exercise of their conscience* and shall be bound only by this Constitution and the laws." This clause is derived from Article 68, paragraph 3, of the so-called MacArthur Draft, submitted to the Cabinet of Japan earlier in 1946. The wording of the latter is similar except for a slight difference of expression which is quite negligible in the context of the present paper.

So far as I know, there is no precedent for this type of provision in the constitutions of other countries or in the old Constitution of Japan of 1889. We can find provisions to the same effect only in constitutions or constitutional drafts of a later date. Among these, the 1947 Constitution of Rheinland-Pfalz and the

---

1. Jerome Hall, "Methods of Sociological Research in Comparative Law," in *Legal Thought in the United States of America under Contemporary Pressures—Reports from the United States of America on topics of major concern as established for the VIII Congress of the International Academy of Comparative Law* 164 (J. N. Hazard & W. J. Wagner eds. 1970).

1948 draft Constitution for the Federal Republic of Germany are particularly noteworthy.[2] The Constitution of Rheinland-Pfalz provides: "The judicial power is exercised by independent judges who are bound only by the Constitution *and their conscience*" (Art. 121).[3] Similarly, the so-called Herrenchiemsee Draft (1948) of the Federal Constitution[4] provided: "The judges are independent and are subject only to the law *and their conscience*" (Art. 132).[5] But the conscience clause contained in this provision was not incorporated into the Bonn Basic Law of 1949 (Art. 97, para. 1).

The conscience clause of the Herrenchiemsee Draft was originally designed to permit the judges to examine the compatibility *(Vereinbarkeit)* of positive law with the unwritten law.[6] Retention of the conscience clause was supported during the debates in Parliament by a member belonging to the Christian Democratic Union, but his opinion was not adopted. The objection urged by another member, who belonged to the German Socialist Party, was that the conscience clause would give the impression that conscience is an independent source of law equivalent or even superior to the positive law.[7] This objection seems to have been the main reason why the conscience clause was not included in the Bonn Basic Law.

---

2. One should also mention the 1948 Constitution of the Republic of Korea and the 1961 Constitution of Turkey. The former, presumably after the model of the Japanese Constitution provides: "The judges shall rule independently *according to their conscience* and in conformity with the Constitution and law" (Art. 98). The latter does not refer to the judges' conscience explicitly but seems to do so implicitly by using the expression "their personal convictions." It provides: "Judges shall be independent in the discharge of their duties. They shall pass judgment in accordance with the Constitution, law, justice and *their personal convictions*" (Art. 132). Both are quoted from 2 A. J. Peaslee, *Constitutions of Nations* (3rd ed. 1965).

3. "Die richterliche Gewalt üben unabhängige, allein der Verfassung *und ihrem Gewissen* unterworfene Richter aus."

4. On the Herrenchiemsee Draft, see Carl J. Friedrich, "Rebuilding the German Constitution," 43 *American Political Science Review* 478 (1949).

5. "Die Richter sind unabhängig und nur dem Gesetz *und ihrem Gewissen* unterworfen."

6. v. Doemming, Füsslein & Matz, "Entstehungsgeschichte der Artikel des Grundgesetzes," 1 *Jahrbuch des öffentlichen Rechts der Gegenwart, N.F.* 716. See also H. J. Abraham & others, *Kommentar zum Bonner Grundgesetz*, Art. 97.

7. Abraham & others, *op. cit.*, Art. 97, at 101.

It should be noted, however, that despite exclusion of an express conscience clause from the Bonn Basic Law, it is possible to argue that such a clause is nonetheless at least tacitly incorporated in the German Judges' Law. Rotberg, for instance, strongly favors this argument, considering the judge's conscience to be the basis for the independence of the judiciary.[8] It is not my intention here to take a position with respect to a dispute in Germany. So far as the Japanese Constitution is concerned, the wording of Article 76, paragraph 3, seems to have been carefully chosen; conscience is mentioned exclusively in connection with judicial independence. In the Japanese provision it is "in the exercise of their conscience" that the judges are independent and it is "only by this Constitution and the law" that they are bound, whereas "law" and "conscience" were treated instead as parallel expressions in the German Draft.

It is well known that the notion of conscience is deeply rooted in English law, especially in the practice of the courts of equity. The Court of Chancery, which played such a large role in the struggle with the Common Law Courts, was a Court of Conscience. In its early stages, equity more closely resembled "natural justice" than a legal system and it was thought to be the duty of the Court to purge the defendant's conscience of its sense of wrongdoing.[9] According to Vinogradoff, Christopher St. Germain, in his *Doctor and Student,* lays down the proposition that equity qualifies and makes exceptions to law on grounds supplied by reason and conscience.[10] Here conscience seems to me to have operated more as a kind of source of law than as a factor promoting judicial independence.

There are, as observed above, very few constitutions that include a conscience clause in a provision concerning the independence of judges. But even under a constitution which lacks such an explicit clause, the question will arise whether the judges, nevertheless, cannot exercise their conscience in discharging their duties. The

8. H. E. Rotberg, *Zu einem Richtergesetz* 12 (1950).

9. Harold Potter, *An Historical Introduction to English Law and Its Institutions* 33 et seq. (3rd ed. 1948).

10. Paul Vinogradoff, "Reason and Conscience in Sixteenth-Century Jurisprudence," 24 *Law Quarterly Review* 379 (1908).

answer must certainly be affirmative, if independence is guaranteed to the judges at all. In this sense, the problem of the judge's conscience is a basic one which transcends any particular provision of the positive law. It is quite understandable, as we have seen, that this problem has been much discussed in the Federal Republic of Germany even under the Bonn Basic Law where a conscience clause was purposefully deleted from the provision safeguarding judicial independence.

There then arises the question of the character of the conscience of the judge: is it subjective or objective?[11]

Cardozo thought the distinction between the subjective or individual and the objective or general conscience is little more than one of words and that it will seldom be decisive for a judge in the practical administration of justice.[12] I admit the distinction is a subtle one. Nonetheless I think it is of utmost significance not only from a theoretical but also from a practical point of view.

As is often mentioned, Lord Nottingham, the father of Modern Equity, once remarked that "With such a conscience as is only *naturalis et interna,* this Court has nothing to do; the conscience by which I am to proceed is merely *civilis et politica,* and tied to certain measures."[13]

Conscience proper is, of course, the innermost voice of each individual. When conscience is referred to, for example, in the New Testament (e.g. I Peter 3:16), it seems to be used in precisely this proper sense. One likewise speaks of the constitutional guarantee of the freedom of conscience. But since the legal order is by its nature objective, it follows that the conscience of the judge, not as a mere citizen but as an organ for interpreting and applying the law, must also be objective. The judge's personal belief, as such, cannot be a criterion used by him in the discharge of his functions as a judge, even if it does derive from the inner voice of conscience. It is easy to imagine the sort of dilemma this

---

11. In Japan there are controversies between the objective and the subjective theories, but for linguistic reasons the references are purposely omitted in the present paper.

12. Cardozo, *The Nature of the Judicial Process* 110 (1921).

13. 6 Holdsworth, *A History of English Law* 547 (reprinted, 1966).

can give rise to when a judge has to deal with cases involving, say, the death penalty, sterilization or castration, euthanasia, abortion or artificial termination of pregnancy, artificial insemination, heart transplants, divorce, political or ideological offense, etc.

In extreme cases recourse may be had to natural law in order to modify or partially nullify the positive law. And in such cases, conscience will play a role in finding what natural law is for the particular case in question.[14] This is precisely what was contemplated in the conscience clause of Article 121 of the German Herrenchiemsee Draft which aimed at enabling the judges to examine the compatibility of positive law with the unwritten or natural law. But here again conscience is not subjective but rather objective because natural law involves much more than a mere personal feeling on the part of the judge.

In saying this I do not mean to suggest that the judge's conscience should be a constructive or fictitious one—that conscience which he ought to have as a judge regardless of the promptings of the inner voice of his own personal conscience. Conscience, so far as it deserves the name at all, cannot be conceived of without reference to its internal side. Thus the term "objective conscience," as I use it, differs from what is called the conscience of society or of the people. For instance, Justice Douglas once remarked that "the judiciary is in a high sense the guardian of the conscience of the people as well as of the law of the land."[15] I quite agree with him. But, he uses the term conscience figuratively, in a sense different from its original one. Saleilles spoke of the *conscience juridique de la collectivité* and of the *conscience populaire*.[16] From the context of his argument, it seems to me that the French word *conscience* is here to be understood as meaning "consciousness" rather than "conscience." Sometimes natural law is called the "conscience of the positive law" *(Gewissen des*

14. According to Dean Pound, the founders of the United States believed in a "natural right of revolution" and argued that conformity to the dictates of the individual conscience was the test of the validity of a law. Pound, *Criminal Justice in America* 52 (1945).

15. William O. Douglas, *We the Judges* 445 (1956).

16. Saleilles, "Ecole historique et droit naturel d'après quelques ouvrages récents," 1 *Revue trimestrielle de droit civil* 108 (1902).

positiven Rechts) or the "conscience of the State" *(Gewissen des Staates).*[17] This is another example of the figurative use of the term "conscience," although it should be remembered that there is an intimate connection between natural law and conscience in its proper sense. *Lex naturae est lex conscientiae* (Wolf).[18]

The conscience of the judge must also be "objective" in the sense that his subjective belief based on an inner voice ought nonetheless to be connected with and have some bearing upon his duty, a duty to interpret and apply the law which, by its nature, must be objective. He has to believe (according to his subjective conscience) that such and such is the right interpretation of the law appropriate to the particular case before him and suitable as a precedent in future cases of a similar nature. The same applies to judicial functions other than that of interpreting law. The Supreme Court of Japan has held that the expression "in the exercise of conscience" "means that the judge is to exercise his own subjective good judgment and moral concepts without yielding to any tangible or intangible pressures or enticements from external sources,"[19] but I do not think that this statement of the Court can be taken positively to deny the objectivity of the judge's conscience, as I have defined it above.

On the one hand, conscience is internal and subjective in the sense that it is a voice speaking from deep within the individual. On the other hand, conscience has a basically social character.[20] It has been pointed out that the Latin word *conscientia* indeed connotes an essential combination of the I and the Other and that, accordingly, it is to be construed as *Mitwissen mit anderen.*[21] Würtenberger has written at length about the social character of conscience. He refers to Baumgarten's emphasizing the fact that, though conscience is that which is inmost in man, it is proved from the first as *geselliges Inneres.* For Heidegger the voice of

---

17. See Heinz Scholler, *Das Gewissen als Gestalt der Freiheit* 83 (1962).

18. Scholler, *op. cit.* at 84 note 18.

19. Dando, *Japanese Criminal Procedure* 70 (B. J. George Jr. transl. 1965).

20. For the following, see Thomas Würtenberger, "Vom rechtschaffenen Gewissen," in *Existenz und Ordnung, Festschrift für Erik Wolf* 342 et seq. (1962).

21. Würtenberger, *op. cit.* at 343. Cf. Heinrich J. Scholler, *Die Freiheit des Gewissens* 212 (1958).

conscience is the call of the *eigenes Selbst* to his *Seinkönnen* and to his *Dasein, d. h. . . . als Mitsein mit anderen.* In Hegel's view, what is called conscience is an *allgemeines Wissen und Wollen, das die Anderen anerkennt . . . und das darum auch von ihnen anerkannt wird* and if conscience is conceived in too subjective a form, as in Kant's theory, it will be dangerous to both law and the community. Del Vecchio also speaks of *coscienza transubiet-tiva* as a specific form of conscience by which one counterposes oneself objectively to others and recognizes oneself as belonging to an order of relations with others.[22] The objectivity of the judge's conscience may also be explained in this sense.

The conscience of the judge is a kind of professional conscience, determined to a large extent by professional ethics.[23] The judge is required, when necessary, to modify a dictate of his purely personal conscience in order to adapt it to his professional duties. In most cases this modification will be an apparent one, for the inner voice itself will order him to perform his official duties in spite of his contrary personal belief. For instance, a judge who conscientiously believes that the distribution of obscene literature should be decriminalized *de lege ferenda* need not feel any pangs of conscience about convicting a defendant of that offense under existing law. Likewise he will be able to satisfy his inner voice in punishing a defendant with whose motives he nonetheless sympathizes, whether for ethical or other reasons.

Professional conscience is a specialized form of conscience proper. It can vary from one profession to another. Suppose a professor of law has become a judge. An opinion he entertained before from a purely academic point of view may well have to be altered when, as a judge, he is now required to render an actual decision. This change of opinion does not mean he is not conscientious. On the contrary, the stronger his conscience, the greater will be the discrepancy between his professional conscience as a scholar and as a judge. In any case, professional conscience has the conscience proper as its nucleus.

22. G. Del Vecchio, *La giustizia* 84 (4th ed. 1951).
23. Cf. Rotberg, *op. cit.* at 13.

At times, though very rarely, the internal conscience of the judge will not yield to the dictates of duty. There is then a real conflict between the conscience proper of the judge and his duty or a conflict between his conscience and the law. In such a situation, the only way for him to resolve the conflict will be either to resign his position or to withdraw from participation in the particular case.[24]

Let us turn now to the problem of the role of the judge's conscience in the administration of criminal justice and then consider its role in the judicial process at large.

The independent exercise of conscience by a judge in the discharge of his functions makes him responsible for what he does.[25] It brings personal elements into the judicial process and makes it rather more like "the hand-made as distinguished from the machine-made product"[26] or as better expressed by Jerome Hall, something more than a mere "impersonal and depersonalized process."[27] This is particularly significant in the administration of criminal justice where not only a scientific but also a humanistic approach is very definitely required.

This is the case in every phase of the criminal process, not only its substantive aspects but also in the trial, the finding of facts, interpretation of law, application of punishment, etc.

The way in which a judge conducts the trial is not without its impact on the defendant. Such procedural matters as, for instance, the acceptance or rejection of witnesses requested by the defense, the manner in which evidence is examined, or the attitude the judge takes toward him, can affect the defendant no less powerfully than does the substantive content of the final judgment. The conscience of the judge, as it is expressed in all these points of detail, can help to establish a favorable human relationship between him and the defendant. It can help to

---

24. Karl Peters, "Das Gewissen des Richters und das Gesetz," in 1 *Gegenwartsprobleme des Rechts* 37 et seq. (Conrad & Kipp eds., Görres-Geseelschaft zur Pflege der Wissenschaft, N.F., Heft 1, 1950). Cf. Wilhelm Pötter, "Richterrecht und richterliches Gewissen," in *Beiträge zum Richterrecht* 50 (the same series, Heft 5, 1968).

25. Peters, supra note 24 at 30.

26. Pound, *An Introduction to the Philosophy of Law* 70 (rev. ed. 1954).

27. See note 1 supra.

arouse the defendant's own conscience and to influence his mind and attitudes and thus contribute to putting him on the path towards resocialization. The rehabilitation of offenders is not the exclusive task of penal and post-penal institutions; it must have its starting point at a much earlier stage, so far as that is compatible with safeguarding the defendant's rights and interests.

Sentencing is another domain where the judge's conscience has a role to play. Generally speaking, the meting out of just punishment involves at once both scientific considerations (derived from criminal policy) and the sense of justice. To borrow Gény's words, "we are to interrogate reason and conscience to discover in our innermost nature the very basis of justice."[28] Thus the judge's conscience will be a particularly important factor where the criminological considerations applicable to ordinary cases are not deemed valid, for instance, in some but not all of the cases of political offenders who have acted out of strong conviction. (In saying this, I do not mean to deny, however, that political criminals are among the major subjects of criminology.)[29]

The conscience of the judge is especially significant as a force in the judicial process at large, whether in criminal or in civil cases.

As has been widely recognized, the application of law is not a mere logical or mechanical process. Whatever its ultimate behavioristic determinants, it does require a value judgment which naturally will vary from one judge to another according to the point of view adopted. It is, indeed, as a German judge puts it, "an act of logic, legal sentiment and conscience."[30] An overly subjective justice is not acceptable; it must necessarily lead to an arbitrary justice which is a *contradictio in adjecto*. On the other hand, an overly objective justice which leaves no room for the judge to appeal to his own conscience will become a stereotyped justice incapable of evolution, incapable of adapting itself to

---

28. 2 Gény, *Methode d'interprétation et sources de droit privé positif* 92 (quoted from Cardozo, supra note 12, at 74).

29. Stephen Schafer, "The Concept of the Political Criminal," 62 *Journal of Criminal Law, Criminology and Police Science* 380 et seq. (1971).

30. Cited by Arthur Kaufman, *Rechtsphilosophie im Wandel* 166 (1972).

the development of society. As was pointed out by Dean Pound, "the certainty attained by mechanical application of fixed rules to human conduct has always been illusory."[31] One has, therefore, to take a middle ground, allowing room for the judge to exercise his conscience but insisting that his conscience must be objective in the sense discussed earlier.

Uniformity and certainty are, of course, among the most important postulates of law. Thus, each legal system has a mechanism, such as an appeals procedure, to maintain the uniformity of law. But legal certainty should not be overemphasized if justice is to be kept sound and progressive. As Cardozo remarked, "the rule of adherence to precedent, though it ought not to be abandoned, ought to be in some degree relaxed."[32] We often see cases in which some seemingly erratic opinion of a lower court has finally prevailed and been approved by the appellate courts, thus modifying precedent and adapting the law to the demands of society. We also see instances in which dissenting opinions in a court of last resort become in course of time the majority opinion.[33] All of this is largely due to the initiative taken by judges acting according to conscience. It may cause confusion at times— but, in the long run, it does contribute to improving the law. Cardozo most exquisitely describes how the eccentricities of judges balance one another, how what is good in the work of a judge endures and how it stands as the foundation on which new structures of law will be built.[34]

Golding harbors, with reason, "a strong suspicion that procedural justice is a 'pluralistic,' rather than a unitary notion."[35] This is especially apt to be true in pluralistic societies like our

---

31. Pound, supra note 26, at 71.

32. Cardozo, supra note 12, at 150.

33. Justice Hughes, referring to dissenting opinions in a court of last resort, remarked that "unanimity which is merely formal . . . is not desirable," because "what must ultimately sustain the court in public confidence is the character and independence of the judges." Charles Evans Hughes, *The Supreme Court of the United States* 67 (1936).

34. Cardozo, supra note 12, at 177 et seq.

35. M. P. Golding, "Preliminaries to the Study of Procedural Justice," in *Law, Reason and Justice* 18 (Graham Hughes ed. 1969).

own. The independence of the judiciary as a whole, *vis-à-vis* other branches of government, is essential to any democratic legal system but even more important is the independence in a pluralistic society of each individual judge.[36] It is here that the role of conscience is particularly vital.[37]

As Felix Cohen once remarked, the problem of conscience can and must be attacked with the methods of science.[38] We agree with him, that conscience is largely a product of the moral teachings of parents, nursemaids, teachers, friends, and judges; and in fact there are many such scientific studies of conscience. Darwin explored its origins from an evolutionary point of view.[39] Würtenberger mentions, as other examples, the "biological" conscience of Monakow, the Freudian view of conscience as a manifestation of superego, and Wellek's psychological-characterological inferences from the ground of *Gemüt*.[40] Nowadays, the formation of conscience during infancy is a particularly favorite subject of science. Nonetheless the problem of conscience does have very deep roots in the religious, ethical and philosophical domain which lies beyond the farthest borders of the territory of science.[41]

In his well known analysis of the judicial process, Jerome Frank criticized the conventional formula, R × F = D (the Rules times the Facts equals the Decision), and replaced it tentatively with another formula, S × P = D (S for the Stimuli that affect the trial judge, P for his Personality). He pointed out that this tentative formula has little value for predictive and critical purposes because the "personality" of the judge represents an exquisitely complicated mass of phenomena.[42] Of course he is

---

36. In Japan, the old Constitution of 1889 (Art. 57) referred only to the independence of the judicial power as a whole, while the new Contsitution, as we have already seen, guarantees explicitly the independence of each individual judge.

37. Pötter, supra note 24, at 39 & 48.

38. *The Legal Conscience: Selected Papers of Felix S. Cohen* 28 (L. K. Cohen ed. 1960).

39. See Heinz Scholler, supra note 17, at 61.

40. Würtenberger, supra note 20, at 339 & 349 et seq.

41. See, *e.g.*, Heidegger's analysis of conscience in his *Sein und Zeit* §§54-60.

42. Jerome Frank, *Courts on Trial* 14 et seq. & 182 (1950).

right. The "personality" factor is not only "complicated," it is comprised of elements which, by their nature, cannot be objectivized. Thus, the judicial process, with the judge's conscience at its heart, must constitute the subject matter of what Jerome Hall calls a "humanistic" sociology of law.[43]

---

43. Jerome Hall, "From Legal Theory to Integrative Jurisprudence," 33 *Cincinnati Law Review* 153 at 191 et seq. (1964).

CHAPTER 3

CESARE BECCARIA, HERBERT MARCUSE AND MODERN YOUTH

J. M. van Bemmelen

Professor Emeritus of Criminal Law, University of Leiden

ALL OVER THE WORLD there is renewed interest in Beccaria and his work and ideas. No doubt the second centennial in 1964 of the publication of his book, *On Crimes and Punishments,* has contributed to this revival of interest.[1] Yet there are probably more important factors which account for it. The principal rea-

1. In 1964 and the years following, several new translations of Beccaria's essay appeared, along with many articles tracing the influence of his book on the criminal law of various countries. A full list of these publications may be found in the Bibliography at the end of the Dutch translation of Beccaria's essay by the Belgian judge, Dr. J. M. Michiels, which also contains a long commentary on Beccaria's life and work. Cesare Beccaria, *Over Misdaden en Straffen,* Antwerp, Standaard Weten-schappelijke Uitgeverij; Zwolle, Tjeenk Willink, 1971. At the request of Dr. Michiels, I had the honor of writing the Foreword to this book. The present article is largely an adaptation and translation of that foreword. Michiels' translation is based on the original Italian text but follows the sequence of chapters introduced by the French translator, the "Abbé" Morellet. Morellet's rearrangement, which had been approved by d'Alembert and Hume, was accepted by Beccaria. However, the anonymous eighteenth century English translation, which is still the standard version of Beccaria's work in English, retained the organization of the earlier Italian editions. There is a relatively recent English translation following Morellet's rearrangement which appears as a "preface" to Alessandro Manzoni, *The Column of Infamy,* K. Foster & J. Grigson transl., London, Oxford University Press, 1964. A set of tables comparing Morellet's order of chapters with the early Italian text may be found in the edition of *Dei delitti e delle pene* edited by Franco Venturi (Torino, Einaudi, 1965), at 103-110. References to Beccaria in the present article are initially to chapters of the Morellet version used by Dr. Michiels, followed by specific page references to the 1964 English translation by Foster & Grigson. Parallel references to chapters of the earlier English translation are given in square brackets, along with specific page references to the 2d American edition (Philadelphia, Philip H. Nicklin, 1819), reprinted by Academic Reprints, Stanford, California, in 1953. Quotations from Beccaria are based on Michiels' Dutch translation which is considerably more modern in flavor than either English version.

25

son may well be the resemblance between the conditions of the present day and those of the second half of the eighteenth century. Once again there is, internationally, a deep-rooted and grievous feeling of discontent with economic, moral and social conditions in the world. As in the days of Beccaria, there has been an enormous alteration in moral conceptions; the authority of the church, state and science are being subjected to doubt and criticism. Young people in particular remonstrate continually against law and order and the effect of their protests is to expose a need for changes in existing legislation, especially in the field of criminal law.

Beccaria's book was a blazing protest against the legislation of his own day, particularly against prevailing criminal law and criminal procedure. His essay is the work of a young man, twenty-five years old, and strongly influenced by a sense of rebellion against the authority of his father. There is yet another resemblance between Beccaria and the protesting young men of today in that Beccaria, when starting to write on his chosen subject, did not know the first thing about it.[2] In spite of that, he wrote a book which became a bestseller immediately upon its publication and which is still quite famous.

One is tempted to draw a comparison between Beccaria and the philosopher, Herbert Marcuse. Marcuse is now over seventy years old but his book, *One Dimensional Man*,[3] has had a great influence on today's protesting youth. There is certainly some similarity between these two thinkers. Both Beccaria and Marcuse rebel against "the maelstrom of misdirected power."[4] In Beccaria's day this misuse of power derived from the fact that a minority could make the laws and impose its convictions and opinions on the masses. Nowadays the end result is practically the same: in our industrialized world the interests of the nation, the "welfare and

---

2. Michiels, *op. cit.* at 36.

3. Herbert Marcuse, *One-Dimensional Man: Studies in the Ideology of Advanced Industrial Society* (Boston, Beacon Press, 1964).

4. Beccaria, chap. 1, p. 12 [Introduction, p. xiii.]; Marcuse, passim. See especially Marcuse's first chapter where he says: "Today political power asserts itself through its power over the machine process and over the technical organization of the apparatus." (p.3).

warfare state," have come to prevail over the interests of the individual and particularly over his freedom. It is no longer a minority which imposes its will on the majority but the industrial system and apparatus which frustrate the freedom of the individual, his freedom of thought and his freedom to arrange his life as he pleases. According to Marcuse, this is true both of capitalism and of communism.

Beccaria's starting point is the premise that the law ought to be based on a thorough knowledge of human nature; that this knowledge can reduce the contradictory activities of the mass of people to one common aim; the only aim in terms of which these activities should be assessed is the greatest happiness of the greatest number.[5] Marcuse takes the position that, in the present-day welfare state, "technological rationality" tends to result in a system of production which imposes itself on everyone and from which it is impossible to escape. It forces men to seek the satisfaction of unnecessary and false needs and it leads, in consequence, to continuous growth of population because a society with permanently increasing production

> needs an ever-increasing number of consumers and supporters; the constantly regenerated excess capacity must be managed. . . . [T]he growing population aggravates the struggle for existence in the face of its possible alleviation. The drive for more "living space" operates not only in international aggressiveness but also *within* the nation. Here, expansion has, in all forms of teamwork, community life, and fun, invaded the inner space of privacy and practically eliminated the possibility of that isolation in which the individual, thrown back on himself alone, can think and question and find.[6]

According to Marcuse, this sort of privacy has become "the most expensive commodity, available only to the very rich (who don't use it)."[7] Marcuse therefore would like to see society turn back or at least convert itself into a community with fewer people but with individuals who will really be free to choose consciously which needs they wish to satisfy and which they do not. He esti-

---

5. Beccaria, chap. 1, p. 11 [Introduction, p. xii.]
6. Marcuse, *op. cit.*, p. 244.
7. *Id.*

mates that the chances for such a turnabout are rather small. His only hope is that, in the long run, there will be men who are prepared to devote their lives to this "Great Refusal." Marcuse does not, therefore, formulate concrete proposals for changes in society, in contrast to Beccaria who was moderately optimistic about the future of society and who made a number of proposals for new legislation. The principal reforms recommended by Beccaria have for the most part been realized in many countries: abolition of the death penalty and of torture, the introduction of a uniform code of criminal law written in the national language of the people to whom it applies, reduction of the general level of punishments and more frequent use of fines, greater safeguards for the position and rights of suspected and accused persons and limitation of the use of pretrial detention.

One might even say the present-day "welfare state" has actually realized Beccaria's central ideal, i.e., reduction of the conflicting activities of the masses to one common aim (the greatest happiness of the greatest number of people). Marcuse criticizes this ideal insofar as it is limited to those nations which have evolved culturally and industrially into welfare states and does not apply to those countries which have not attained this status. Beccaria still thinks in terms of separate states, whereas Marcuse tries to embrace the whole world in his aspirations. A second and more important difference between Beccaria and Marcuse is that the first hopes to achieve his aims by spreading the light of "Reason" to the masses, while the latter sets his hope on the free and critical thinking of individuals. This difference is less fundamental than one might be inclined to think at first glance. Beccaria already foresaw the danger, that as the territory of a state is enlarged, its power increases proportionately and so does the possibility of that power being abused. According to Beccaria, this danger can be averted only by dividing the big states into a number of smaller ones and forming these into a federation.[8]

History has not borne Beccaria out on all points. His argument that a judge should not be allowed to interpret the law has been passed by in the evolution of the administration of justice. It is,

---

8. Beccaria, chap. 39, p. 89 [Chap. 26, p. 92.]

however, very seldom that judges act in opposition to the clear wording of the law and Beccaria did particularly stress the importance of a clear and comprehensible statutory text. Analogical application of the criminal law is still taboo in most continental law systems and we have Beccaria to thank—among others—that the *nulla poena sine lege* rule has become a fundamental human right.

Beccaria's opposition to the criminal law of his time differs in two ways from the protests of the youth of today. In the first place, he is optimistic in his conviction that "Reason" will ultimately lead humanity to greater felicity. He looks forward to that "blessed time when truth will be within the reach of the great masses as error has been hitherto."[9] And towards the end of his work he again manifests his confidence that there will come a time in the faraway future when everyone will be happy.[10]

The second way in which Beccaria differs from today's youth is that, although he protests against tyranny and tyrants who abuse the criminal law for their own purposes, he never propagates anarchical sentiments. At the very beginning of his book he says emphatically that his aim is to serve and to promote lawful authority.[11] One does, however, get the impression every now and then, that this is all lip service thrown in for the purpose of making his ideas acceptable to the authorities of his own time. Had his ideas really been accepted, it would have meant a sort of revolution. Like Marcuse, he preaches that attention should be paid "to the lamentations of so many defenseless and helpless men who are sacrificed to the bloodthirstiness of narrow-minded fanatics and the indifference of the possessing classes."[12] In this respect there is a similarity between Beccaria and Marcuse. The latter writes at the end of his book:

> However, underneath the conservative popular base is the substratum
> of the outcasts and outsiders, the exploited and persecuted of other

---

9. Beccaria, chap. 16, p. 51 [Chap. 28, p. 107.]

10. Beccaria, chap. 41, pp. 91-96 [Chaps. 41-45, pp. 148-57.] See Michiels, *op. cit.*, p. 165.

11. Beccaria, To the Reader, p. 7. [Beccaria's foreword "to the reader" does not appear in the earlier English version.]

12. Beccaria, chap. 1, p. 12 [Introduction, p. xiii.]

races and colors, the unemployed and the unemployable. They exist outside the democratic process; in their life the most immediate and the most real need is for ending intolerable conditions and institutions. Thus their opposition is revolutionary even if their consciousness is not.[13]

Although Beccaria could not anticipate the developments of the nineteenth and twentieth centuries, he might in our time have written the same. He even gives the following warning:

I wish to restrict myself to drawing attention to the most important general principles and to the most frequently occurring and most disastrous forms of abuses, in order to open the eyes of those, who out of an ill-conceived love for freedom, want to plunge society into anarchy, and of those who strive to subject humanity to a discipline and order such as we find in a cloister of monks.[14]

Beccaria attached great importance to the equality of all men before the law and particularly to equality in application of the criminal law. In so many words he demands that penal sanctions be the same for the top-ranking citizen as for the lowliest. Differences of social rank or of wealth can be justified only in accordance with the initial supposition of equality before the law, which treats all those subject to it as standing on an equal footing.[15] Marcuse, on the other hand, is not sure this equality before the law will necessarily result in happiness for the masses. Equality, he says, is not one of those terms "which do not require development of their meaning, such as the terms designating the objects and implements of daily life, visible nature, vital needs and wants. These terms are generally understood so that their mere appearance produces a response (linguistic or operational) adequate to the pragmatic context in which they are spoken."[16] According to him, "[t]he situation is very different with respect to terms which denote things or occurrences beyond this non-controversial context. Here, the functionalization of language expresses an abridgement of meaning which has a political connotation."[17]

13. Marcuse, *op. cit.,* p. 256.
14. Beccaria, chap. 1, p. 12 [Chap. 8, p. 36.]
15. Beccaria, chap. 27, p. 68 [Chap. 21, p. 80.]
16. Marcuse, *op. cit.,* p. 87.
17. *Id.*

Marcuse is of the opinion that "equality" belongs to this second set of terms, along with words such as "freedom," "democracy," and "peace." In practice these have a different meaning in the East and in the West. "Thus, the fact that the prevailing mode of freedom is servitude and the prevailing mode of equality is superimposed inequality is barred from expression by the closed definition of these concepts in terms of the powers which shape the respective universe of discourse. The result is the familiar Orwellian language ("peace is war" and "war is peace," etc.) which is by no means that of terroristic totalitarianism only."[18] This may be true to some extent, but Marcuse neglects to mention that *ab origine* men are not equal. From birth onwards, they differ intellectually, temperamentally and in character. This is inevitable under any form of society. We may try to make conditions of education and opportunities to obtain work and welfare as equal as possible but we cannot eliminate the original inequality of men.

Beccaria did realize that great differences do exist between men with regard to their intellect, temperament and character. He recognizes that not all men are endowed with a superabundance of effusive energy,[19] that there are too few courageous personalities in society[20] and that there are wide differences in human intellect.[21] He realizes, too, that "[t]he equality of punishment can never be more than external, since its effectiveness differs with each individual."[22] But at the same time that Beccaria speaks of the fact that most men lack "a superabundance of effusive energy," he also mentions that it is such superabundant energy which causes the gravest criminality as well as the most spectacular instances of courage and virtue. According to him, history teaches that both phenomena will always occur simultaneously in those nations which have to sustain themselves by unremitting governmental activity and a common concern for the public welfare. But here again we see a certain similarity between Beccaria

---

18. *Ibid.*, p. 88.
19. Beccaria, chap. 13, p. 40 [Chap. 31, p. 116.]
20. Beccaria, chap. 14, p. 41 [Chap. 37, p. 139.]
21. Beccaria, chap. 19, p. 56 [Chap. 19, pp. 75-76.]
22. Beccaria, chap. 27, p. 69 [Chap. 21, p. 81.]

and Marcuse—Beccaria is of the opinion that in countries with vast territories or consistently good laws, interest in the general welfare of the people tends to be weaker. In these countries, concern is focused more on maintenance of the existing regime than on its improvment. From this Beccaria draws the conclusion that a high rate of crime does not necessarily prove that a particular country is in a state of decay or decline.[23]

Despite Beccaria's realization of great psychological differences between people and the possibility that these may underlie the various sorts of delinquency, criminal psychology and psychiatry were still a closed book to him. He speaks of these differences in mentality as obscure and infinite. He says:

> If it were possible to apply mathematical measurement and logic to the obscure and infinite motivations which determine human actions, it ought to be possible to draw up a mathematical scale of corresponding punishments, varying from very severe to very light. If it were possible to draw up such an exact and universal tariff of crimes and punishments, we would at the same time have at our disposal a trustworthy yardstick for the freedom-loving or tyrannical character of the political regime in the various countries and for moral character traits or the criminal tendencies of their population. But for the wise legislator it will be sufficient to indicate the great principles in order to reach a desirable balance and to avoid the danger of punishing the most serious crimes with the lightest sanctions.[24]

It seems as if Beccaria was prophesying methods of measurement of criminality like those nowadays proposed by Sellin and Wolfgang[25] and, in The Netherlands, by C. J. Dessaur.[26]

In his chapter on sentencing policy, Beccaria says in the first sentence that the gravity of a crime is essentially determined by the harm it causes to society.[27] In his opposition to differentiation of punishment on psychological grounds, Beccaria goes so far as to say he considers it wrong to suppose—as some authors do—

---

23. Beccaria, chap. 13, p. 40 [Chap. 31, pp. 116-17.]
24. Beccaria, chap. 23, p. 63 [Chap. 6, p. 30.]
25. Thorsten Sellin & M. E. Wolfgang, *The Measurement of Delinquency* (New York: John Wiley & Sons, 1964).
26. Catharina I. Dessaur, "Foundations of theory—formation: a methodological analysis," Leiden University thesis, 1971.
27. Beccaria, chap. 24, p. 63 [Chap. 7, p. 33.]

that the evil intention of the criminal is the true measure of the seriousness of his crime. "Intent," according to Beccaria, "depends on external, temporary circumstances and on one's own previous disposition. These factors vary from one person to another and even for the same person they change from moment to moment in a quick succession of thoughts, passions or external influences. If one were to take all these factors into consideration it would not only be necessary to draw up a separate code for every citizen, but to make a new law for every crime committed."[28] Beccaria is a convinced opponent of individualization of punishment. The terms "responsibility" and "imputability" are simply not used in Beccaria's book. Even infancy as a ground of nonresponsibility is not mentioned. It is difficult to reproach Beccaria for this. Medical science did not yet have a clear conception of the different mental disorders, let alone the capacity to see the connection between these disorders and specific forms of criminality. The idea that a child is not merely a grown-up person in miniature only gained ground a century later. The harm or injury to society is, according to Beccaria, not the only measure of the gravity of the crime. He also takes into account the attraction which a certain kind of crime has for all people. In Italian he speaks of *"la misura delle spinte che li portano ai delitti."*[29]

In spite of his progressive conceptions, Beccaria was in many respects a child of his time and of his class, the nobility. The masses he describes in a chapter on "social parasitism" as "the dense common herd, which admires those who only grab for themselves and never sacrifice anything."[30] By way of contrast, in his first chapter, he sees the enlightenment brought about particularly by the printing press, as teaching men the real relations which ought to exist between sovereigns and their subjects, between the government and the common people and between vari-

---

28. *Ibid.*, p. 63 [Chap. 7, p. 33.]

29. Beccaria, *Dei delitti e delle pene* (Venturi ed., 1965), p. 19 [Chap. 6, p. 28]. W. P. J. Pompe, "Beccaria a-t-il encore un message pour les criminalistes de notre temps?" [1964] *Tijdschrift voor Strafrecht*, p. 199, points out that in the French text Morellet translated this line rather freely as "et peut devenir plus commun."

30. Beccaria, chap. 34, pp. 77-78 [Chap. 24, p. 85.]

ous nations.[31] His short chapter on parasitism deserves comparison with the ideas of Marcuse. There is one point of similarity. Both consider it very important that people with leisure have the opportunity to think about ways in which to obtain freedom and other human rights for all classes. But Beccaria assumes that a number of rich people will do this and that they will assure that food and the means of subsistence are available to the working poor in order to enable them to fight the silent war which the working class wages against the exaggerated opulence of others, instead of fighting an uncertain and bloody battle with force and weapons.[32] Marcuse does not trust the rich to perform this task. As already mentioned, he says that "privacy—the sole condition that, on the basis of satisfied vital needs, can give meaning to freedom and independence of thought—has long since become the most expensive commodity, available only to the very rich (who don't use it). In this respect, too, 'culture' reveals its feudal origins and limitations. It can become democratic only through the abolition of mass democracy, i.e., if society has succeeded in restoring the prerogatives of privacy by granting them to all and protecting them for each."[33] But Marcuse is far from optimistic about the possibility of achieving this goal: "The degree to which the population is allowed to break the peace wherever there still is peace and silence . . . is frightening. It is frightening because it expresses the lawful and even organized effort to reject the Other in his own right."[34]

If Beccaria were writing today he might have said the same.

---

31. Beccaria, chap. 1, p. 11 [Introduction, p. xii.]
32. Beccaria, chap. 34, p. 78 [Chap. 24, p. 85.]
33. Marcuse, *op. cit.*, p. 244.
34. *Ibid.*, p. 245.

CHAPTER 4

WAR CRIMES AND CRIMINAL LAW

EDWARD M. WISE

Professor of Law, Wayne State University

I PROPOSE IN THIS PAPER to offer a few comments on certain problems connected with the prosecution of international offenses and particularly war crimes, which have come up in the context of the Indochina war. My main theme is taken from an article on international criminal law published some fifteen years ago by Jerome Hall.[1] Due perhaps to its publication in a relatively inaccessible collection of essays, Hall's article has not had the direct influence it deserves, even amongst cognoscenti in what, after all, is still a somewhat esoteric field. Nevertheless, its basic thesis is one that bears reiteration.

Hall's thesis is simply this: anyone who would construct a system of international criminal law would do well not to neglect the vast body of traditional knowledge that has been developed in connection with domestic criminal law. It is reasonable to expect that any effort to enforce precepts of international behavior through the specific medium of criminal prosecution must necessarily be complicated and qualified by the peculiar nature of the criminal law itself. People who make it their business to talk about responsibility for international crimes might profitably devote at least some attention to the conditions and prerequisites of criminal responsibility generally.

Hall's article was framed, in large part, as a critique of the "Draft Code of Offenses Against the Peace and Security of Man-

---

1. Hall, "International Criminal Law from the Perspective of American Law and the Science of Criminal Law," in 1 *Aktuelle Probleme des Internationalen Rechts* 82 (R. Laun & D. S. Constantopoulos eds., 1957).

kind," drawn up by the International Law Commission in 1954.[2] It is surely safe to say that this particular draft by now is moribund.[3] There have, however, been more recent efforts to revive the idea of a convention on international crime.[4] Although more sophisticated in many ways than earlier proposals, I am afraid these efforts may also be found to fall somewhat short of Hall's exacting standards.

I have elsewhere tried, in effect, to show the applicability of Hall's thesis to the law of extradition and to the so-called question of jurisdiction over crime—indeed, to the whole body of problems that come up when national authorities are required to deal with crimes involving a foreign element.[5] A similar point has been made, at least in connection with questions of jurisdiction, by Professor Fitzgerald: "in discussing the present topic" he says, "we must beware of forgetting our criminology."[6]

At present, my concern is neither with the classic problems of extradition and jurisdiction, nor with proposals for the construction of a code of international crimes, but rather with the pertinence of "criminology" to situations in which States are more or less bound under existing international law to prosecute individuals who engage in certain specified forms of behavior, such as the commission of war crimes.

---

2. General Assembly Official Records, IX, Supp. 9 (A/2693) 11-12 (1954), reprinted in G. O. W. Mueller & E. M. Wise, *International Criminal Law* 594-96 (1965).

3. See Wise, "The Present Prospect for an International Criminal Court," *Newsletter of the American Section of the Int'l Assn. of Penal Law*, No. 2, at 5 (1968).

4. See J. Stone & R. K. Woetzel, *Toward a Feasible International Criminal Court* (1970); Foundation for the Establishment of an International Criminal Court, *The Establishment of an International Criminal Court: A Report on the First International Criminal Law Conference* (1971); Foundation for the Establishment of an International Criminal Court, *The Establishment of an International Criminal Court: A Report on the First and Second International Criminal Law Conferences* (R. K. Woetzel ed., 1973).

5. See Wise, "Prolegomenon to the Principles of International Criminal Law," 16 *N. Y. Law Forum* 562 (1970). See also Wise, "Some Problems of Extradition," 15 *Wayne L. Rev.* 709 (1969).

6. Fitzgerald, "The Territorial Principle in Penal Law: An Attempted Justification," 1 *Ga. J. Int'l & Comp. L.* 29 (1970).

The obligation to prosecute war crimes has a textual basis in the 1949 Geneva Conventions,[7] each of which requires that real steps be taken to bring to trial anyone to whom "grave breaches" of these conventions are attributable. The question of how far this obligation extends came up in connection with the much publicized trial of Lt. William Calley. One of the witnesses called against Calley was a former member of his company, Mr. Meadlo, whose revelations on television about the killings at My Lai helped considerably to project the case into public prominence. Mr. Meadlo claimed his privilege against self-incrimination and declined to testify unless he was given a formal grant of immunity from future prosecution by the federal government. This was duly done. But the question has been raised, of whether the government's grant of immunity in this instance did not amount to a breach of its international obligations?[8]

There is a preliminary problem of whether the South Vietnamese civilians killed at My Lai were really "protected persons" under the Geneva Conventions. It is true that Article 3 of each convention sets out rules requiring civilized behavior towards noncombatants in situations of civil war. It is doubtful, however, how far this article in itself applies to a conflict which both sides agreed—no doubt for different reasons—to be of an international character; and there is no technical obligation under the conventions to prosecute for breaches of Article 3. One might think civilians must surely be protected by the Convention on the Protection of Civilian Persons; but Article 4 of that Convention specifically prescribes that "nationals of a cobelligerent state shall not be regarded as protected persons while the State of which they are nationals has normal diplomatic representation in the state in whose hands they are." The argument that this excludes

---

7. Convention for the Amelioration of the Condition of the Wounded and Sick in Armed Forces in the Field, 75 U.N.T.S. 31; Convention for the Amelioration of the Wounded, Sick and Shipwrecked Members of the Armed Forces at Sea, 75 U.N.T.S. 85; Convention Relative to the Treatment of Prisoners of War, 75 U.N.T.S. 135; Convention Relative to the Protection of Civilian Persons in Time of War, 75 U.N.T.S. 287.

8. See Comment, "Punishment for War Crimes: Duty—or Discretion?" 69 *Mich. L. Rev.* 1312 (1971).

only those who are able to rely effectively on normal diplomatic protection seems to have been quite definitely rejected in the *traveaux preparatoires* of the Geneva Conference. This has led some commentators to treat the civilians killed at My Lai as coming under the Convention on Prisoners of War. Their argument is based on Article 5 of that convention which extends protection to those whose status as prisoners of war is somehow in doubt.[9] I am not persuaded by this argument, which incidentally seems to say that the more obviously innocent the victim, the less he is entitled to protection. I am also puzzled by the underlying assumption that there is no obligation to prosecute war crimes independent of the Geneva Conventions. All this strained effort to invoke those conventions attests, no doubt, to the good guardianship of them by the International Red Cross. But it may also reflect a rather exaggerated and, in ways, unhappy emphasis on the observance of textual precepts as constituting the entire sum and substance of international duty: a variation of our peculiarly modern notion that morality is wholly a matter of following explicit rules, as opposed to customary modes and decent habits of behavior not easily reducible to rule. There were laws of war before Geneva. The slaughter of innocents, at least in hostile territory, falls under the Hague Conventions and is a breach of those residual laws of humanity to which the Hague Rules refer. It is true that the old Hague Conventions do not specifically make provision for criminal prosecution. But there is a whole body of international law on state liability for injuries to aliens which does impose a very definite obligation to prevent or else punish flagrant offenses against the person and property of foreign nationals.[10] In principle, at least, this obligation is no less compelling than one imposed under the Geneva Conventions.

Assuming an obligation to prosecute, a case can be made out for saying that the Geneva Conventions—and customary law almost *a fortiori*—have to be interpreted as allowing grants of immunity such as that extended to Mr. Meadlo. This is one of those matters left to be determined by local law.[11] It is hard to see how

9. See Note, 12 *Harv. Int'l L. J.* 345, 347-49 (1971).

10. See Wise, "Note on International Standards of Criminal Law and Administration," in G. O. W. Mueller & E. M. Wise, supra note 2, at 135.

11. See Comment, supra note 8.

it could be otherwise. Given, for instance, the peculiarities of American rules of evidence, there are sometimes facts that can only be brought out by promising not to proceed against one of the culprits. To disallow the purchase of proof on these terms may mean that other offenders will effectively escape prosecution. The possibility that someone may at sometime have to be granted immunity is surely an unavoidable qualification to any international obligation to prosecute undertaken by the United States.

The objection, of course, is that States should not be able to carve out exceptions to an international obligation by invoking deficiencies or idiosyncracies of local procedure; that a refusal to prosecute remains a refusal to prosecute, no matter what justifications may be urged in its favor; that individual responsibility for what is supposed to be an international offense ought not to turn on peculiar national modes of dealing with crime.[12] But certainly some allowance for the fact that local procedures will operate unevenly must be taken to be implied in the initial decision to rely on national agencies of prosecution; this is an inevitable consequence of placing prosecution in local hands. It is realistically recognized as such in the 1970 Hague Convention on the Unlawful Seizure of Aircraft.[13] There was strong pressure at the time to cast a duty to prosecute hijackers in unconditional terms and this perhaps accounts for a clear statement of something that is usually left to implication: that the only duty which can fairly be demanded of states is the duty to treat the offense in question in the same manner as other cases of serious crime appearing in the ordinary domestic calendar. The obligation to prosecute, in other words, is qualified to the extent that local tradition generally permits the authorities to abstain from prosecution.[14] This makes individual liability for an "international offense" turn on innumerable national variations in criminal pro-

---

12. Paust, "My Lai and Vietnam: Norms, Myths and Leader Responsibility," 57 *Military L. Rev.* 99, at 121-23 (1972).

13. I.C.A.O. Document 8920 (1970).

14. Cf. Samuels, "A Symposium on the Unlawful Seizure of Aircraft—The Legal Problems: An Introduction," 37 *J. Air L. & Comm.* 163, at 167-68 (1971); Mankiewicz, "The 1970 Hague Convention," *id.* 195, at 204-06; Guillaume, La Convention de la Haye du 16 Décembre 1970 pour La Répression de la Capture Illicite d'Aéronefs," [1970] Ann. Français de Droit International 36, at 51-53.

cedure. But because certain conduct has been loosely characterized as an "international crime" does not necessarily mean states
are obligated to deal with it according to a uniform procedure.
In a sense, this is the reason the Geneva Conventions deliberately
speak of "grave breaches" rather than "war crimes"—so as not to
prejudge the issue of whether an international criminal law
stricto sensu may be said to exist. So long as there is reliance on
local prosecution, any international undertaking to repress particular conduct must necessarily be complicated, qualified, modified, and even distorted, by the whole system of national law
through which it is forced.

It is partly this consideration that makes me somewhat skeptical about speaking of "international criminal law" in the sense
of a body of international law comparable more or less to the
domestic criminal law of particular states—which Schwarzenberger has called the "proper" or "material sense" of the term,[15]
the sense which would be rendered in German as *Völkerstrafrecht.*[16] I am not sure there is actually in being any body of international law which will bear a respectably close analogy to our
systems of domestic criminal law.[17] This is not simply because an
international criminal court does not exist. The argument for the
reality of an international criminal law does not necessarily depend on assertions about similarities of formal structure. The
claim seems rather to be that, despite dissimilarities of form,
there is still a very fruitful analogy of content and function between the two fields[18] in that international law does, on occasion,
declare certain conduct to be an offense, provides that the offender is liable to be tried and punished and has as its purpose
in so doing the suppression of individual acts which are supposed

15. Schwarzenberger, "The Problem of an International Criminal Law," 3 *Current
Legal Prob.* 263 (1950), reprinted in G. O. W. Mueller & E. M. Wise, supra note
2, at 3.

16. Cf. Zlataríc, "Erwägungen zum Abkommen über strafbare und bestimmte
andere Handlungen an Bord von Luftfahrzeugen vom 14. September 1963," in
Aktuelle Probleme des Internationalen Stafrechts 160, at 161-63 (D. Oehler &
P.-G. Pötz eds., 1970).

17. Cf. Hall, supra note 1, at 83-84.

18. For this distinction in another, related context, see H. L. A. Hart, *The Concept of Law* 226-31 (1961).

to be injurious to the entire community. However, there are two grounds for doubting that this is actually the case. One is the question of whether it is really plausible to speak of a genuine "international community."[19] The second has to do with the fact that the concept of crime in municipal law not only implies a developed institutional tradition on which the distinction between civil and criminal law depends, but also a complex web of settled associations and partly tacit appreciations about the differences between culpable and justifiable and excusable actions. Where all this is lacking, one cannot easily speak of a system of criminal law.

In one of his *Essais,* Montaigne refers to the system of law as "a structure of various parts so closely interconnected that it is impossible to disturb one without the whole body feeling it."[20] There are dangers to be sure, in exaggerating the character of the criminal law as a *systéme juridique.* But so long as one does not lose sight of hard facts and standards of value, it can be quite fruitful—as Jerome Hall's own work has shown more than once —to consider the criminal law in precisely this character, as a system of interlocking and tightly related elements. One then comes to see how the content and sense of a particular rule may be vitally affected by the whole context in which it is applied and how expectations about the setting in which it will be applied have a considerable influence on the shape and substance of a rule itself. An especially striking instance is the great difficulty which has been experienced in Japan in trying to combine an essentially German criminal law with an essentially American criminal procedure.[21] One can expect to encounter similar difficulties in any effort to enforce international rules through the medium of diverse local procedures. There are not only local peculiarities with respect to matters which may wholly cut a case off, such as

---

19. See Wise, supra, note 5, 16 *N.Y. Law Forum* at 570-71; cf. C. de Visscher, *Theory and Reality in Public International Law* 89-101 (rev. ed. P. Corbett transl. 1968).

20. Montaigne, *Oeuves Complètes* 118 (ed. de la Pléiade, 1962).

21. Hirano, "Some Aspects of Japanese Criminal Law," in A. T. von Mehren, *Law in Japan,* 274-75 (1963). Cf. Dando, "Interrelation of Criminal Law and Procedure," 2 *Japan. Ann. of Law & Politics* 163 (1953).

prosecutorial discretion[22] or prescription.[23] There are also diverse dispositions with respect to modes of proceeding and proof and in the composition of courts which may have a substantial influence on the outcome of a case, which may significantly affect the result—something we should be keenly aware of in the United States in consequence of the problems arising under *Eire v. Tompkins*.[24] There is a sense in which the presence of local variations may affect the very substance of the rules themselves.

There is an important illustration of this point to be drawn out of the argument of Telford Taylor's book on *Nuremberg and Vietnam*.[25]

Taylor begins with a very limited conception of what constitutes a violation of the laws of war. There are not, in his view, any absolute prohibitions. The laws of war are rather a matter of saying certain conduct is so distantly related to any reasonable military objective that it ought not be engaged in. They are ultimately based, in other words, on a principle of circumstantial reasonableness or proportionality; they are inspired, as the preamble to the Hague Rules says, "by the desire to diminish the evils of war, as far as military requirements permit" and they do not forbid anything that may be proximately demanded by military necessity.

This is an extremely narrow view of the nature of the laws of war, although one peculiarly congenial, perhaps, to an age notable for its distrust of absolutes and for its uncertainty about the validity even of elementary decencies. Much of the force of Taylor's book derives from his finding nonetheless that the American conduct of the war in Vietnam was, by and large, unlawful. Still, this view of the laws of war as imposing no more than a

---

22. For national variations in this regard, see Symposium, "Prosecutorial Discretion," 18 *Am. J. Comp. L.* 483-548 (1970).

23. Cf. Miller, "The Convention on the Non-Applicability of Statutory Limitations to War Crimes and Crimes Against Humanity," 65 *Am. J. Int'l L.* 476 (1971); Lerner, "The Convention on the Non-Applicability of Statutory Limitations to War Crimes," 4 *Israel L. Rev.* 512 (1969).

24. *Erie R.R. v. Tompkins*, 304 U.S. 64 (1938). See especially the remarks of Mr. Justice Frankfurter in *Guaranty Trust Co. v. York*, 326 U.S. 99 (1945).

25. T. Taylor, *Nuremberg and Vietnam: An American Tragedy* (1970).

rule of reason, has been severely criticized.[26] It is insisted, with considerable truth, that the laws of war ought and do contain some fairly inflexible prohibitions against inhumanity in the conduct of war and it is no objection that these make the winning of battles more difficult; any more than it is a valid objection to say that prohibiting barbarity by the police makes the catching of criminals less certain.

It may be that Taylor's extraordinary emphasis on proportionality rests on far too rigid an assumption that any more demanding rule must necessarily be ineffective and by that token, invalid. It seems to me to be accounted for by certain other, related assumptions. One is Professor Taylor's premise that any violation of the laws of war is necessarily a war crime.[27] It is by no means obvious that this should be the case. We have painfully learned in the United States how disastrous it can be to insist that every bit of undesirable behavior ought to be subject to criminal sanctions.[28] Schwarzenberger puts the point, that a permissible form of this premise, "any breach of the rules of warfare may be punished by the enemy as a war crime," is justified by the fact that strong, individualized reprisals are virtually the only means available during the anarchic course of hostilities to insure the rules of war will continue to be observed; that reprisal, therefore, "is the foundation of war crimes jurisdiction under international customary law and the basis of the substantial law in this field." Schwarzenberger does recognize that certain limitations on the exercise of war crimes jurisdiction, such as a requirement of some form of guilt on the part of those punished, may be imposed by countervailing standards of "civilization." But he rightly concludes that insofar as the punishment of "war crimes" is

---

26. See, *e.g.*, Wasserstrom, "Criminal Behavior," *N.Y. Rev. of Books*, June 3, 1971, p. 8; Cohen, "Taylor's Conception of the Laws of War," 80 *Yale L. J.* 1492 (1971).

27. Taylor, supra, note 25, at 19. See also U.S. Dept. of Army, *Field Manual 27-10, The Law of Land Warfare* 178 (1956).

28. Cf. Kadish, "The Crisis of Overcriminalization," 374 *Annals* 157 (1967); H. Packer, *The Limits of Criminal Sanction* 249-366 (1968); N. Morris & G. Hawkins, *The Honest Politician's Guide to Crime Control* 1-28 (1969).

a species of reprisal, it represents a very rudimentary form of law which will not sustain a respectable analogy to a developed system of domestic criminal law.[29] Any domestic system of criminal law imports a whole tradition of limiting conditions partly aimed at drawing a distinction between the question of whether or not an act conforms to the law and the question of whether or not it constitutes a crime. Whether or not the act amounts to a crime turns on the applicability of certain justifications and excuses. There are, of course, differences between legal systems as to how far precisely criminal liability will be qualified by these considerations. One of the most important distinguishing characteristics of a particular system of criminal law is the extent to which it admits or disallows certain defenses. One of the real difficulties in framing definitions of crimes in international agreements is that nothing can be taken for granted about what qualifications will be admitted once the definition comes to be applied in a national forum. The result is a very decided tendency in the drafting of international instruments to compensate for that fact by trying to work into the definition of particular crimes those qualifications which a ripe system of criminal law would leave to be determined as a matter of general principle. I suspect the same tendency may underlie Taylor's very flexible conception of what constitutes a breach of the laws of war.

The Nuremberg Tribunal was sensitive, to a degree, to this tradition of limitation which is bound up with the notion of criminal law. Herbert Wechsler characterized its judgment as a judgment of limitation—a judgment which, as the criminal law generally once was supposed to do, set measured bounds to demands for the exaction of vengeance.[30] It should suggest to those who urge the pertinence of Nuremberg that it is not enough simply to assert the principle of individual responsibility on every possible occasion. What is also needed is a more careful specification of the conditions that limit individual responsibility. A system of international criminal law requires both. It is important that attempts to say hypothetically how the Nuremberg Principles

29. G. Schwarzenberger, 2 *International Law as Applied by International Courts and Tribunals: The Law of Armed Conflicts* 13-14, 453-55, 478, 520-21 (1968).

30. Wechsler, "The Issues of the Nuremberg Trial," 62 *Pol. Sci. Q.* 11 (1947).

would apply to the circumstances of the Indochina war should not lose sight of the fact that if those principles had actually become part of a concrete tradition of international criminal law, they might well have been accompanied by a limitation of some of the more dubious doctrines which were bandied about at the end of World War II, by a more painstaking statement of the law of complicity and causation and perhaps by the qualification of much that was said then about conspiracy and command responsibility.

This need not to forget our "criminology" is particularly apparent in connection with the problem of superior orders. There are differences of opinion on how the problem shall be treated. The key lies in Lauterpacht's suggestion, that "it is necessary to approach the problem of superior orders on the basis of general principles of criminal law, namely as an element in ascertaining the existence of *mens rea* as a condition of accountability."[31] Lauterpacht himself concluded that a man will not be excused for obeying a patently illegal order which he stupidly believes to be lawful. What he has done, I suspect, is to assume that in the criminal law itself unreasonable mistakes can never normally excuse. This in fact is sometimes the case in Anglo-American law; insofar as it is the case, people are punished, in effect, for negligence. One has to beware of the trap of supposing the law one is familiar with must be the law everywhere, of assuming, for instance, there are no circumstances under which error of law can properly operate as an excuse. In some systems this is true. It is not in others.[32]

One has also to take these national differences as given and recognize they are not entirely accidental. For example, insofar as American law permits convictions for what is in effect negligence, it is to some extent compensating for procedural restrictions on proof of the accused's mental state. Without lifting

---

31. Lauterpacht, "The Law of Nations and the Punishment of War Criminals," 21 *Brit. Yb. Int'l L.* 58, 87 (1944). See also Y. Dinstein, *The Defense of "Obedience to Superior Orders" in International Law* 87-90 (1965). Cf. Meltzer, "Some Uneasy Reflections on the Calley Case," in U. Chi. Law School, *The Law School Record* 13, at 15-16 (Spring, 1971).

32. See Ryu & Silving, "Error Juris: A Comparative Study," 24 *U. Chi. L. Rev.* 421 (1957).

these restrictions, there is considerable question about the capacity of American criminal law to take full account of the grada-
tions of culpability that another system might treat as a matter
of course.[33] There is also the fact that Anglo-American law in assessing problems of guilt, tends to emphasize questions of knowledge, where other systems emphasize questions of will—an emphasis paralleled in the English philosophic tradition and, to some
extent, implicit in the structure of ordinary English speech. Giv-
en these practically unavoidable peculiarities, one has to recognize that even so fundamental a matter as the level of culpability
associated with international crimes is necessarily subject to national variation.

I have referred to criminal law as importing a tradition of
limitation. In this it more or less mirrors the state of common
sentiment about the circumstances under which people are or are
not to be blamed for what they do. By the same token, as we
have found in the United States, nothing but trouble results
from trying to suppress through criminal prosecution conduct
which a sizeable segment of the community does not regard as de-
serving of punishment. It is all well and good to urge this as a
reason for erasing from the statute book attempts at controlling
through the criminal law those vices which one does not find personally uncongenial. Must one not also recognize it to be an equally cogent reason for at least skepticism about the value of any effort to set the criminal law against conduct one personally is sure
constitutes a great evil?

These are matters of degree. There is a sense in which the very
function of criminal law is to impose on dissidents the opinions
and standards of those who dominate or are ascendant in a society, just as there is a point beyond which the criminal law is a
uniquely inappropriate instrument for pitting one prevalent set
of opinions against another. There are further complications
having to do with how one defines the pertinent community and
with the intricate interrelation between the different intensities

33. Cf. National Commission on Reform of Federal Criminal Laws, *Final Report:
A Proposed New Federal Criminal Code,* Comment to §302, at 29 (1971).

and levels at which particular opinions are entertained.[34] However, as was said in connection with earlier efforts to establish an international court, "if half the members of a society believe the other half is actually or potentially criminal, conditions are unfavorable for the functioning of a system of criminal law. . . ."[35] The converse is also true and goes far to account for why certain men of light and leading in this country to whom not only war crimes but "crimes" against peace and against humanity—"deeds that demand not only condemnation, but *damnation*"[36]—have been plausibly attributed are not likely to be tried for them. One has to recognize that the Nuremberg Principles have not entirely prevailed. Richard Falk suggests we are still "in a situation of transition from one world order system to another, from a statist logic"—what he calls the "Westphalia tradition"—"which is no longer adequate to a normative logic associated with the United Nations Charter and the Nuremberg Principles that does not yet pertain."[37] Arguing from the imperatives of a system of appreciations that does not yet pertain is not, as Falk in effect recognizes, a very satisfactory basis for imposing specifically criminal liability. One would first have to have a radical alternation of sentiment and public consciousness.[38]

What Falk depreciates as the Westphalia tradition did in fact form habits of honour and restraint which for a long while made impossible a reversion to the butchery and brutality endemic in the earlier European wars of religion. In the seventeenth century, one sees this new sensibility prefigured not only in Grotius' *De jure belli et pacis* but most vividly in Velasquez' painting of the Surrender at Breda—as much a portent of things to come as Picasso's painting of Guernica in our own century.

---

34. On the latter, cf. H. Arendt, "On Responsibility for Evil," in R. A. Falk, G. Kolko & R. J. Lifton, *Crimes of War* 486 (1971).

35. Q. Wright, "Proposals for an International Criminal Court," 46 *Am. J. Int'l L.* 64, 65 (1952).

36. P. L. Berger, *A Rumor of Angels* 67 (Anchor Books ed. 1970); Berger uses this expression, it is only fair to say, in another context.

37. Falk, "Nuremberg: Past, Present and Future," 80 *Yale L. J.* 1501, 1511 (1971).

38. *Id.* 1528. See also Falk, "The Question of War Crimes: A Statement of Perspective," in Falk, Kolko & Lifton, supra note 34, at 3-10.

Conventions of courtesy in the conduct of war are not entirely, as they often are said to be, Quixotic vestiges of medieval chivalry, but rather a half-conscious construction of the century that followed the Treaty of Westphalia. To be sure, there were very severe economic as well as intellectual restraints which account for the relatively moderate temper of war in the late seventeenth, the eighteenth and even the nineteenth century.[39] There are also dark places in the civilization of those centuries which, in retrospect, appear as symptoms of a serious malaise; precise models of previous culture are not of much help to us.[40] Nonetheless, I think an important part of the state of consciousness that is required if the world is to be perceptibly improved must be that strong sense of moderation and civility which characterizes the culture that came to prevail in Europe some three centuries ago. Since punishment is in essence a species of public violence, I am not sure these rather unheroic qualities can be cultivated through the medium of criminal law, except perhaps incidentally by laying stress on the extent to which it embodies a tradition of limitation and restraint.

39. See John U. Nef's studies on *War and Human Progress* (1950) and *Cultural Foundations of Industrial Civilization* (1958).

40. Cf. G. Steiner, *In Bluebeard's Castle: Some Notes Towards the Redefinition of Culture* (1972).

PART II

CODIFICATION AND REFORM OF THE CRIMINAL LAW SYSTEM

CHAPTER 5

THE BACKGROUND OF CURRENT ITALIAN PENAL LAW REFORM*

GIULIANO VASSALLI

Professor of Criminal Law, University of Rome

T HE PRESENT ITALIAN PENAL CODE has been in effect for over forty years. It entered into force on July 1, 1931, together with a new code of criminal procedure, a new set of penitentiary regulations (Rules for Institutions of Prevention and Punishment, Decree of July 18, 1931, No. 787), a new set of consolidated laws on public safety (Decree of June 18, 1931, No. 773) and the law of January 7, 1929, No. 4, which contains the general rules for the repression of violations of revenue laws and which also includes all fiscal offenses.

Forty years is not in itself an exceptionally long life-span for a penal code. One can easily think of other penal codes which have survived profound political and social change in this century as well as in the century past. It has apparently been sufficient now and then simply to amend provisions of a distinctively political character (e.g. crimes against the security of the state), or to enact special legislation dealing with particular offenses (e.g. the sale and possession of narcotic drugs, tax fraud, etc.), or to establish, again through special laws, institutions whose effectiveness was realized only at a later time (e.g. juvenile courts, probation, and the like). The French and German codes are, of course, among the most obvious and significant European examples. The French Penal Code is still the Napoleonic codification of 1810, despite the continual superimposition of special laws; the German Penal Code of 1871 has lasted for a hundred years.

What is somewhat surprising, however, about the longevity of

---

* Translated by E. M. Wise.

the Italian Penal Code is the fact that it originated as the avowed and deliberate product of a totalitarian regime, i.e. the Fascist regime of 1922-1943, but has nonetheless endured long after the overthrow of that regime and its replacement by one which is avowedly opposed to Fascism and committed to eliminate all vestiges of it. The code of 1930, defined as "Fascist" at the time it was written and entered into force, has governed Italy through twelve years of Fascism and through almost thirty years of a democratic and avowedly "anti-Fascist" regime. One need only recall that Italy was governed from June 1944 to December 1945 by a coalition of six anti-Fascist parties (the Liberal, Christian Democratic, Labor Democratic, Communist, Socialist and Action parties; the last two were not formally in the Government between October 1944 and May 1945). From January 1946 to June 1947 Italy was governed by a coalition of the Christian Democrats, Socialists, and Communists (during which time the Minister of Justice was always a Communist—for several months, the party chief, Togliatti). The governing party after June 1947 was either the Christian Democratic Party alone or a coalition in which the Christian Democrats were always the dominant partner; sometimes together with Republicans, Social Democrats, and Liberals and sometimes together with Socialists, Social Democrats, and Republicans (respectively the so-called governments of the centre, centre-right, and centre-left). Never, except for the briefest periods, were any of these governments supported by latter-day exponents of Fascism. The German Code of 1871, mentioned above, was a product of the age of Wilhelm I and Bismarck and a symbol of the unity of a recently reunited country. It was not fundamentally altered by Nazi legislation in the period 1933-1945, which was tacked on to the code only for ten or twelve years and afterwards, with the fall of Nazism, almost wholly repudiated. The situation was a very different one from that in Italy.

It may be helpful to indicate briefly some of the more general reasons why the Italian code has lasted so long without much change in its main provisions or basic structure.

First of all, the 1930 penal code forms part of an impressive complex of laws with which it is closely bound up and coordinated. We have previously mentioned the basic penal and parapenal legislation which took effect at the same time as the penal code. These laws comprise a rather imposing piece of handiwork, of the sort which is produced somewhat more easily under a vigorous authoritarian regime and which a traditional parliamentary democracy, such as Italy has had since 1946, finds it very difficult, both for structural and functional reasons, to undo in a short period of time. The Republic of Italy has sought throughout the last few decades to confront these various problems, but progress has been slow. Nothing or virtually nothing has been changed in the general law on the repression of fiscal offenses, and very little in the laws on public safety (despite a number of attempts to do so). After two legislative terms, a bill has almost been completed, authorizing the government to write a new code of criminal procedure along the lines specified in the bill. The approval of one house of Parliament has been obtained for the draft of a new penitentiary law (criticized by some as a very inadequate reform) and for the draft of a partial reform of the general part of the penal code.

Secondly, the draftsmen of the 1930 code did achieve a high technical level and perfection of statement that has induced all serious reformers to be somewhat cautious and even timorous about meddling with provisions which have become an integral part of the whole dogmatic scheme with which students of Italian criminal law are now familiar.

Thirdly, the 1930 code did, in its way, represent an advance over the preceding code of 1889. Unlike the authors of the earlier code, those of the 1930 code took into account, although in a wholly aberrant and often eccentric fashion, the radical changes produced in criminal law by the doctrines of the positivist school (e.g. with the classification of offenders, and with certain security measures) and also of new developments appearing in legislation towards the end of the last and the beginning of the present century (e.g. suspended sentences, conditional liberty, judicial pardon for juveniles). This gave the 1930 code a sufficiently fresh and modern flavor even years after its passage and in any event rendered inconceivable the pure and simple reversion to the earlier code which was expected by some in the years 1944-1945.

Fourth, there is the fact that with the passage of time the generation of lawyers and particularly magistrates who had practiced under pre-Fascist legislation (the Penal Code of 1889 and the Criminal Procedure Code of 1913) began gradually to disappear after the Second World War, so that the overwhelming majority of judges and lawyers is easily made up of those who have been educated under the code of 1930 and who are by now thoroughly habituated to its system and its mentality, even if not always fully in favor of its contents.

Finally, until a few years ago the Italian economic and social system (class structure especially) had not undergone any really profound transformation. Thus, a code worked out in the period between the two world wars has not in some respects seemed entirely ill-adapted to Italian postwar society; particularly so since apart from distinctively political provisions, it did take account, decades in advance, of certain of the changes which have been wrought in this century.

But if it takes some explaining to show why a code derived from the Fascist period has lasted throughout the life of the democratic Republic, one can more easily understand why it has been felt since 1944 that a new code or at least a major revision of the old one is definitely required.

It is true that like what was brought about a year later in Germany by the Allied Control Council, a law of 1944 (Law of July 27, 1944, No. 159, Art. 1) did provide in general terms for "the abrogation of all penal provisions enacted under auspices of institutions and political organs established by Fascism." Since 1944 the death penalty for common crimes (introduced in Italy by the 1930 code) has been abolished and characteristic features of the liberal regime abolished by Fascism in the code of 1930 have been restored; such as provision for general extenuating circumstances, allowance of the defense that a public officer was acting arbitrarily (in cases of force or threats, resistance and insults directed against public officials), and limited allowance for the "proof of truth" in cases of insult and defamation. Nevertheless, the code of 1930 was still felt by practically everyone to be unsuited to the new political and social conditions of the country and it was not merely for the sake of principle or simply to keep up appearances that it was thought necessary to have a new penal code for the newly restored Italian democracy. On August 31, 1944, while war and civil war were still raging in many parts of Italian territory, the Rome Government used its legislative authority to make provision "for the reform of the criminal laws and for the drafting of a new penal code and a new code of criminal procedure fully conforming to the legal traditions of the Italian people." On January 2, 1945, a ministerial committee for revision of the penal code was appointed.

Since that time there has been a long succession of proposals and reform projects.[1] These have been sometimes for complete, sometimes for partial revision of the code; sometimes on government, sometimes on private members initiative (the latter only for partial revision). These have all led up, after more than a quarter of a century, to the current reform bill. Although limited to the general part of the penal code, it is the first draft to have gained the approval of a house of Parliament, the Senate. It has therefore a fairly good chance of being enacted into law during the sixth Legislature, which opened in 1972.

Indeed, since 1944-1945, the case for reform can only have been strengthened. What at first were merely formal reasons have become substantial reasons for reform. One need only point to the following facts:

(1) The fact that the courts have become increasingly uncertain about how to interpret the effects of the explicit and implicit abrogation of institutions and rules introduced by the Fascist regime. This has created a conspicuous and often dangerous state of uncertainty in the law, e.g. in connection with charges of a political character (unlawful associations, unlaw-

---

1. For detailed information about government-sponsored projects up to 1960, see my entry under "Codice penale" in 7 *Enciclopedia del diritto* 227 (1960). For an analysis of the same, see Dean, "Die Entwurfe zur Aenderung des Codice Penale vol. 1949/50, 1956 und 1960 im Lichte der italienischen Strafrechtswissenschaft." 75 *Zeitschrift für die Gesamte Strafrechtswissenschaft* 1, 131.

ful propaganda) or of an economic character (strikes, lock-outs, disruption of public services, etc.).

(2) The new Constitution which was approved by the Constituent Assembly in 1947 and which took effect on January 1, 1948, contains certain basic rules of criminal law which conflict in several respects with unrepealed and unreformed provisions of the 1930 Code, e.g. those pertaining to criminal responsibility for the acts of others, to the purposes of punishment, to extradition, and to political offenses.

(3) Experience with certain basic institutions has shown they are badly adapted to the war against crime and the treatment of delinquency and that there is need to find new rules and new methods of treatment.

(4) The fact that new forms of criminality have appeared and the consequent necessity of bringing up to date many of the sections of the special part of the penal code.

The reform bill now being considered in Parliament is responsive to most of these exigencies (even if it is not a wholly adequate response).

As previously pointed out, the predecessor of the current Italian code dated from 1889 and was in force for about forty years —from January 1, 1890 to July 1, 1931. It was referred to as the Zanardelli Code after the Minister of Justice who introduced the final draft on which it was based and who was also one of the chief proponents of reform during the decade which preceded it. It is still known and cited by this name not only in Italy but also in other countries which, like Turkey, adopted it almost in toto or in which it was profoundly influential, as it was in many states of Latin America. The Zanardelli Code was the first criminal code for Unified Italy. Even so, it took eleven drafts and nearly thirty years of work and was only enacted twenty-nine years after Italian unification (1861) and twenty-four years after the effective date of the new civil code (1865) and of the first code of criminal procedure (1865).

Despite a certain modernity, its balanced and equitable structure, and the crystal clarity of its provisions which were the work of a generation of great jurists, experienced practitioners and of eminent political men, this code, not only because of the long labor which went into it, was not born young. It fell short of the level reached by those new currents which galvanized criminal law towards the end of the nineteenth century. For example, it virtually ignored all criminological typologies and made no provision either for the conditional suspension of punishment (which was not introduced in Italy until 1904) or for the judicial pardon of juveniles who it subjected to criminal punishment if they had reached the age of nine and acted "with discernment." Even if there had not been a radical change of political regime as there was in 1922 and the substitution of a totalitarian for a liberal-democratic system, and a dictator like Mussolini, anxious to leave his own name on new legislation, the Zanardelli Code would have been revised sometime or other after the First World War. Ferri's famous draft of 1921, well-known as one of the leading products of the Positivist School, was not drawn up as the isolated and abstract work of a celebrated scholar but rather upon the instructions of the Government of the day acting on the basis of a Royal Decree of 1919 which had appointed a ministerial commission "for reform of the criminal laws in harmony with rational principles and methods for the defense of society against crime in general and more effective and reliable protection against habitual delinquency." Lawmakers of the Fascist period therefore found the ground was already prepared for reform of the penal code for reasons having nothing to do with the shift in political system or the peculiar needs of the Fascist regime in fighting its political enemies. This last set of needs, moreover, was quickly met with the law of November 25, 1926, No. 2008, which introduced a series of formerly unknown political offenses, the death penalty for the more serious political crimes, and the "Special Tribunal for the Defense of the State" (that is, for the defense of the Fascist regime).

The Minister of Justice, Alfredo Rocco (from whom the Italian Code of 1930 traditionally takes its name),[2] did in fact point to these general considerations when in 1925 he requested

---

2. From now on I will refer to the code of 1889 as the Zanardelli code and to the code of 1930 as the Rocco code. With regard to the latter code, it is, however, only fair to mention that one of its principal architects—particularly so far as technical matters are concerned—was Professor Arturo Rocco, brother of the Minister and a professor of criminal law (the Minister Rocco was a professor of commercial law).

authorization from Parliament to reform the penal code. In his report to the Chamber and the Senate he referred particularly to the "not unimportant increase in criminality during past years, especially in the postwar period, owing to causes . . . difficult to discover in their whole complexity, but which all derive ultimately from the profound changes produced in the psychology and spirit of the individual and the community and in the conditions of economic and social life as a consequence of the Great War" and to the consequent "necessity of putting into the hands of the State more adequate legal means for conducting the war against crime."

Among the defects of the criminal law in force up to that time he mentioned specifically "the absolute unfitness of punishments to counteract the serious and worrying phenomena of habitual delinquency, juvenile delinquency, and the delinquency of the dangerously mentally ill." This was taken to indicate "the need to provide in the penal code not only the usual and traditional measures of repression but also new and more carefully contrived means for preventing criminality" and particularly the need to bring into being certain auxiliary institutions which would serve as a substitute for traditional punishments: all of which seems to be in line with the teachings of the positivist school and with other modern criminological tendencies.

The inspiration of the Rocco reform was thus twofold. On the one hand it aimed at a very great severity in dealing with delinquency. This was justified in terms of the defense of the State and of those individual and communal interests which were held worthy of penal protection. On the other hand it introduced new institutions which were thought to reflect more up-to-date notions about the prevention of crime, such as measures of security and other complementary provisions, like the judicial pardon for juveniles. It envisioned a close merger of the penal and the penitentiary systems, and sought to promote "rationality" in criminal justice by simultaneous abolition of both the popular jury and the unreasoned verdict.

These two sources of inspiration nonetheless worked in the same direction—towards greater severity of treatment. The great harshness of the Rocco Code as compared with the Zanardelli

Code, can be traced basically to three general tendencies: (1) to increase both the minimum and maximum punishment provided for a single offense, to increase the number of aggravating circumstances set out both in the general and in the special part of the code, and particularly to drastically increase punishment in cases of multiple infractions of the penal law; (2) to resort to so-called objective criminal responsibility; (3) the insistence that measures of security should be added on to the punishment of a responsible or partially responsible delinquent, rather than allowing the one to serve in lieu of the other. A system of punishments even more severe than the one which preceded it was juxtaposed beside a system of measures of security which could be imposed on responsible offenders only together with punishment and which was thus harsher than punishment standing alone. The single exception, although this unfortunately is mostly theoretical, was the juvenile criminal law. The Rocco Code raised the age of criminal capacity (i.e., the age at which punishments may be imposed in cases of recognizable maturity) from nine to fourteen years. It expressly authorized detentive punishment aimed solely at the child's moral reeducation and it permitted judicial pardon of the first offense attributable to minors up to eighteen years in cases where a detentive punishment not exceeding one year would otherwise be imposed.[3]

The authors of the Rocco Code did explicitly declare that they were inspired by a eclectic vision rather than by the teachings of any particular criminological school and that they aimed at taking "from each school only that part of it which is sound and true, not caring much to create a logically perfect statutory system which carries one-sided theoretical principles to extreme limits, but very much concerned, instead, to frame a system which will draw all the schools together into the unity of a higher organism fit to serve the real needs and actual exigencies of the life of society and of the State."[4] This avowed eclecticism is apparent in

3. In the subsequent law of July 20, 1934, No. 1404, the possibility of judicial pardon was extended to cases in which a detentive punishment not exceeding two years would otherwise be imposed.

4. Relazione del ministro Rocco al Re, §1, in VII *Lavori preparatori del codice penale e del codice di procedura penale* n. 13 (Roma, 1930).

a great number of the code's basic provisions. Nevertheless, it is a very singular eclecticism which almost always involves trying to lay the postulates of different schools side by side in order ultimately to arrive at intimidative punishment and to enable the war against crime and the fear of crime to be fought with every available means and without quarter.

What seems particularly interesting about this "eclecticism" with regard to criminological schools is the use to which the authors of the Rocco Code put the proposals of the positivist school. The positivists had called for a more concentrated and determined fight against criminality which would take account of personal dangerousness and of the offense as a symptom of dangerousness; but at the same time they also called for individualized treatment, which they proposed again and again to substitute for traditional punishments, even though it would result in a more rigorous regime and in indeterminate "criminal sanctions." The Rocco Code instead combines the special prevention of dangerousness through measures of security with the imposition of retributive punishment, without allowing for any reciprocal interconnection between the two.[5] The positivist school had proposed placing greater emphasis on the individual's state of mind, so far as it bears on his dangerousness. The Rocco Code enlarges the sphere of punishable activity by carrying it back in time to incidents of mere preparation: it punishes political conspiracies which consist only of an agreement not followed by any overt act (Art. 304) and it extends the scope of punishable attempts (Art. 56), but it wholly disregards the symptomatic character of the act and simply applies the ordinary and traditional tests of punishability. The positivist school had emphasized the

---

5. An extreme instance of the absurdity to which the lack of any osmosis between punishment and security measures can be carried is Article 148; according to this provision, if a convicted person (who was responsible at the time of the offense) becomes mentally ill after sentence is imposed or in the course of the execution of a punishment and must consequently be transferred to a mental hospital, once he has recovered he must then be returned to prison to resume serving the detentive punishment at the point at which it was interrupted, without any possibility of being credited (except through pardon) with the time he was deprived of liberty in the mental hospital, which may have been, as happens in not a few cases, a considerable period of time.

concept of "social responsibility" in order to underscore the un-acceptability of criteria for combating crime based on a distinction between responsible and irresponsible persons and to direct the attention of legislators and judges to criminal acts committed by irresponsible individuals—all with the idea of promoting carefully individualized treatment. The Rocco Code turns this into a reason for applying ordinary standards of punishment even to the acts of incapacitated individuals, e.g., acts committed by persons who are totally intoxicated at the time of the offense.

The positivist school had called attention, if not strictly speaking, to the "born delinquent," to those who have a tendency to delinquency and emphasized that they too required integrated and individualized treatment. The Rocco Code created the curious figure of the "delinquent by tendency" (in connection with crimes of violence) who is fully responsible but subjected first to punishment and then to measures of security in a house of labor or an agricultural colony (Art. 108 and 216).

Finally, the positivist school had insisted on the need to exercise continuing supervision over an offender after the criminal sanction had been carried out. The Rocco Code drew from this a justification for the stringent imposition of supervised liberty on those released after serving long detentive punishments (Art. 230, No. 1), for attaching high penalties to recidivism and for subjecting habitual delinquents to practically indeterminate sentences.

The sort of criticism of the Rocco Code which we have outlined in no way diminishes the genuine strengths and great merits which it does have. These are seen particularly in its scrupulous respect for the principle of legality in the specification of crimes and punishments,[6] its sensitivity to the problems of international cooperation in penal matters, in the clarity of most of its provisions with regard to offenses in general and its definitions of the particular offenses contained in the special part, in its informed craftsmanship, its careful internal and external correlations, the

---

6. It was this feature (condemned as "liberal" by certain German writers during the Nazi era) which in 1945 led prominent jurists to favor retaining the Rocco Code.

modernity of its language, and in the sense of criminal law scholarship which it reflects. The weak spot of the code lies rather in
its system of sanctions—in the means with which it chooses to
fight crime and to treat offenders. But it is this very fact which
makes it so difficult to bring about a genuine reform of the
code. Such a reform will have to be guided by an even more systematic and ideologically current vision than that which inspired
the Rocco Code and will have to be supported by new institutions
for the adequate treatment of offenders—of the sort which
Rocco himself anticipated in criticizing the defects of the system
in effect under the Zanardelli Code, but which in Italy are still a
long way from being anything other than a paper reality.

The current reform was preceded by many earlier projects, as
to which there is an authoritative literature.[7] The present proposals are largely taken from ministerial drafts of 1956 and
1960, but turn these into only a partial reform of the penal code,
as well as from some of the more important proposals which
originated in Parliament in the form of private member bills.
The basic source of the current reform is Bill No. 351, introduced in the Senate on November 19, 1968, by the Minister of
Justice, Dr. Gonella (at which time the President of the
Council of Ministers was the current President of the Republic,
the criminal law scholar Professor Leone). Only the "general
part" of the bill was considered by the Senate during the course
of the fifth Legislature (1968-1972). After preliminary consideration, the bill was divided into two parts: Bill 351 A on
"Amendments to the first book and to Articles 576 and 577 of the
Penal Code," and Bill 351 B dealing with the special part of the
code, i.e., with all offenses other than aggravated homicide
(which is the subject of Articles 576 and 577). The first part of
this reform (Bill 351 A) was approved by the Senate in July
1971, but the Chamber of Deputies was not able to consider the

---

7. Besides Dean's paper, cited in note 1, *supra*, see also the important study by
Nuvolone, "Alle soglie di una riforma," [1964] *Rivista italiana di diritto e procedura
penale* 365, which deals particularly with the 1963 government bill, which was
ultimately lost.

project at all due to the early dissolution of the legislature.[8] The Senate itself did not get around to examining Bill 351 B during the fifth Legislature. At the beginning of the sixth Legislature in the late spring of 1972, the Andreotti Government reintroduced in the new Senate (with the new designation of Bill No. 372) the text of the bill (No. 351 A) which had been approved by the Senate during the preceding year, together with the recommendation that account be taken of the amendments to that bill which I myself, as reporter for the Chamber of Deputies, had proposed in my working paper of October, 1971, but which the Chamber had not been able to consider. Between August 1972 and January 1973, the Senate worked rather quickly through the new bill and the amendments to it, taking advantage of the "abbreviated procedure" permitted by its rules for projects already approved by the same house of Parliament during a preceding Legislature. The formal text passed the Senate and was sent to the Chamber of Deputies on February 2, 1973, although the Chamber has not yet been able to take it up. The Government at the end of the summer of 1973 had not reintroduced in the sixth Legislature any project dealing with the special part of the Code. Therefore with regard to the special part, one has to rely primarily on the original bill of 1968 although account must also be taken, in connection with certain political offenses and offenses having political overtones, of another bill which represents a very decided improvement over that of 1968 and which was put ahead of the rest of the reform of the special part and even approved by the Senate of the Republic in 1971.[9] The bill

---

8. In the Chamber of Deputies, during the fifth Legislature, matters did not advance beyond the submission of a working paper by the author of the present article, which also suggested a series of amendments of a technical character. In the Chamber of Deputies, throughout the fifth Legislature, Senate Bill No. 351 A was assigned No. 3499. The equivalent bills in the sixth Legislature have been assigned No. 372 in the Senate and No. 1614 in the Chamber.

9. This bill also was not brought up for consideration by the Chamber of Deputies before the dissolution of the fifth Legislature. In connection with this bill, too, the present writer was able to prepare a report for the Chamber, which recommended its passage without amendment. In the Chamber of Deputies, throughout the fifth Legislature, this bill was assigned No. 3705. It has not been reintroduced by the Government during the current Legislature, but is before the Senate (as Bill No. 54) on the initiative of the parliamentary members of the Socialist Party.

referred to—Senate Bill No. 1445, on the "abrogation and modification of certain provisions of the Penal Code"—was introduced by the center-left government in 1971 and partly adopted certain proposals put forward by the parties of the left and by a wing of the Christian Democrats. Since it already met with the approval of one house of Parliament during the last Legislature, it is probable that the text of this bill will ultimately form part of the official program for reform of the Penal Code.

These are the official proposals current in Italy at the beginning of the sixth republican Legislature. Since this Legislature is supposed to last for five years, presumably these proposals will run the full legislative gamut. They are worth careful study. Some are truly innovative. Nonetheless, one has ultimately to conclude that on the whole and for the reasons mentioned above, the revision of the penal code which is now in progress in Italy scarcely approaches anything that might be considered a definitive and truly satisfactory reform. The current effort aims to adapt the code to changed political, constitutional and international circumstances, to round out certain imperfect rules, to eliminate obvious or incontestable defects, to soften somewhat its severity, and to bring it closer to the principles of responsibility based on fault and of actual dangerousness on the part of persons deemed dangerous. But a true reform would require precisely what is lacking in Italy: on the one hand a clear conception of the most effective means of preventing crime; on the other the existence of modern penal establishments and devices for the individualization of treatment and the resocialization of offenders —let alone an adequate system of other institutions and services. The reform presently in progress must be regarded as a stop-gap measure, which will have a positive effect only if followed up with further penal legislation (like the long-awaited statute on probation) and with suitable institutions for the realization of a rational and clearly articulated penal policy.

CHAPTER 6

A GUIDE TO STATE CRIMINAL CODE REVISION

B. J. GEORGE, JR.

Professor of Law and Director of the Center for the Administration of Justice, Wayne State University

THE NEED FOR CRIMINAL CODE REVISION

WELL INTO THE NINETEENTH CENTURY the criminal law of the United States was basically common law, augmented by piecemeal statutes to cover some of the most obvious gaps and inadequacies. The common law system was one under which definitions of crime evolved out of a mass of judicial decisions. If changes in definition were required, judges accomplished them through new decisions which were retroactive as far as the particular defendant was concerned. The process of the common law thus was "one of blundering along from case to case and hoping gradually to achieve certainty."[1]

In the midnineteenth century with New York and California the leading examples, a majority of the states, particularly those west of the Mississippi River, codified their criminal law, at the same time abolishing common law crimes. However, by the last quarter of the nineteenth century, the force of the codification movement was largely spent. Few states thereafter joined the ranks of code states; for the most part the revisions that took place were cosmetic only. Meanwhile, successive legislatures in each state reacted to new problems not by a thorough recodification but by individual statutes to meet specific cases. These statutes tended increasingly to overlap one another, to carry incompatible punishments, and to use words in inconsistent fashion. Many states began to arrange criminal statutes alphabetically ac-

---

1. Miller, "Criminal Law—An Agency for Social Control," 43 *Yale L. J.* 691, 702 (1934).

cording to the names of the crimes; such an arrangement inevitably obscures the kinds of harms aimed at by the criminal law and the relationship that one crime bears to others in terms of seriousness or degree. In addition, the welter of criminal statutes still lacked the virtue of comprehensiveness. Definitions of important basic matters like intent, causation, mental defect, intoxication, mistake and self-defense rarely were included, so that for all practical purposes decisional law had to be resorted to fully as much as in the common law era.

This is the condition in many states of the criminal law today. However, the nation is in the midst of a new codification movement that in the latter part of this century can transform the criminal law at least as much as last century's codifications did through abrogation of the common law. The greatest single force behind the new revisions is undoubtedly the American Law Institute's Model Penal Code.[2] Intended as a model on which states might pattern their own statutes, it covers the four major areas of (1) general concepts of criminality, (2) specific definitions of crime, (3) treatment and correction, and (4) organization of corrections. Particularly the first two segments have had substantial influence on new state codes and drafts.

Ten states[3] had revised criminal codes in effect by the close of 1972 and four others[4] had enacted revisions to take effect in 1973 or later. Twelve jurisdictions[5] had completed revisions not yet approved by legislatures, eleven others[6] had revision projects under way, while in four states[7] revision studies had been authorized.

---

2. *Model Penal Code* (Proposed Official Draft, 1962) .

3. Colorado, Connecticut, Georgia, Illinois, Kansas, Louisiana, Minnesota, New Mexico, New York and Wisconsin. The Illinois, Louisiana, Minnesota and Wisconsin codes were enacted before the influence of the Model Penal Code was felt. Idaho approved a revised code in 1972 but repealed it four months later.

4. Hawaii, Kentucky, New Hampshire and Oregon.

5. Alaska, Delaware, Maryland, Massachusetts, Michigan, Montana, Pennsylvania, Puerto Rico, Texas, Vermont, Washington and the proposed Federal Criminal Code.

6. Alabama, California, Florida, Iowa, Missouri, Nebraska, New Jersey, North Carolina, Ohio, Rhode Island and South Carolina.

7. Arizona, North Dakota, Oklahoma and Virginia.

DRAFTING ORGANIZATIONS

Effective code revision requires an appropriate drafting group eligible to receive federal or state funding and supplementary foundation or private support. Several alternatives exist: A special legislative commission (as in California and New York), an augmented legislative committee (as in Colorado), an executive commission convened by the governor (as in Delaware and Massachusetts) or by the attorney general (as in Missouri and North Carolina), a state bar committee (as in Illinois, Michigan and Texas), or a committee sponsored by the judiciary (as in Arkansas and Hawaii).

At an early stage, those who create the drafting organization must decide the scope of the revision effort. The easiest path may appear to be a limited or partial modernization of the criminal law. However, few definitions of crimes exist in isolation, so that a fundamental change in the definition of larceny, for example, may have great impact on crimes like robbery, fraudulent obtaining of property and receiving. Alteration of the language of a homicide statute may affect the scope of traditional defenses like self-defense. Code revision like pregnancy usually goes to term.

The decision about the scope of criminal code revision will dictate in large measure the choice of drafting agency. If a modest partial revision is the objective, then perhaps a legislative subcommittee is the most economical device. If a complete revision is projected in a state of any size and wealth, a legislative or executive commission is the better choice. An adequately-funded special commission is the only device through which a comprehensively revised criminal code can be drafted within a fairly short period of time.

The process of creating a drafting organization also serves to test the degree of actual interest on the part of policy makers in code reform. Indeed, the principal advantage of a legislative commission is that its creation requires at least tentative legislative commitment to criminal code revision; while this is no guarantee of the result, there seems to be a substantial correlation between legislative creation of the drafting agency and ultimate acceptance of its proposals.

The selection of the membership of the drafting organ is the single most critical stage as far as the code project itself is concerned. Designation of the chairperson is likewise momentous. Critical policy decisions must also be reached about drafting responsibilities.

If a code revision project is to be completed within two years, two full-time reporters (usually law professors) are an essential minimum and three are preferable. In some states, all drafts are discussed by the entire commission. In others, the commission is divided into drafting subcommittees to work with individual reporters. A subcommittee structure may expedite the revision process provided each smaller committee is representative of the commission as a whole, and each commission member is willing to accept the drafts of other subcommittees than his own as presumptively valid. If everything is exhaustively redone in plenary commission meetings, then the subcommittee structure may delay rather than accelerate completion of the project.

TECHNIQUES OF EFFECTIVE STATUTE DRAFTING
Scope of the Drafting Effort

Even if the decision is to make a complete revision, the commission must still decide at the outset how "total" that will be. Some limitations surely will be placed on the coverage of the new code. Obvious candidates for exclusion include the motor vehicle code, securities regulations, pure food and drug laws, and building construction codes. Firearms control is another area that may be selected for exclusion, as is the regulation of drugs in a state that has enacted the Uniform Controlled Substances Act corresponding to the Federal Controlled Substances Act of 1971. Therapeutic abortion, one of the most controversial subjects a drafting commission will face, can be left for special handling as a bill affecting medical licensure.[8] A drafting commission that rec-

---

8. An approach strongly impelled by the United States Supreme Court's decisions on constitutional requirements for valid abortion legislation. *Roe v. Wade*, 410 U.S. 113 (1973) ; *Doe v. Bolton*, 410 U.S. 179 (1973) .

ognizes danger as it starts, acts prudently if it promptly discards its losers.

An important mechanical task that should be performed immediately is a section-by-section study of the entire body of statute law of the state to extract and photocopy in multiple copies every statute that carries criminal penalties. Only in this way can the reporters decide which existing provisions can be merged into new consolidated sections, and which must be preserved as individual sections in the new code or in other statutes. If cross-indexed files showing the recommended disposition of each section are maintained, most of the necessary work will have been performed to compile a list of statutes that must be repealed or amended by the time the new code goes into effect. These files are also valuable aids in preparing section commentaries. Case law need not be compiled this systematically because the new code itself should replace inconsistent precedent. A reporter, however, should research cases for inclusion in his commentary, as well as the history and interpretation of individual sections.

Structure and Style

The reporters should prepare a projected table of contents for the code as an early order of priority. As related earlier, many older codes arrange crimes alphabetically by title. The new drafts uniformly organize provisions into two main heads, the so-called "General Part" in which provisions applicable to all crimes are placed, and the "Special Part" in which individual crimes are to be found. Chapter headings in the general part often include culpability, parties, justification, responsibility, inchoate crimes, disposition of offenders, probation, imprisonment, fines, and general definitions. The special part is organized according to the harms which related crimes are designed to prevent. For example, offenses involving danger to the person will include homicide, assaults, kidnapping and violent sex offenses. Offenses involving damage to and intrusion upon property comprise burglary and trespass, criminal damage to property, and arson. Theft offenses are drawn together, as are crimes of forgery and fraud. An examination of chapters and sections within a title reveals clearly how many offenses work together comprehensively to control harmful conduct.

The contemporary code pattern also is to relate offenses within a given chapter in a degree gradation, the first-degree category bearing the heaviest penalty. Functionally speaking, the lowest degree of an offense is the least complicated, with the fewest elements and least specific mental element, while the highest degree is usually characterized by narrowly drawn requirements and specific intent or knowledge. For example, third-degree burglary may be defined as knowing entry into or unlawful remaining in a building with intent to commit there a crime against person or property, while first-degree burglary requires that the building be a dwelling and the criminal armed.

Hierarchies of sections may in turn be related in ascending and descending order to one another. For example, ascending degrees of criminal trespass blend into additional degrees of burglary, while degrees of false imprisonment meld into degrees of kidnapping. Perhaps a majority of sections defining crimes will carry this sort of reciprocal relationship.

There are practical advantages in this. As far as the code itself is concerned, a degree format minimizes overlap between criminal statutes and so eliminates the possibility that a prosecutor can cumulate charges for what essentially is a single act or transaction. The degree arrangement also facilitates plea negotiations. The availability of lesser degrees enables the negotiators to rank the possible pleas and control the outside limits of punishment that can be imposed. The scope of a jury's power to render a valid verdict is also more evident under a topical degree system than it is under a code arranged alphabetically.

There is no need for statutes to be phrased in cumbersome, repetitive, archaic language, and there are several helpful techniques a draftsman may use to achieve clarity. One is to provide definitional sections whenever possible. Many existing statutes at least appear unintelligible because definitions of terms are run into the text immediately after those terms. The definitional section avoids this. Some terms that appear frequently throughout the code can be defined in the general part. Definitions common to a chapter can be placed in a separate section at the beginning of that chapter, those controlling a series of sections at the beginning of the series, and those affecting a single section as a separate subsection within it. Indexing is of course important to the ultimate user of a code constructed in this way and a reader may need to examine two or three sections before he understands what is intended, but the fact that a definition of crime has been stripped down into its component parts by the drafter is of great help.

In the same way, exceptions from coverage are usually clearer when they are set apart either in separate sections toward the end of a chapter or series of sections, or made a separate subsection. Examples are consent to some kinds of sexual activity, marital status in theft, and belief of eligibility to remarry in bigamy. As a variation of this, if a traditional exception is to be eliminated, for example, a claim of right to property taken at gunpoint, an appropriate subsection will begin, "It is no defense in a prosecution under this section that. . . ."

Simplicity of definition sometimes is enhanced through cross-references to other parts of the code or to other statutes. For example, what is "property" for theft becomes "property" for robbery through a suitable cross-reference. If "snowmobile" is defined at length in a licensing statute, there is no need to develop another definition for a criminal code section on unauthorized use of a vehicle; a cross-reference to the existing statute suffices.

The purpose of a statute should be to inform those who read it about what the legislative draftsmen wanted them to know. Therefore, simple, direct words usually are best. Instead of "carnal knowledge," the phrase "sexual intercourse" will do nicely; instead of "the abominable and detestable crime against nature" for sodomy, the term "deviate sexual intercourse" serves well, particularly when that phrase is further defined as "any act of sexual gratification involving the sex organs of one person and the mouth or anus of another." Someone of delicate sensibilities may not like the definition, but at least he knows the meaning.

The meaning of words constantly shifts. If one were to solicit definitions for the word "malice" from a lay group it is unlikely that the legal definition, "intent," would be found among them. The word "lunatic" probably would receive a wider array of potential applications than lawyers or judges might accord it. Because many inherited words relate to the mental element of crime, the universal response of code drafters, following the example of the Model Penal Code, is to select four terms for criminal intent—intentionally (or purposely), knowingly, recklessly, and with criminal negligence, define them as precisely as possible in lay terms, and use them consistently throughout the code. Many archaic terms are eliminated in this way.

Sometimes new lay terms are selected to prevent inherited legal doctrines from being incorporated in the new law. For example, the traditional common-law definition of "larceny" has been "the taking and carrying away of personal property in the legal possession of another with intent to deprive the owner permanently of his property." Each component carries with it a gloss of thousands of decisions which together often provide inadequate protection against theft. If "larceny" is used in a new code, judges and lawyers may prefer to assume that the new statute incorporates the old law, rather than to read the new text. Use of the word "theft," which has no established common-law meaning, may curb this tendency. As another illustration, if the term "false pretenses" has been construed to exclude promissory fraud, statements of future acts or events that the actor does not believe will occur but wishes to encourage his victim to expect, then it is better to substitute the word "deception" in the new code and define it.

Naturally, statutes as communications can be no more explicit than the language permits. No one can provide a precise definition for words like "reasonable," "substantial," "serious," "protracted" or "unjustifiable." They nevertheless must be used because no clear-cut line can be drawn between some kinds of harmful acts, usually unintended, that merit criminal penalties and others that can be left to private compensatory actions. Words like these are a formal invitation to juries to use their common sense and to decide in the particular case on behalf of the community how far penal sanctions will extend. Carried too far, use of undefinable words may invite an attack on grounds of constitutional vagueness, but a certain number of them are appropriate and even necessary.

Commentaries play an especially important role in this regard because they serve as a helpful source of explanation and illustration. With them, a court may be persuaded a term has meaning that otherwise it would tend to find impermissibly vague.

In the final analysis, the best guarantee against vagueness is for the drafter to know what he wishes to say before he begins to say it. If a commission or drafting subcommittee can first list tentatively the acts it would like to penalize and those it would exclude from coverage, and characterize the state of mind an offender should have, the draftsman's task is much simplified. If objectives are unclear, statutory language also will be unclear.

The matter of selection of statutory structure and language is not as difficult for a commission that begins its work today as it would have been a decade ago. The early revisers had few examples; those today have many. While the background work of extracting criminal statutes from the entire body of legislation and deciding on the scope of the revised code must be done anew in each state, the draftsman has several excellent examples from which he can draw his initial drafts. This alone may enable a draft to be completed in less than two years, while even five years ago three years might have been required.

MAJOR PROBLEMS OF SUBSTANTIVE COVERAGE

A code revision commission, if it carefully studies the codes prepared by its predecessors in other states, can identify the areas which will consume most of its time. Most of the major ones follow.

Jurisdiction

"Jurisdiction" as a legal term covers a great many things. For purposes of the criminal code, it means the competence of the legislature to penalize activity. A particularly serious problem concerns the extent to which a state may penalize persons who act beyond its borders to threaten or work harm within. The power of a state to regulate the activities of anyone physically present within its boundaries is clear; some traditional statements of law seem also to say that presence within the state is required (so-called territorial jurisdiction), and that no further power exists. However, it is generally accepted today that a state has the power, if it wishes to exercise it, to penalize those who act beyond its borders to commit harm within and to control the acts of its own residents wherever they are.

Several of the new proposals, therefore, follow the pattern of Model Penal Code §1.03 by recognizing that acts outside a state may be punishable under the appropriate penal provision if they work harm within the state's borders. This accentuates a problem that has long existed, the possibility of punishment imposed by two governments for the same act or transaction. An example is an interstate automobile theft. There is at present no constitutional bar to three prosecutions of the thief: (1) larceny of the automobile in the state in which it was taken; (2) larceny in the state to which it was taken; and (3) federal transportation of a stolen vehicle in interstate commerce. If three prosecutions do not in fact occur, it is because of the exercise of administrative discretion. Other examples of the same thing include robbery of a bank within the Federal Reserve System, interstate transportation of prostitutes, narcotics transactions, and any crime on a federal reservation over which the state has not absolutely ceded its powers.

If a state legislates on the pattern of the Model Penal Code, it increases the scope of overlap. A fraudulent scheme taking effect in Michigan or Arizona, for example, could be prosecuted in Canada or the United States or Mexico as well, if the conspirators met there. A similar scheme launched in Ohio to take effect in Colorado could be prosecuted in both states.

The draftsman's response, patterned on Model Penal Code §1.10, is to make earlier prosecution by one of the governments having concurrent power to prosecute (jurisdiction) pleadable as a reason for nonprosecution by the others. Although this may do violence to traditional theory, it has strong support as a fairer approach to prosecution.

Culpability

"Culpability" refers to the states of mind or attitudes of those whose actions, objectively speaking, fit within a definition of crime. It covers the mental element of crime, what classically is referred to as mens rea.

Inherited criminal statutes are inconsistent in their descriptions of the mental attitude a person must have before his physical acts violate them. Part of the problem is archaic language ("malice," "abandoned and malignant heart"). But the greater part stems from a legislative failure to be consistent. Some very minor offenses may have a lengthy epithetical description of the mental state required, while heavily-punished felony statutes may express no required state of mind at all. As a result, the actual task of defining the state of mind appropriate to each crime has been largely that of the courts.

The new codes consistently use only four categories of mental state or culpability: (1) intentionally (or purposely), which means the actor has the conscious objective of acting or producing the prohibited harm; (2) knowingly, which means that the actor is aware that he is acting or that circumstances defined in the specific criminal statute exist; (3) recklessly, in that the actor is aware that his projected activity poses a substantial and unjustifiable risk of harm or injury, but proceeds anyway; and (4) with criminal negligence, which indicates that the actor did not in fact see the potentially harmful consequences of activity he was about to engage in, although a person of average or standard perception would have, so that the defendant's failure amounted to "a gross deviation" from the normal standard of care. As each specific definition of crime is drafted, one or more of the culpability alternatives are written in; degree grading of related offenses also rests in large part on the culpability elements included.

A major purpose of the new codes is to limit so-called "strict liability" offenses, by creating in effect a presumption that one of the culpability alternatives attaches to every criminal statute, whether in the criminal code or elsewhere in the state's compiled laws. Under a strict liability statute, one whose acts contravene a statute is held responsible even though he was unaware that the specific act occurred, and fully intended and expected to comply with the law. Laws regulating business activities and commodities are commonly strict liability offenses. Strict liability is absolutely necessary to effective enforcement of certain standards.

However, a code revision commission may do well to view every instance in which strict liability is necessary to enforcement as also prime for decriminalization. Any person or business operating under a license or other form of administrative supervision can be assessed penalties for violation of regulations, receive suspension of his license or have it revoked entirely. These are effective sanctions that can be imposed swiftly through administrative action reviewable in a civil action on the same basis as any other administrative decision. If greater use is made of administrative penalties, the burden on courts of minor criminal jurisdiction can be measurably eased. Criminal sanctions can then be reserved for chronic, deliberate violators whose culpable state of mind can readily be proven.

There are four other factors that also bear on culpability: mistake, mental condition, intoxication and immaturity. All are likely to be troublesome.

Mistake

The inherited common-law tradition gave only limited recognition to mistaken belief on the part of one whose acts cause harm. Mistakes of law fell into two categories. Error about the coverage of the statute under which one was prosecuted, or indeed unawareness of its very existence, was legally immaterial: "ignorance of the law is no excuse." This rule held even though the defendant had no way to find out about the enactment of the statute under which he was punished (for example, he was at sea at the time), or had received advice of counsel to act as he did. Nor could he rely on an administrative decision or lower court ruling. If, however, his mistake went to some other area of law, for example, the law governing ownership of property, and that error negated a required specific purpose or intent, then evidence of the mistake could be heard by the jury as a "collateral mistake of law." Larceny of property thought mistakenly to be one's own has been a classic illustration.

Mistakes of fact were less hedged by restrictions. The basic test was whether the defendant's belief that facts existed which did not indeed exist negated specific intent or knowledge required under the statute. If the defendant donned in a restaurant a coat, identical in make, color and size to his own, which later turned out to belong to someone else, his intent could hardly have been to "deprive the owner of his property." One conceptually troubling limitation found in the law of some states, however, was that the mistaken belief had to be "reasonable." One who was "unreasonable" became criminal. Since criminal negligence in effect involves an unreasonable mistake about the true situation, this meant that many crimes could become commitable through criminal negligence, which usually was not intended to be the case.

The new proposals generally accept any mistake of fact if it bears on the culpability element in the criminal statute, collateral mistake of law on the same basis, and even mistakes about the criminal statute under which the prosecution is brought if the defendant has relied on advice or a ruling by a government officer or agency qualified to interpret the provision. This should eliminate some of the unfair results reached in the past. Reasonableness also generally is not a limitation on mistake.

Mental Condition

Perhaps the most consistently troublesome problem in criminal law has been the extent to which abnormal mental condition should relieve one from amenability to criminal processes. Judges and legislatures have struggled for generations to formulate a test meaningful to jurors, under which those whose mental condition precludes choice or control can be diverted from the criminal justice system by an acquittal based on abnormal mental condition ("insanity"). Until recently, most states followed the so-called *M'Naghten Rule,* set forth by the English House of Lords in 1843, which defines "insanity" (a legal, not a medical term) as either lack of awareness that the defendant is acting, or a lack of awareness based on his mental condition, that the act performed is "wrong." The *M'Naghten* opinion itself, and a few American states that relied on it, also had an "insane delusion" alternative under which the actor was to be acquitted if the situation as the defendant deludedly thought it was would have warranted his act. Other American states added an "irresistible impulse" test, which asked the jury to find that the defendant was irresistibly impelled to do the act even though he knew it was wrong.

Dissatisfaction with the more traditional tests has brought into being two more contemporary alternatives. One is the so-called *Durham* rule[9] which asks whether the otherwise criminal act is the product of mental disease or disorder. If it is, the defendant should be acquitted. The second, usually called the ALI-*Currens* rule,[10] inquires into the defendant's substantial capacity to conform his conduct to the requirements of the law, granted his mental condition. The primary purpose of both tests is to allow the jury to hear a medically sound diagnosis of the defendant's mental condition, unfettered by arbitrary legal terms like "know" and "wrong."

Resolution of the issue of how a revised criminal code is to treat mental disease or defect is one of the most difficult tasks a code revision commission faces. The reasons again largely lie beneath the surface and are seldom articulated. One is a nearly universal psychological antipathy toward mentally-ill persons. Average citizens fear "crazy" persons. They want them put away—anywhere, on whatever basis. Since popular mythology has it that prisons hold inmates longer than mental hospitals, most people feel safer if killers, for example, go to prison rather than to a mental institution. This attitude is compounded by an attitude of disbelief in psychiatry and distrust of psychiatrists and psychologists. The premise that a modernized test for abnormal

---

9. So-called because first enunciated in *Durham v. United States*, 94 U.S. App. D.C. 228, 214 F.2d 862 (1954). It has since been replaced in the District of Columbia by the A.L.I. test. *United States v. Brawner*, 471 F.2d 969 (D.C.Cir. 1972).

10. Because one version of it is found in Model Penal Code §4.01 and a similar one in *United States v. Currens*, 290 F.2d 751, 774 (3d Cir. 1961).

mental condition negating culpability is necessary so that mental health experts can practice their profession without arbitrary legal restrictions hardly will gain universal acceptance.

Difficulties in resolving the issue have also been compounded, in states having capital punishment, by the fact that the defense of insanity has most often been raised in capital cases. If emotional conflicts over the death penalty swirl together with emotional fears of mentally abnormal persons, rational resolution of the criminal code problem is not easy.[11]

It probably behooves a drafter to stress that many mentally-ill persons are first identified only because they happened to be arrested, or taken into custody by the police who have no apparent legal alternative to booking them on criminal charges. Traditional law recognizes two ways only to divert such a person from the criminal justice system: (1) finding him incompetent to stand trial; and (2) acquitting him. The first alternative has recently come under strict constitutional regulation.[12] The second can be furthered somewhat by any new statutory test that lets the jury hear as much about the defendant's mental condition as possible. But the most pressing need is revision of criminal procedure law so that police, prosecutors and trial judges can divert mental cases out of the criminal justice system at any stage they are identified.[13]

Intoxication

The common-law treatment of drunken criminals was harsh. Only if the defendant were "involuntarily" intoxicated could he claim an absolute defense to a criminal charge and judges rarely have found any involuntariness, even in contemporary instances in which a defendant suffered the synergistic effect of, for example, a small amount of barbiturates on top of a moderate

---

11. Capital punishment in its traditional format of course was ruled unconstitutional in *Furman v. Georgia,* 408 U.S. 238 (1972). Enactment of several state statutes in 1973 restoring a mandatory death penalty shows, however, that the issue still confronts code revisers in many states.

12. *Jackson v. Indiana,* 406 U.S. 715 (1972). See also *McNeil v. Director, Patuxent Institution,* 407 U.S. 245 (1972); *Humphrey v. Cady,* 405 U.S. 504 (1972).

13. See U.S. National Advisory Commission on Criminal Justice Standards and Goals, *Report on Courts* [hereinafter referred to as Courts Report] 27-41 (1973).

amount of alcohol, an effect of which he was unaware. However, the *fact* of intoxication might be relevant in either of two ways. One was when the defendant's intoxicated condition made it unlikely that he could maintain a specific criminal intent, e.g., the intent to deprive another of his property. The second was as a form of alibi evidence. If the crime as committed evidenced a high degree of physical coordination, the defendant's proof that he was staggering drunk tended to show that someone else must have committed the crime.

None of these rules protected a chronic alcoholic, particularly an indigent, from repeated arrests for public intoxication. Nor did brief sentences of imprisonment serve any rehabilitative purpose.

The new codes on the pattern of Model Penal Code §2.08 modify the common-law rules. They preserve the evidentiary relevance of intoxication to any issue in a criminal prosecution but in addition provide that either non-self-induced or pathological intoxication is a legal defense to crime, provided it destroyed the defendant's capacity to conform his conduct to the requirements of the law (a test identical to that used in the context of mental incapacity). Self-induced intoxication is defined as the knowing introduction of substances (a term including drugs or narcotics) into a person's body which he knows or ought to know will cause intoxication—unless either he takes them on medical advice or the circumstances otherwise would afford a defense to crime (for example, coercion by someone else). Pathological intoxication is defined in effect to govern instances of synergistic effect not expected by a defendant.

Modernized provisions of this sort soften the harsher aspects of traditional criminal law and make it unlikely that a person will be punished solely as an addict or chronic alcoholic.[14] However, none of the new statutes effectively governs the principal problem; the diversion of alcoholics out of the criminal justice system. If a state or community provides treatment facilities ade-

---

14. Compare *Robinson v. California*, 370 U.S. 660 (1962) (punishment of addict as such is cruel and unusual punishment) and *Powell v. Texas*, 392 U.S. 514 (1968) (public drunkenness may be punished) .

quate to accommodate its alcoholics who transgress the criminal law or otherwise come to the attention of authorities, then procedure law must be amended to permit protective custody rather than criminal arrest, immediate transfer of an alcoholic to a medical facility rather than a jail and civil commitment proceedings under strict definitions of alcohol addiction by governing due process procedural guarantees. A uniform act to accomplish this has been drafted.[15] Unless the needed facilities are built and staffed however, legal changes of this sort make no functional difference.

Immaturity

The common law dealt with the problem of amenability of children to the criminal law in a rudimentary way, through presumptions. Those under seven were conclusively presumed incapable of formulating a criminal intent, those between seven and fourteen presumed incapable (although the presumption could be rebutted by proof of capacity), while those fourteen and over were fully responsible.

All states now have special juvenile courts and procedures. A contemporary substantive code should therefore be drafted so the minimum age of criminal responsibility is the minimum age at which the jurisdiction of an adult criminal court attaches, either directly or after waiver from a juvenile court. Juvenile codes themselves are almost always in dire need of revision and many of the purported standards of delinquency or eligibility for waiver to an adult court are perilously vague. These problems must be cured by a tightening up of the language of juvenile codes and modifications of criminal procedure law to promote effective diversion and cross-transfer of juveniles. The criminal code itself is only peripherally affected.

Defenses (Justification)

Inherited criminal law recognizes several instances in which deadly force can lawfully be used, if apparently it is the only reasonable response to protect life: (1) self-defense, (2) de-

---

15. See also Courts Report.

fense of others to whom the defendant is closely related, (3) prevention of (serious) felonies and (4) effectuation of a felony arrest. A survey of judicial decisions over generations shows that in almost every situation in which the defendant was found to qualify under one or more of these defenses, his own or another's life was or appeared to be in mortal danger.

New criminal codes to a large extent restate the thrust of the traditional law. In two aspects the new provisions appear to be more restrictively drawn and both are likely to arouse great controversy.

One is the amount of force a householder may use to defend his property against criminal intrusions. Few cases over the years have approved the use of deadly force to prevent forced entries unless an occupant's life is endangered or the intruder is about to (or reasonably appears about to) commit a crime of violence against the occupants or the structure itself. The new codes generally require either a self-defense situation or the commission or apparent commission of a limited number of crimes like arson, burglary and theft. Nevertheless, many citizens firmly believe that they have a broader right to keep and use firearms to protect the integrity of their homes, and so treat the proposed code provision as a limitation on what they view (mistakenly as a matter of constitutional law) to be their right to keep and bear arms. Because volatile emotional issues are thus present, neither legal precedent nor logic will likely prevail. This may be one issue on which code drafters need to compromise, perhaps by lengthening the list of crimes motivating the repelled entry.

The second concerns the power of police to use deadly force in arresting and preventing escape. In the comparatively few appellate decisions reviewing convictions of police officers for excessive use of deadly force in making a felony arrest or preventing an escape, courts usually have limited the use of such force to self-defense or arrests for felonies that obviously threaten public safety, like homicide, dangerous assault, arson, nighttime burglary, rape or robbery. Following this judicial tradition, the new proposals have restricted the use of life-endangering force on the part of police officers to self-defense or defense of others against actual or apparent deadly attack, to arrests for felonies involving the actual or threatened use of deadly force, or to escape attempts evincing immediate or potential serious physical injury or death to others unless the escaping felon is immediately retaken through the use of deadly physical force.

Provisions thus limited invariably come under strong attack from law enforcement groups, who maintain that line police officers cannot make sophisticated evaluations of this kind in a situation of stress and that use or threatened use of deadly force is necessary to control hardened criminals. This, too, is an area in which code proponents may be well advised to compromise (over the strong but generally less well organized objection of civil libertarian groups) by expanding the list of felonies concerning which police may use deadly force to arrest or retain custody to include all those involving force against person or property. Since the deadly force used always must be reasonable, courts and prosecutors can still punish cases of excessive force if they will.

Criminalization and Decriminalization

In one dimension, decriminalization can mean simplification: sheer reduction in the number of penal sections in a state's laws. A survey of existing statute law may well show 2,500 to 5,000 sections defining criminal activity. A well-drafted modern statute can accomplish equivalent protection in 350 to 400 sections and promote clear understanding of the criminal law in the process. This might be called decriminalization through reduction of statutory inventory.

In another application, decriminalization can involve line-drawing between criminal and noncriminal conduct. At what point does overenthusiastic huckstering of merchandise end and criminal liability for fraud or deception begin? Is absolute accuracy required of all information supplied by anyone to any governmental office or employee? Should a creditor be able to threaten his debtor with criminal prosecution unless he pays immediately in cash or should this be called extortion? Should he be able to collect immediately at gunpoint in the belief he has a legal right to do so? In each instance, when the legislature expands or contracts the coverage of criminal law, it either criminalizes or decriminalizes conduct.

In its most common usage, decriminalization means the exclusion of entire classes of citizens or activities from criminal law coverage. Almost without exception, substantial conflict arises whenever specific traditional crimes are singled out for elimination from the coverage of criminal law. Relief from the sheer burden of criminal cases flooding criminal courts in some instances may vastly outweigh any theoretical objections advanced to decriminalization. In others, a strong majority may favor change and so override the dissent. But in still others, controversy will rage. The crimes that will probably create the greatest conflict are vehicle offenses, licensed or regulated activities, tax crimes, alcoholism, narcotics usage, gambling, abortion, consensual sex activity, patronizing prostitutes, pornography and vagrancy.

Sentencing

Perhaps the greatest contribution a criminal code revision can make to effective administration of the criminal justice system is through the creation of functional penalties rationally related and realistically implemented. There are several areas that offer considerable difficulty in drafting.

Life Imprisonment

Most experts in penology concede that some convicts are so dangerous they must be kept in custody for life. The question for the code drafter is how these cases can be provided for without at the same time subjecting persons who might safely be released to the same harsh sanction.

Almost all codes authorize a maximum life sentence for a few dangerous crimes, usually murder and the most aggravated forms of arson, burglary, kidnapping and rape. What of the highly dangerous person who commits some other crime bearing a maximum term less than life? At times a record of past convictions may warrant an enhanced term up to life for recidivism. Occasionally civil commitment proceedings at the end of the maximum prison term may serve. Otherwise, a clearly dangerous person must go free even under the new codes.

A more troublesome problem for the drafter, however, is the elimination of mandatory life terms, usually in murder cases. Despite the fact that murderers as a class are likely to be better candidates for early release than, for example, check forgers, there is certain to be strong resistance to fairly early parole eligibility for murder convicts. In only one other area has a high mandatory minimum sentence been encountered frequently (a multiple offender conviction for narcotics sale), and the advocacy for that is comparatively slight today in view of the penalty structures of the Federal Controlled Substances Act of 1971 and the Uniform Controlled Substances Act adopted in several states.

Capital Punishment

Consideration of the scope of aggravated murder and the extent of nonculpability because of mental disease or disorder will be more difficult in a state with the death penalty than in one in which the death penalty already has been abolished. However, the character of the debate is markedly different today, in light of the Supreme Court's decision that capital punishment in its pre-*Furman* form constitutes a denial of equal protection and cruel and unusual punishment.[16] Under *Furman,* the only option open to a legislature appears to be to require capital punishment for all persons convicted for the crime to which it attaches, without any exercise of discretion. During 1973 several states indeed enacted such a draconic sanction, although not as a part of a general code revision.

Concurrent Terms

Some jurisdictions have long permitted the trial judge a choice between concurrent sentences, in which separate penalties imposed for different crimes run at the same time, or consecutive, in which sentence maxima and minima are added together for a total that in some instances is the functional equivalent of a life

---

16. *Furman v. Georgia,* 408 U.S. 238 (1972).

sentence (and may be so intended). Parole eligibility will accrue much earlier under concurrent sentencing than consecutive.

Revised criminal codes frequently adopt concurrent sentencing as the standard. This reflects in part the belief that most cumulated crimes arise from one transaction or set of transactions, so the most serious offense committed is likely to provide a satisfactory maximum term of imprisonment. The assumption also is that early parole eligibility is needed if rehabilitation is to be even a slight possibility. If some defendants must be segregated for long periods, then the appropriate statutory alternatives are higher maximum sentences for dangerous crimes or recidivism statutes authorizing enhanced maximum penalties for confirmed criminals.

Only one special context seems to call for the possibility of cumulated sentences: crimes committed during imprisonment, the crime of escape from prison and crimes committed during escape. If most or all the period of imprisonment assessed for these crimes is to be served concurrently with a sentence imposed earlier, there is little deterrent to prison crime or escape efforts, particularly on the part of those sentenced originally to long prison terms. Therefore, cumulative sentences are standard in the escape context. But even cumulated terms mean nothing to a convict under a mandatory life sentence; in this case one confronts again the question of the death penalty.

Disposition of the Mentally-Ill Offender

Defendants acquitted as not culpable because of their mental condition traditionally have been committed immediately to a mental institution, often designated for the "criminally insane." Although affluent ex-defendants frequently obtain their release on habeas corpus because they are not presently dangerous to themselves or others, many unrepresented persons have been held in what amounted to maximum security penal detention for years or even for life.

A few statutory revisions provide for an immediate special hearing governed by the mental health civil commitment statute, to determine whether the acquitted defendant is commitable.

Release is then governed by the same statute. A recent Supreme Court decision[17] strongly suggests that such a procedure is constitutionally mandated.[18]

Presentence Reports

If sentencing alternatives under a new code are to be invoked intelligently by a trial judge, he should have substantial background information about the offender. Therefore, it is common to require presentence investigations for all first offenders, and to authorize them in all other cases.

Another device to promote informed sentencing is a diagnostic commitment to a prison intake facility, medical or psychiatric diagnostic center, or both. This not only enhances the data available to the judge but also enables prison officials or staff physicians to indicate beforehand whether the defendant is a suitable inmate.

Appellate Review of Sentences

As long as only one judge has control over the content and length of sentence, excessive prison terms are probable in some cases. Removal of the power to impose binding minimum sentences is one means of control over the judge, although it creates a new need to review parole-granting procedures.

As an alternative, an increasing number of jurisdictions now experiment with some form of sentence review, whether by a special panel of trial judges or regular appellate review.[19] However, the most usual setting for innovation is the criminal procedure law, not the criminal code.

THE IMPERATIVE OF CONTINUAL REVISION

The above discussion is offered as guide to the procedures by which criminal codes can be modernized and the principal areas of coverage that require special attention. Much of the benefit realized through revision is likely to be lost unless revision is a

---

17. *Humphrey v. Cady,* 405 U.S. 504 (1972).

18. See *Wilson v. State,* 287 N.E.2d 875 (Ind. 1972); cf. *United States v. Brown,* 478 F.2d 606 (D.C.Cir. 1973).

19. Courts Report at 122-125.

continuing process, through which omissions or duplications in coverage can be remedied, defects in administration cured and even more important, the inevitable urge to pass new statutes resisted to the utmost.

What is needed is a permanent commission that drafts legislation on request and researches existing law to see whether it is adequate to meet the problem underlying a request for a draft bill. If unneeded legislation is enacted, the governor may use the commission opinion as a basis for a decision whether or not to veto. The placement of such a commission within the structure of government probably should vary from state to state. Perhaps all that can be done initially is to urge the necessity of a continuing review body, leaving it to political processes to determine to whom such a body should be directly responsible.

Not entirely facetiously, one might also advocate the wisdom of a "self-destruct" policy by which legislation older than a specified number of years is legally viewed as repealed. Obsolescence of criminal laws like other statutes is probable as community views of what conduct is and is not proper change and as the problems of earlier years fade to nothing. Automatic repeal has the merit of requiring periodic appraisal and reapproval of criminal (and other) statutes in light of current needs and past experience.

CHAPTER 7

ALTERNATIVES TO IMPRISONMENT IN THE NEW POLISH PENAL CODE

K. Poklewski-Koziell

A NEW POLISH PENAL CODE was finally adopted in 1969[1] to replace the Code of 1932. Before enactment into law it was widely discussed not only by lawyers but also by the daily press, radio and television. It came into force on January 1, 1970.

Discussion of the entire Code would necessarily involve an oversimplification of many complex issues. Concentration on any single legal concept embodied in the Code would, on the other hand, risk losing its broader ideas amid a welter of detail. To avoid taking either too broad or too narrow an approach, I propose to concentrate in this paper on those provisions of the new Code which establish alternatives to deprivation of liberty as part of the correctional process. The development of sanctions which do not require imprisonment in my opinion constitutes a sound trend in modern penal legislation.

Criminologists are no longer as confident as they used to be about the advantages of isolating or imprisoning offenders. Such confidence rested on a metaphysical analysis of human behavior and on doctrines about sin. But waning faith in the advantages of imprisonment has not necessarily been accompanied by a complete change in attitudes towards criminals and towards crime. Even in the supposedly sophisticated second half of the twen-

---

1. This Penal Code forms part of a larger codification of Polish law. Two other codes were adopted by the Sejm (Parliament) at the same time: the Code of Criminal Procedure and the Code relating to Execution of Criminal Sanctions. See *Dziennik Ustaw* (Official Publication) No. 13, 1969. A French translation of the Penal Code by the present author was published in Warsaw by Wydawnictwo Prawnicze in 1970. An English translation is being prepared by William S. Kenney, Esq., of Washington, D.C., and will be published in the American Series of Foreign Penal Codes.

tieth century, we are surrounded by relics of a darker, unscientific past. Celebration of the two hundredth anniversary of Cesare Beccaria's famous essay *On Crimes and Punishments* has served as a reminder of how far we still are from the full realization of Beccaria's main principles and irrefutable ideas. It is possible that the eighteenth century may turn out to be too modern for our hyper-advanced epoch. Warnings by legal scholars[2] especially and the observation of specific social phenomena support the contention that our own times are still too often caught in the grip of antiquity. Many jurists are still guided by preconceptions based on completely fictitious and unrealistic principles. In the clash which thus frequently results from the presence of opposed and conflicting tendencies in the legal doctrine, legislation and practices of a given country, every jurist has a duty to advance and support the ideas he considers right.

The system of sanctions contained in the new Polish Penal Code was influenced to some extent by the tendency to seek alternatives to imprisonment which one also sees manifested in the United Nations Congress on the Prevention of Crime and the Treatment of Offenders and especially by the evident failure of short-term prison sentences. The Code contains a number of provisions which empower the courts to dispense with incarceration of a convicted offender. In place of imprisonment—although of course only under certain limited conditions—the court may instead order (1) a fine, (2) the penalty of restricted liberty, (3) a suspended sentence (i.e. conditional suspension of execution of a penalty) or (4) conditional dismissal of the proceedings.

1. The fine in the Polish law (Articles 36 and 37 of the Penal Code) is similar to the fine in most other penal systems. Perhaps it need only be noted that very often a fine cannot be effectively imposed in lieu of a prison sentence because of the financial po-

---

2. Especially noteworthy among more recent works making this point are Gerhard O. W. Mueller, *Crime, Law and the Scholars* (1969) and N. Morris & G. Hawkins, *The Honest Politician's Guide to Crime Control* (1970). Cf. S.-C. Versele, "Public Participation in the Administration of Criminal Justice," *International Review of Criminal Policy* No. 27 (1969) at 9: "The administration of justice is . . . complacently isolated in an ivory tower, clothing a moralizing approach in logical garb. It prides itself on a haughty independence which causes it to turn its back on society."

sition of the offender; in many cases, imposition of a fine would create a greater hardship for his family than it would for the convicted person himself.

2. Restricted liberty is, on the other hand, a relatively new measure. It is not designed to be used in dealing with grave offenses but rather for offenses such as slander, battery and petty theft. It can be imposed pursuant to the general part of the Penal Code (a) whenever there are grounds for the extraordinary mitigation of a penalty or (b) whenever a crime is subject solely to a penalty of deprivation of liberty (the form of penalty which in the new Code, replaces imprisonment and arrest) of which the minimum term would not exceed three months, the maximum meted out would not exceed six months and the court believes that even this penalty is not justified (Art. 54, §1). It can also be imposed in connection with particular offenses pursuant to certain provisions of the special part of the code. Such provisions in the special part permit the imposition of restricted liberty (a) as an alternative to deprivation of liberty for up to two years in connection with offenses such as the performance in a state of intoxication of duties designed to insure traffic safety (Art. 147) and offenses against the religious beliefs of others (Art. 198); (b) where an otherwise serious crime is perpetrated unintentionally (e.g. endangering life under Art. 160, §3); and (c) where the crime, in certain circumstances, is considered to be of minor importance (e.g. unlawful appropriations under Art. 199, §2).

Restricted liberty may be imposed for a period of from three months to two years. During this period the convicted offender is subject to the following restrictions: (1) he may not change his place of residence without the court's permission, (2) he is obliged to perform work as prescribed by the court, (3) he is not allowed to occupy any responsible position in a social organization and (4) he must furnish the court with complete information concerning his compliance with the terms of its sentence. The court is also empowered to order restitution by a convicted person for the damage caused by his offense or to have the offender tender an apology to the injured party.

The obligation to perform work as prescribed by court order entails working without pay and under supervision for the public good, from twenty to fifty hours per month. If the offender is already employed in a socialized institution, the court can order in lieu of his duty to perform work that from 10 to 25 percent of his salary shall be withheld for the benefit of the public Treasury or for a public purpose designated by the court. While the convicted person is subject to restricted liberty he cannot terminate his employment without the court's consent; nor may he be promoted or have his salary increased. If the offender is unemployed at the time of his conviction, the court may assign him to perform his prescribed work for an appropriate socialized institution, subject to obligations and restrictions previously mentioned.

These measures may give rise to certain doubts and reservations, especially so far as concerns the difference between a fine and the withholding of a percentage of the offender's salary. The object of the latter is probably to adjust punishment more exactly to the professional status of the offender, to establish a close connection between the amount of the penalty and his earnings so as to avoid any excessive financial burden. It also enables the court to direct application of the withheld sums to a specific purpose.

The obligation to perform work for the public good without receiving remuneration is in some respects a very vague and open measure; the precise character of this type of punishment must largely depend upon an individual's circumstances. The judges have to scrutinize the various implications of such a penalty and tailor it to the specific traits of the offender. The obligation to work for a couple of hours at cleaning streets in a small town would, for instance, be a relatively mild sanction for a manual worker but would probably be equivalent to the medieval pillory for the local doctor or lawyer.

3. Suspended sentences are so closely bound up with an established probation system in the United States that Americans may find it difficult to understand the obstacles encountered in introducing this measure in continental Europe. The famous Massachusetts experiment[3] in the middle of the last century, of sus-

_____

3. See Mueller, op. cit. at 77.

pending sentences for purposes of placing the offender on probation, was gradually adopted by the other States of the Union with relative ease, as it was in England. On the European continent the predominance of statutory law prevented the gradual judicial development of conditionally suspended punishments. Such a system could only be developed through legislation and only after the doctrinal controversies it engendered had been resolved. France provides a perfect example. At the end of the last century Senator Bérenger's bill, which provided for the institution of conditional sentences, was vehemently criticized by many jurists, although it was adopted in France in 1891, as a similar law had been enacted in Belgium in 1888. Its distinguishing feature was that it provided for suspension of the *execution* of a sentence rather than suspension of its *imposition*. It did not entail any measures of supervision or assistance to the convicted person such as are implicit in the probation system. The concept of probation gradually gathered yet greater support but even after World War II the French Parliament rejected bills proposing to introduce a probation system. It was only in 1958, under the forceful de Gaulle government, that genuine probation as an optional alternative to the *sursis simple* (which is the suspended sentence without supervision) came into being in France.

The concept of a suspended sentence leads to passionate doctrinal disputes between the partisans of a criminal policy based on the theory of special prevention and those who are committed, above all, to a theory of general deterrence. It also clearly illustrates the financial and organizational problems involved in the introduction and application of really dynamic measures of criminal justice administration.

In Poland, the Code of 1932 provided that "in case of conditional suspension of the execution of a penalty, the court may place the convicted person on probation during the period of suspension. The court shall entrust the supervision of probation to reliable persons or institutions." This provision, however, was not practically enforced and with rare exceptions, it remained a dead letter.

In the years following World War II, the attitude of the

Polish authorities towards the suspended sentence was inextricably tied up with political considerations. During the Stalinist era the supposed "abuse" of this measure by the courts was severely condemned and its pernicious leniency was strongly criticized. There were no attempts, however, to show objectively, by statistics and other means, why the suspended sentence comprises such a grave social danger. The data proved just the opposite. Revocation of conditional suspension of the execution of punishment appeared necessary in a relatively small percentage of cases. But excessive faith in the efficacy of the deterrent aspect of punishment nonetheless had an influence on official attitudes towards the administration of justice.[4]

Although this situation has changed, one must agree that it would be undesirable for both justice and for the victims of crime if the suspended sentence were regarded as equivalent to an acquittal. It is precisely a probation system that can perhaps help to avoid this extreme. It is essential that no one should consider the first commission of an offense as a circumstance requiring automatic release. The sufficiently onerous conditions attached to probation may further convince offenders that crime does not pay and that such a sanction is by no means mild, thus also providing an element of deterrence.

Under the present Polish Penal Code (Arts. 73-79) the court may direct conditional suspension of the execution of a punishment involving no more than two years' deprivation of liberty in the case of an intentional offense and of punishments not exceeding three years' deprivation of liberty if the offender acted

---

4. For a contrary view, see *e.g.*, A. Gubinski & J. Sawicki, "Rzeczywista a pozorna rola prewencji generalnej i specjalnej (The effective and apparent role of general and special prevention)," *Panstwo i Prawo* No. 10 (1958). The authors state that conditional suspension of the execution of a sentence has a specific purpose which is irreconcilable with principles of retribution and general prevention. The judge who is presented with such a conflict must be guided by existing legislation. In light of all the purposes of the penalty, the gravity of the crime and the nature of the criminal, the law does exclude many acts and many offenders from the privilege of receiving a suspended sentence. However, when the statute provides for its applicability and the court concludes that the particular case falls within the purview of the statute, then the judge must be guided by the objective of special prevention.

unintentionally. In deciding to suspend punishment, the court has to take into consideration the character and personal circumstances of the offender, his past behavior and all other factors which justify the conclusion that even though the penalty will not be executed, the offender will lead a law-abiding life and will not, in particular, commit another crime. The court has also to consider whether the social advantages to be gained from punishment do not militate against the case for conditional suspension.

Execution of the sentence may be suspended for a period of from two to five years. The court may make it a condition of such an order of suspension that the offender is to (1) make reparation of the damage caused by his offense, (2) tender an apology to the injured party, (3) support his own dependents, (4) perform specified work or services for a public purpose, (5) perform remunerative work or pursue a course of study or of vocational training that will equip him for remunerative employment, (6) refrain from excessive consumption of alcohol, (7) undergo medical treatment, (8) refrain from frequenting certain places or from associating with certain persons or groups or (9) observe such other rules of conduct during the period of suspension as will prevent the commission of another offense.

The court may specify in detail how long a particular obligation is to last and how it is to be carried out. During the period in which a sentence is suspended, the judge may adjust these conditions to conform to modified correctional considerations. The suspension of a sentence may be made to depend on a guarantee by a social organization, institution or trustworthy person that they will undertake to ensure that the offender observes the law and does not commit further crimes. In practice, however, this rather vague provision is not easily applied because organizations are not very eager to accept the burden which this involves in matters unrelated to their business.

Genuine probation is provided for in a passage of the Code which reads: "In suspending execution of the penalty, the court may place the convict, for the term of probation, under the supervision of a designated person, institution or social organization." This measure is optional if the offender is an adult, but *obligatory* if the accused is under the age of twenty-one years. Thus the Polish law accepts as a general rule the French pattern of permitting a penalty to be suspended either with or without supervision but, taking account of their particular traits, requires supervision for young persons. The situation as regards probation is very different from what it was under the Code of 1932, not so much because of changes in the text of the code, but because Poland now has a staff of trained probation officers and volunteer supervisors who can ensure that this measure is really effective.

Revocation of a suspended sentence is in some instances mandatory and in others left to the discretion of the court. The court is obliged to reinstate the penalty if during the period of suspension the convicted person commits an intentional offense for which he is sentenced to deprivation of liberty or if he has not made reparation of damage caused by his offense to a socialized institution. The court may order reinstatement of the penalty if the convicted person has otherwise violated the legal order and if, in particular, he has committed an offense not punished by deprivation of liberty or has not paid a fine or has evaded the obligations imposed on him. Reinstatement of the penalty can be ordered only during the period of suspension or during the six months following. Six months after the end of the period of suspension the conviction is annulled by virtue of law.

4. The conditional dismissal of criminal proceedings (Arts. 27-29) is a new measure in Polish penal law and a relatively original one.[5] It represents a progressive step toward achieving reformation of the offender and the prevention of recidivism without invoking strong repressive measures.

In certain cases, from the point of view of the offender's interests and even from that of rational criminal policy, it is not enough simply to suspend the execution of a sentence. Conviction by a court requires a criminal record be placed on file, and this can cause harmful and irreparable damage to the individual.

---

5. This subject was analyzed in greater detail in my article "Non-lieu conditionnel, nouvelle institution du droit pénal polonais," *Revue de Science Criminelle et de Droit Pénal Comparé* No. 2 (1971).

At the same time, it is advantageous for the administration of justice if phases of procedure that are not essential can be avoided. Conditional dismissal is a device for realizing the aims of the suspended sentence but at an earlier stage of the criminal process. It occupies an intermediate position between the absolute withdrawal of charges (which may afford insufficient security for the future conduct of the offender) and the conditional sentence (which, by requiring that the offender be put on trial, may in itself cause unnecessary hardship).

This concept derives from Norwegian law.[6] It is discussed in the 1951 United Nations publication on *Probation and Related Measures*.[7] Widely divergent views have been expressed with respect to the advantages and the applicability of conditional dismissal or suspension of prosecution. There have been some efforts to formulate its ideal limits. In the first place, it has been suggested that this measure should be confined to simple kinds of offenses and to cases of juvenile delinquency. It is also said that each case should be selected on the basis of the improbability of the recurrence of an offense. In the second place it is thought desirable to restrict the practice to cases in which it will be adequate to place on the offender both fewer and more simple conditions than are used in connection with the conditional or suspended sentence. Finally, it has been suggested that in the interests of general prevention, the use of this procedure must not become the predominant method of dealing with criminal cases. It should be noted, however, that it is felt in Norway that the conditional suspension of prosecution has indeed satisfactorily proved to be efficacious. Neither the criminal courts nor the officers charged with the practical administration of the measure have expressed any need to restrict the scope of its application.

As an alternative to the suspended sentence, the Polish Penal Code provides that it is possible to *conditionally dismiss* penal proceedings when (1) the social danger of the act is not considerable, (2) the circumstances of its commission are not in doubt, (3) the offender has no prior convictions, and (4) the position

---

6. See Marc Ancel & Ivar Strahl eds., *Le Droit Pénal des Pays Scandinaves* (Paris, 1969).

7. *Probation and Related Measures* 191, 192 (New York, 1951).

of the offender and his past behavior warrant the conclusion that even though the proceedings will be dismissed, he will lead a law-abiding life and will not commit another crime.

Conditional dismissal of criminal proceedings can be used in any case where the applicable penalty would otherwise be a fine, restricted liberty, or deprivation of liberty for not more than three years.

The conditional dismissal may be made to depend on a guarantee that steps will be taken to insure that the offender will not commit another crime. Such a guarantee can be given by an organization to which the offender belongs or a group of persons with whom he is working, serving or studying. The guarantee may also be given by a trustworthy person.

When proceedings are conditionally dismissed, the accused can be required (1) to make reparation for the damage caused by his offense, (2) to tender an apology to the injured party and (3) to perform specified work or to contribute goods or services for a public purpose. The total duration of the work required to be performed may not exceed, as is also the case with a suspended sentence, twenty hours.

Proceedings may be suspended for a period of from one to two years. They are to be resumed only when the offender evades his obligations during this period, violates the legal order or, in particular, commits another offense.

The penal code does not specify who can order the conditional dismissal of proceedings. This important question is settled by provisions of the code of criminal procedure which confer such a power not only on the court but also on the prosecutor. The question is one which caused some controversy and which was extensively discussed in the course of debate on the recent codification in Poland. Many jurists, especially judges, were opposed to conferring on the prosecutor a power which is considered, in a certain sense, to be a prerogative of the judiciary. It is true that before proceedings may be conditionally dismissed it is necessary to decide the question of who is the author of the offense and to resolve problems of guilt, responsibility, and so on; and this is certainly a judicial function.

On the other hand, the measure is applicable only to offenses of which the social danger is not considerable. This means that it is applicable to cases of petty offenses. The purposes for which this measure is resorted to are above all, practical purposes and speed of procedure is here particularly important. The person concerned has a right to appeal from the decision to dismiss conditionally if, for instance, he wishes to establish his full innocence. In such a case the decision will be automatically repealed.

Conditional dismissal of penal proceedings can also affect the interests of the injured party. The code of criminal procedure confers upon an injured party the right to appeal from a decision dismissing proceedings but this right to appeal extends only to the conditions imposed upon the offender. It seems, in this respect, that the victim's interests are not sufficiently protected. The victim should also have the right to appeal from the decision as a whole and not only with regard to its conditions; he may have a definite interest in bringing about the conviction of the offender.

The court has the power to order conditional dismissal at any phase of the proceedings after an indictment has been filed, and may do so even at the judgment stage. In this last case it is of course not the time-saving element which will be decisive, but rather considerations of rational criminal policy. Dismissal at this point may, in particular, spare the offender such harm as results from a formal conviction and from the burden of a criminal record.

An important difficulty in connection with conditional dismissal arises in determining precisely when the social danger of the act is not considerable. The notion of the social danger of an act is a fundamental one in the penal law of the Socialist countries. The so-called material conception of crime contemplates penal responsibility only in the case of an act considered socially dangerous. This conception is emphasized in the first article of the Polish Penal Code. We also find it provided (in Article 26) that "the act which presents a minor social danger does not constitute an offense." This gives rise to certain subtle considerations. For instance, is the danger of the act determined only by its objective appearance or also by the attitude, the intention and personality of the offender? These questions are debated by theorists, but the judge in his everyday practice has also to decide when an act presents a minor social danger and when its social danger is not considerable. In the first case the author of the act must be acquitted irrespective of the penalty applicable to the deed. In the second case—if the act is not subject to a penalty exceeding three years of deprivation of liberty—the court can resort to conditional dismissal of proceedings.

The provisions of every penal code have a particular background embodying more or less clearly rationalized conceptions about the ends of criminal justice and of punishment. It seems that in our field, as in many others, elements of primitive emotion or irrational belief can be classified as retrograde. The tendency to replace to the largest possible extent the traditional penalty of short-term imprisonment with substitute measures which allow the offender to remain at liberty and to promote, at the same time, reeducation as the main purpose of criminal justice, can be considered as progressive. But realistic assessment of the requirements of organized society should not permit us to forget there is little chance that deterrent and even retributive elements of punishment will wholly disappear from the criminal law. To equate the treatment of criminals completely with the treatment of the sick would after all, be yet another type of irrationalism. The situation of these two categories of individuals is basically distinguishable. At least in the more simple cases the difference is, perhaps, that the sick person has a problem which concerns mainly his own self, and needs the help of specialists; the criminal, besides his own problem has created a situation which involves a victim, his and his family's misery, as well as the legitimate anger of the public which will not tolerate impunity for the crime.

Short-term imprisonment is not entirely dispensable. Certain penologists have argued that when reeducation in a strict sense cannot be achieved imprisonment constitutes a necessary measure, imposing a desirable psychological shock.

From the point of view of comparative law, it is particularly interesting to note the legislative solutions reported and the opinions expressed in the course of the congresses on the prevention of crime and treatment of offenders which are organized every five years by the United Nations. The second congress which took place in London in 1960 set out the following considerations as bearing on certain of its recommendations:

1. The Congress recognizes that in many cases short-term imprisonment may be harmful in that it may expose the offender to contamination, and that it allows little or no opportunity for constructive training, and would, therefore, regard its wide application as undesirable. The Congress recognizes, however, that in some cases the ends of justice may require the imposition of a short sentence of imprisonment.

2. In view of this fundamental situation, the Congress realizes that the total abolition of short-term imprisonment is not feasible in practice, and that a realistic solution of this problem can be achieved only by a reduction of the frequency of its use in those cases where it is inappropriate and particularly where the offense is trivial or technical or imprisonment is used in default of payment of a fine without consideration of the offender's means.

3. This gradual reduction must be brought about primarily by the increased use of substitutes for short-term imprisonment, such as suspended sentences, probation, fines, extramural labour, and other measures that do not involve the deprivation of liberty.

4. In the cases where short-term imprisonment is the only suitable disposition of the offender, sentences should be served in proper institutions with provision for segregation from long-term prisoners, and treatment should be as constructive and as individualized as possible during the period of the detention. Wherever practicable, preference should be given to open institutions as places where sentences are served.

It seems to us that this point of view is a realistic one and provides a clear summary of the problems involved in seeking alternatives to imprisonment. As we have seen, the Polish legislature has made substantial efforts to take account of the main points contained in these suggestions.

There is, of course, frequently a certain gap between the legislative enactment of a legal norm and its realization in judicial practice.

In Poland, the year or so since codification has been character-ized by close study of the activities of the courts by authorities and institutions concerned with the administration of law and by their efforts to aid judicial practice.

One of these agencies is the Supreme Court. It has in Poland, apart from the traditional task of supervising other courts through the review of specific cases, the power to promulgate guidelines for the administration of justice. These guidelines are supposed to elaborate and interpret particular rules. Sometimes these interpretations which are binding on the courts, come very close to being amendments of the law. The Supreme Court has published guidelines relating to the conditional dismissal of criminal proceedings. Those concerning the general rules for ju-dicial sentencing are still in the course of preparation.

Statistical data compiled during the first year of the new Code's operation (1970) are of course available, but these sta-tistics do not always provide enough detail with respect to matters of current interest. Thus, to provide further data with regard to penal measures not involving deprivation of liberty, the Minis-try of Justice, the Office of the Attorney General and the Insti-tute of Legal Sciences are presently engaged in analyzing, from their respective points of view, representative samples of several hundred cases.

Much of the information now available concerns subtleties more likely to obscure than to elucidate the principal topics in question. I propose, therefore, to draw on these materials only so far as they bear on a limited number of problems which ade-quately illustrate the expectations and difficulties connected with three measures: (1) restricted liberty, (2) conditional suspension of punishment, and (3) conditional dismissal of criminal pro-ceedings.

1. In 1970, 14,058 persons were sentenced to a term of restrict-ed liberty.[8] Since this measure is new, it is not surprising that it was imposed in the first half year only on 3,838 persons and that

---

8. W. Michalski, "Kara ograniczenia wolnosci w praktyce orzecznictwa (The penalty of restriction of liberty as applied by the courts)," *Panstwo i Prawo* No. 8-9 (1971) .

the number rose rapidly in the remainder of this period. So far as percentages are concerned, restricted liberty was imposed in 6.8 percent of all those criminal cases which ended in conviction, while 40.7 percent resulted in a suspended sentence of deprivation of liberty, 33.0 percent in deprivation of liberty without suspension, 19.1 percent in imposition of fine, and 0.4 percent in supplementary penalties assessed independently.

As mentioned above, restricted liberty can be imposed under provisions of both the general part and the special part of the Code. The 1970 data demonstrate that the courts have not often applied the provisions of the general part (they have done so in 12% of the cases only) but have largely relied on the provisions of the special part.

The penalty of restricted liberty appears most often in connection with convictions for minor misappropriation of social property (59.9%), minor theft (10.5%), insults to a public officer (27.9%) and infringement of traffic rules resulting in harm (19.7%).

As to the kind of work prescribed by the courts in connection with restricted liberty, withholding of a certain percentage of salary constitutes the majority (51.9%) of cases. In second place are sentences prescribing the obligation to perform work for the public good without remuneration (43.9%) and the smallest number of cases is composed of those in which an unemployed offender is assigned by the court to an appropriate socialized institution to perform prescribed work subject to certain requirements and restrictions (4.3%).

The value of the measure itself, as carried out in practice, cannot be assessed solely on the basis of statistical data. The Institute of Legal Sciences has therefore undertaken a study in depth of 700 files chosen from the whole country and forming a representative sample of cases in which a sentence of restricted liberty was imposed. The preliminary findings provide little ground for unrestrained satisfaction with the immediate success of this measure. The main obstacle to its effectiveness seems to be a lack of proper means and organization for carrying out a complicated system of prescribed duties. Especially in small localities where the public officer is acquainted with nearly every citizen, the duties imposed by the courts may often be performed only on paper. Shortcomings in the existing administrative apparatus that is called upon to carry out the obligations imposed by the courts may well lead to de facto impunity for convicted offenders.

2. Conditional suspension of the execution of penalty was resorted to, as mentioned above, in 40.7 percent of all criminal cases ending in conviction; this corresponds to nearly 60 percent of the cases in which deprivation of liberty was initially ordered.

It is understandable that the proportion of suspensions varies considerably in relation to different crimes. For instance, execution of a sentence to deprivation of liberty was suspended in 95 percent of all cases involving personal and material harm resulting from the infringement of traffic rules (Art. 145, §1); in 47.2 percent of all cases of theft (Art. 203, §1); and in 12.6 percent of all cases of rape (Art. 168, §1).

In 1970, 73,180 persons were sentenced to deprivation of liberty but had the execution of this penalty suspended.

The periods of deprivation of liberty involved in cases where it was suspended were as follows: up to 6 months, in 18,589 or 25.3 percent; from 6 months to 1 year in 45,940 or 62.7 percent; from 1-2 years in 8,615 or 11.7 percent; from 2-3 years (in exceptional cases) in 36 or 0.3 percent of these cases.

Of those 73,180 persons, 22,671 (31.0%) were put under supervision (which may be ordered when the convicted person is an adult and which must be done when he is a youth of less than twenty-one years).

Specific obligations were only imposed on 24,698 persons (33.7%). The total number of such obligations was 32,628 (since one person can be subjected to more than one obligation). These breakdown as follows:

Reparation of damage	8,092
Work or services for a public purpose	7,771
Refraining from excessive consumption of alcohol	6,376
Support of dependents	3,419
Remunerative work or vocational training	2,681

Apology	2,482
Medical treatment	959
Refraining from frequenting certain places	336
Others	512

The problem of probation can be illustrated by the following data:

On December 31, 1970, 38,994 persons were under supervision (naturally, this figure also covers sentences dating from before January 1, 1970):

By probation officers or volunteers	33,223
By various institutions	2,961
By social organizations	2,810

During 1970, 13,710 supervisions were brought to an end due to:

Expiration of the term	5,477
Early release for good behavior	6,357
A decision to execute the penalty (for a new crime committed, for bad behavior, etc.)	1,876

It is perhaps also worth mentioning that in 1970 the suspension of the execution of a penalty was withdrawn in 3,268 cases.

An analysis of judicial practice in this field leads to some critical observations. It is evident that the courts are not using the provision which enables them to make the suspension of a penalty dependent on a guarantee given by a social organization, institution or a trustworthy person. Moreover, the conditions of suspension are not specified fully enough and—as with restricted liberty—it is often difficult to ensure compliance with these conditions. Nevertheless, it seems that much may be expected of this particular measure.

3. The conditional dismissal of proceedings may be ordered, as mentioned above, either by the court or by the prosecutor.

In 1970 the courts applied this measure to 8,591 persons (with imposition of conditions in 60% of these cases and with no conditions in 40%). The conditions imposed consisted of performing specified work or making a contribution of goods or services for a public purpose in 82.3 percent of these cases, reparation of damage in 12.1 percent and apology to the injured party in 5.6 percent. During the same period, prosecutors applied this measure to 25,493 persons.

Further data concerning the conditional dismissal of proceedings appears in the analysis of sets of files prepared by the Ministry of Justice and by the Office of Attorney General. From this data it seems the measure has been used both by the courts and by the prosecutors mainly in cases of theft, infringement of traffic rules involving injury or damage to property, infringement of provisions of the act on the prevention of alcoholism, of the building regulations and of regulations regarding sanitary conditions in food production, etc.

As regards the conditions imposed on offenders, practice was not yet stabilized in 1970. Certain courts and prosecutors limited themselves to ordering "services for a public purpose" for a definite number of hours. Others, by contrast, were meticulous in specifying detailed conditions. For instance, a mender of shoes who had cheated customers was obliged to repair shoes for a certain period of time in the local penitentiary; a physician who had driven after drinking vodka was required to deliver twenty one-hour public lectures on the harmful effects of alcohol.

Those who have studied the operation of this new measure have formulated several objections to the way in which it is used: the possibility of making conditional dismissal dependent on a guarantee given by an institution is practically ignored; conditions are either not imposed often enough or they are not fully specified; once imposed, compliance with them is not efficiently supervised; the personality of the offender is only superficially examined; provisions pertinent to the suspension of penalty are misapplied to the conditional dismissal and vice versa.

Nevertheless, we may hope since the concept itself is sound, it will prove successful in practice after an initial period of "trial and error."

PART III

DEALING WITH VIOLENCE WITHIN THE CRIMINAL LAW SYSTEM

CHAPTER 8

CRIMINAL VIOLENCE AND ITS CONTROL IN THE GERMAN FEDERAL REPUBLIC

DIETRICH OEHLER

Professor of Criminal Law, University of Cologne

INCREASE OF CRIMINAL VIOLENCE

IN RECENT YEARS crimes of violence committed in the Federal Republic of Germany have been increasing at an extraordinary rate. This is true not only of the typical major felonies—murder, extortion, robbery, rape, kidnapping—but also of acts of violence committed for political reasons against the police, politicians, professors, and others and of acts of violence against property as well. In saying this, however, an interesting statistic should be noted. While the crime rate for adults has not changed very much from 1900 to 1969, the rate for juveniles between fourteen and seventeen increased sharply in the fifties and continues to accelerate. In comparison to the fifties, murder has gone up by one-third and rape and robbery by one-half. The rate for adolescents between eighteen and twenty-one reached its highest point in 1962 and has since declined a bit. The reasons for the sudden increase in the number of acts of violence against persons and property are manifold and I can enumerate but a few of them here.

One reason for the increase in violence has been the intensification of political antagonisms. During the last six or seven years the members of the radical political wing learned, contrary to their earlier belief, they could not overcome the establishment by joining it, but had instead to use the opposite means, namely, violence. This began with the big demonstrations against the universities and the state. The demonstrations were then extended to the large newspaper publishing houses which had opposed the radical wing. This resulted in the destruction of some buildings and the burning of cars belonging to these publishing houses. Warehouses were set ablaze to attract people's attention to the radicals. Moreover, an initial aggressive resistance to the demonstrators gradually diminished as the police and other administrative officials found themselves isolated. Prosecutions of violent crimes arising from political motives were no longer pursued as intensively as before. The provisions of the penal code containing the various so-called "crimes of demonstration" were reduced in number and mitigated as to sanction. Thus greater spheres of freedom were created, which the radicals mistook for a greater license to use violence. The many successful hijackings, political extortions through the taking of hostages and the frequent depictions of violence, as it is used in present warlike encounters all over the world, deadened perception of the evil of violence.

Disapproval of violence for the purpose of altering social oppression—even by clerical authorities—confounds many persons, who, thinking themselves the executors of a superior order, claim the use of violence as a right. In this connection, I must call attention to a change in the modern concept of life. The conditions of life have become so complicated that many people are inclined to solve personal conflicts, even those for which they are themselves to some extent responsible, in the simplest manner, namely, by the use of violence. Sometimes these conflicts arise from the impulse to become wealthy and attain respect quickly. But most of all, many people seize this simple way to solve conflicts in their personal lives; for example, with respect to marriage, family and friendship. Today the often-mentioned restraining structures of family, school and work which were far more pervasive in former times, are of less importance. I think one can say despite the traditional antagonism toward violence in former times, one will find that resort to violence is nowadays the most likely sort of solution of conflict situations. The criminal law has only very limited possibilities for controlling the inclinations of this new type of man.

A state which is organized in a liberal and democratic manner certainly has to tolerate more crimes than a state which is dictatorially governed. If, however, a citizen has the impression that the state does not sufficiently protect him from violence, a precarious necessity develops for the citizen to defend himself, as he had to do in times long ago. Certainly a state such as the Federal Republic of Germany could not overcome such conflicts between its citizenry without great convulsions, should they last for any period of time. In the last few years during which the development of violent criminality has rapidly advanced, the law of criminal procedure and the penal law of the Federal Republic of Germany have very clearly undergone a change; from a system which was first oriented in a liberal direction, to a much more stringent system of law. Naturally, even this greater stringency does not favor the ideas of a single political party, for all sides of the political spectrum are trying to tackle the problems of modern criminal violence.

CRIMINAL POLICE ORGANIZATION

First of all, the organization of the criminal police has been changed. Although police organization is the business of the individual states of the Federal Republic, the police do have at their disposal certain central institutions which enable them to use investigative resources in a more rational manner. The examination of fingerprints, *modus operandi,* ballistic evidence and in general, the examination of all matters which aid in detecting crime and the criminal are being standardized. Thus records of previous convictions (criminal records) are kept current for the whole of the Federal Republic by one central authority. North Rhine-Westphalia, the largest state of the Federal Republic, is training sharp-shooters for the police, who will be used in putting criminals out of action without endangering others, for example, where hostages have been taken. The possibility of having suddenly to check on certain groups of persons all over the Federal Republic is being provided for, the training of the police is being improved, equipment is being modernized and the number of policemen is being increased. Especially for purposes of fighting criminal violence, the law of criminal procedure has recently been amended and will soon be further amended.

WIRE TAPPING

In 1968, the German authorities were given the power to wire tap in criminal cases, thus succeeding to the rights of the three western Allied Forces with respect to the Federal Republic. Up to that time, under the German Code of Criminal Procedure, neither the judge nor the prosecutor was entitled to tap the telephone of a suspect or to have it tapped through judicial proceedings. Today, apart from cases of political and certain other extraordinary crimes, wire tapping is also authorized in cases of suspicion of murder, manslaughter, robbery, extortion, kidnapping, political abduction, abduction of minors, certain crimes endangering the public or an extortion completed, attempted or devised through a means for which punishment is provided. Wire tapping is to be ordered only if the investigation would otherwise be substantially impeded. Wire tapping may be ordered not only with respect to the suspect but also with respect to any other person who receives or forwards information on his behalf or who engages in comparable acts. Wire tapping and the recording of telephone calls may be ordered only by a judge, except that in cases where there is danger in delay, the prosecutor is authorized to order it. The police are not entitled to act on their own. In some cases this innovation in the Code of Criminal Procedure will help to prevent the violent criminal from carrying out his plans. After commission of the crime, wire tapping is at least likely to facilitate proof of a defendant's guilt.

PRELIMINARY DETENTION

There is a current controversy as to whether the provisions relating to preliminary detention should be amended to include an additional ground for its use. Ever since the enactment of the Code of Criminal Procedure in 1877, it had been the case that preliminary detention can only be ordered by a judge against a person who is strongly suspected of a punishable act and then only if there is the danger of flight or of tampering with the evidence. In 1964 the law on preliminary detention was liberalized. The duration of preliminary detention was to some extent curtailed and, most important of all, it was required that there had to be "definite facts" to indicate the danger of flight or the danger that proofs would be tampered with. Because of this requirement of the existence of definite facts, German judges nowadays ordinarily refuse to detain an accused who has a fixed place of residence, since they assume that in such cases there is no danger of flight. On many occasions this has had the result that the accused commits new and serious crimes of violence prior to his trial, with considerable impunity since German law requires a compound sentence for all crimes *sub judice*. This compound sentence does not consist of consecutive sentences for each offense but only of the most severe punishment incurred for any single offense. For example: If the perpetrator after his first robbery, and prior to trial, commits ten other grand larcenies, robberies or similar offenses, he will be sentenced to five years' imprisonment for the most serious robbery and, in addition, to one or two years' imprisonment for all the other crimes. Research conducted by the government of North Rhine-Westphalia examined five hundred such cases of serious crime to substantiate the demands for amendment of the law governing preliminary detention. The Ministers of the Interior of the States of the Federal Republic of Germany and recently the Bundesrat, the body representing the States of the Federal Republic, took the initiative in proposing such an amendment of the Code of Criminal Procedure. A bill is pending before parliament calling for the insertion of a provision which will extend "danger of flight" as a ground of detention to include the possibility of flight despite the existence of a fixed place of residence or abode in the Federal Republic of Germany. Furthermore, the danger that the offense will be repeated is also included as a ground for ordering preliminary detention. Along with the general changes in the prerequisites for preliminary detention which were made in 1964, detention on the ground of danger that the offense will be repeated as well as on the grounds of danger of flight and of tampering with the proofs was newly introduced with respect to crimes against morality and decency. That is, preliminary detention may now be ordered against a person who is accused of having committed such a crime if definite facts support a belief that the accused before final conviction will commit a further crime of the designated kind and that the preliminary detention is necessary to avert the threatened danger. In the future, this ground of detention (danger of repetition) is to be extended to dangerous assault and battery, mayhem, larceny, larceny committed by a number of persons, robbery, extortion, arson and other crimes. The danger of repetition may be presumed on the basis of the repeated commission of such crimes in the past and *definite facts* which support a conclusion that the accused, before conviction, will commit further serious crimes of the designated kind.

With the aid of these two projected amendments of the Code of Criminal Procedure, criminal violence hopefully will be restrained—a result which will be particularly helped along by the fact that in Germany, preliminary detention is likely to last for a long time (sometimes for two or three years) because all connected crimes of which the accused is charged have to be adjudicated in one trial.

FETTERING RECALCITRANT DEFENDANTS

According to a new provision of the Code of Criminal Procedure a detained person may be manacled if there is danger that he will use force against persons or property, if he resists, or if he attempts to flee. Though this measure may be imposed by the warden, or other official who has charge of the defendant, it requires in every case the approval of a judge. If there are strong grounds for thinking that a person has committed an offense while in a condition of irresponsibility or of diminished responsibility and that his commitment to an institution for cure and care will be ordered, the judge may direct that he be temporarily committed, if the public security so requires. The persons concerned are frequently irresponsible violent criminals.

CONSENSUAL STERILIZATION

In substantive penal law several provisions concerning violent criminals have recently been introduced. According to the so-called castration act, a man who has an abnormal sexual instinct and whose personality and life indicate he is likely to commit violent crimes against morality and decency or murder, homicide, and assault and battery may be castrated to avert the danger of the commission of further acts of violence and to help the person concerned to live a normal life. The person concerned must give his consent and must be over twenty-five. A group of medical experts participates in the proceedings. This measure, above all, is supposed to contribute to curbing acts of violence arising from abnormal sexual instinct.

SENTENCING

With regard to the legal consequences of violent crime, i.e. punishments and measures of safety and rehabilitation, some substantial alterations have been made recently in the criminal law. Other amendments of a more general kind have also had an impact on violent offenders. In 1969 basic criteria governing the imposition of sentences were introduced into the code. The court in imposing sentence is to take into consideration, among other factors, the motives and aims of the perpetrator, his state of mind and the effort or volition exercised by him. Thus the statutory law requires a judge to consider the intensity of will or effort, or an offender's violent attitude. Such has always been good judicial practice, but today the judge's attention is especially called to the necessity for considering these circumstances when imposing sentence. The criteria used in imposing sentence according to recent case law are subject to appeal; that is, the convict as well as the prosecution has the right to take an appeal from a sentence allegedly fixed in violation of the controlling principles.

PROTECTIVE CUSTODY

Protective custody which, being a measure of safety follows the execution of punishment, is especially directed against violent offenders. Protective custody is ordered by the court in addition to punishment: if the offender has been convicted twice of intentional crimes punished by deprivation of liberty for at least one year, if he has served at least two years of confinement and if an overall evaluation of his deeds proves that in consequence of his inclination to commit serious crime, particularly crimes in which the victim incurs physically or psychologically grievous harm or by which serious economic damage is caused, he is dangerous to the public. A foreign sentence is to be treated as a German sentence if the act involved is an intentional crime under German law as well. Since commitment to protective custody is fixed at ten years when ordered for the first time, it is feared by offenders. Protective custody has become a rigorous measure for segregating dangerous violent criminals from the public after their regular sentences have been served. At present, approximately one thousand persons are confined in protective custody. The provision with respect to protective custody that the most offensive crimes are those in which the victims incur physically or psychologically grievous harm or serious damage to property, is new and is especially directed against violent criminals who again and again violate the penal laws. The institution of protective custody has now existed in Germany for about forty years. The new formulation of this provision was introduced to make the conditions for commitment to protective custody as clear as possible and above all to discriminate positively between violent offenders and unimportant offenders whose criminality is minor. The imperfections of the hitherto existing provisions regarding protective custody derived from the fact that habitual offenders, whether they committed serious, average or minor criminal acts, were liable to be treated more or less equally. Nowadays only the violent perpetrator is supposed to be confined in protective custody.

SOCIAL THERAPEUTIC INSTITUTIONS

The new General Part of the Penal Code which will become effective on January 15, 1974 provides for commitment to a *social therapeutic institution*. This measure will be especially important in dealing with violent offenders as well as with those who commit crimes against morality and decency. The social therapeutic institution is to exist side by side with the psychiatric hospital to which certain irresponsible persons or persons of diminished responsibility are committed and is in addition to the institution for chronic alcoholics. An offender whose character is seriously defective is supposed to be judicially committed to such a social therapeutic institution, in addition to punishment, if he is sentenced to at least two years imprisonment, was sentenced to imprisonment of definite duraton twice before, and is deemed likely to commit serious unlawful acts. This measure is also applicable to a person whose intentional crime was based on his sexual instincts, who has been sentenced to imprisonment of at least one year, and who is likely to commit serious unlawful acts again because of his sexual instincts. A person who is sentenced for an intentional act to at least one year's imprisonment before completing his twenty-seventh year, who has committed certain punishable acts before, and who is likely to develop into a habitual criminal, may also be committed to such a social therapeutic institution. The social therapeutic institution is then a measure of confinement which aims at the resocialization of violent offenders of different kinds and ages.

THE LAW OF DEMONSTRATIONS

The trend in legislation to enact measures which deal with criminal violence directly is also evidenced by certain amendments governing the law of demonstrations. This concept is new and was coined some years ago on the occasion of the big demonstrations against the enactment of the "emergency law" in the Federal Republic of Germany, although it does not itself occur anywhere in the statutes. In 1970, together with these innovations, the two provisions concerning unlawful assembly and failure to disperse were repealed. Those sections made punishable the failure to disperse at a public assembly in the course of which acts of resisting a peace officer or a government functionary are committed after being requested to do so by an authorized official. The provision concerning riot was severely restricted. Today only those who commit acts of violence in the course of a demonstration or who induce a crowd to do so are punishable for riot, but not those who merely take part in a violent demonstration or who remain present while it occurs. But it is very difficult nowadays to identify which participants in a violent demonstration are meant to be covered by the new law. Those at whom the law is aimed are usually surrounded by other demonstrators whose presence prevents them from being identified by the police. Those among the surrounding crowd of demonstrators who intentionally assist violent criminals are naturally punished for doing so, but they too cannot always be identified by the police in the excitement of the situation. This reform was introduced in line with the trend to gradually abolish the remaining features of the authoritarian state and to secure a larger sphere of freedom for peaceful demonstration.

RESISTING LAW ENFORCEMENT OFFICERS

In this connection another change in the penal code is important. Until now anyone resisting an officer charged with the execution of the law was punished, even if he thought he was acting justifiably. His liability to punishment depended exclusively on the objective justification for the policeman's action at the moment. Nowadays the judge is entitled to mitigate punishment or to forego the imposition of punishment altogether. Moreover, he is not permitted to impose punishment at all according to this penal statute, if the perpetrator erroneously thought that the official did not act justifiably. This is a commendable legal innovation which has been urged for a hundred years and which will distinguish those individuals who objectively use force against the authorities from those who are truly criminally violent.

The effects of this amendment of the penal code have been extraordinarily controversial with the public. It is very difficult to evaluate them. According to the information supplied by the Federal Ministry of Justice based on compilations by the Federal Ministry of the Interior in 1971, the first full year after the new provisions came into force, one-eighth of all demonstrations did not come off peacefully; that is without the commission of punishable acts. During the last half of the year before the amendment came into force the number of nonpeaceful demonstrations had not increased. But in a most spectacular manner, the number of demonstrations throughout the Federal Republic of Germany increased by a third after the amendment of the Penal Code. In part the increase in some states is twice or three times that amount. Compared with these figures, the number of nonpeaceful demonstrations increased in some states.

In evaluating figures about the number of nonpeaceful demonstrations, one has of course to consider the fact that several acts, up until now punishable, are no longer offenses. The inclination of the police to keep watch at demonstrations in order to spot crimes has diminished. The lack of support for the police revealed by the press and television and the insignificance of the protection afforded by state and government, did not strengthen the devotion of the police to their tasks during demonstrations. One has to consider that in some areas the law is no longer enforced, so that regular islands of violence have been formed. These do not come to the surface only because their victims evade or ignore violence. Within the university this can be perceived very clearly. These institutions ignore the use of violence by radical students in different ways. For instance, the election of the rector or a session of the faculty or of the senate may be transferred at short notice to a safe place, even several times, to avoid intimidation. Charges concerning the violent occupation of the rooms of the rector, of an institute, or the faculty are no longer pursued. Violent bodily attacks against professors are not brought to the notice of the authorities at all, as no substantial success from prosecution is to be expected. One does not oppose the usurpation of authority by evading the use of violence. This avoidance of the potential use of violence has to be taken into account as a factor in the fight against violent criminality.

PROHIBITION OF DEPICTIONS OF VIOLENCE

At present there is a lively discussion going on in Germany as to whether the pictorial representation of violence ought to be prohibited. Along with amendments to the proscriptions concerning pornography the government has submitted an amendment on this subject to the Penal Law Committee of the Bundestag which passed it in the closing days of last year. It is ultimately likely to become law. Under this bill anyone who produces documentary or phonographic or photographic recordings or representations which depict violence perpetrated against other men in a cruel or otherwise inhuman manner or which incite race hatred, commits a punishable offense. Anyone who disseminates such a representation—and this includes live broadcasts—is likewise punishable. This prohibition does not apply if the violence is depicted in connection with the reporting of current or historical events. I do not want to go into differing scientific opinions on the effects upon adults and children of representations of violence on the radio or television. These are in many ways contradictory. The effects of the representation of violence are not really clearly documented. One must conclude from much that has been written that there is at least a short term effect on children and adults produced by the depiction of violence in the communications media. Under certain circumstances its stimulating effect on aggressive attitudes cannot be denied. That depictions of violence by the media have long term effects is not scientifically proven. It is possible and not at all unlikely that there has been a consequent weakening of the perception of ordinary violence, a certain habituation to the everyday use of violence and a change in attitudes towards violence as a means for pursuing personal aims or for solving conflicts. The latest investigations on behalf of the Bundestag (the Federal Parliament) confirm this surmise. This research which was completed during the closing weeks of 1971 demonstrates that representations of violence through the media of press, film, and television may constitute a precipitating impulse for antisocial conduct if they encounter certain predispositions on the part of the viewer. The very frequent representation of the use of violence seems to change perceptions of the negative value of violence, even for persons who initially have rejected violence. In recent years there is certainly a noticeable correlation between a spectacular number of representations of violence and an increase of criminal violence. Consequently, it is the government's policy that the sources which conceivably encourage criminal violence and which are amenable to control should be brought under control.

EXTORTION CRIMES

Two provisions which impose severe punishment for the kidnapping of a person for purposes of extortion or compulsion are wholly new. Such actions which occur nowadays with appalling frequency in the Federal Republic show that evil examples evoke imitations. When extortions, first abroad and then in Germany, proved successful they occurred more and more frequently, just as ransom demands reached more and more astronomical heights. That these new provisions will serve their deterrent purpose seems to me to be very doubtful. The severity of the threatened punishment certainly will not prevent any cold blooded criminal from carrying out his plan. Extortion, duress and other uses of violence in any event have always been severely punished.

AIR PIRACY

A penal provision against air piracy is also new. This crime is subject to the principle of universality; it may be prosecuted in the Federal Republic even when committed by a foreigner abroad if he has been arrested in the Federal Republic of Germany. A problem is met which up til now had long constituted a gap in the penal law. This provision is in line with an international convention of 1970.

It is likely that the fight against criminal violence will entail in the future, amendments and improvements in substantive penal provisions. The problem of restricting criminal violence is also tied up with another problem—the maintenance of the democratic constitutional state in the Federal Republic of Germany. In other countries other considerations which often cannot easily be compared may well be more important. For the effective restriction of criminal violence, it is crucial that the state be able and willing to enforce the laws it has enacted. The volume of criminal violence will increase if the violent criminal can count on a particularly great chance of not being apprehended by the police or of escaping quickly from preliminary detention or from prison either by force or by court decree or by an act of grace. Under these circumstances, the confidence of the population in the administration of justice is shaken. The Minister of the Interior of the State of North Rhine-Westphalia recently said, referring to his state: "In the glare of publicity and along with a largely passive attitude on the part of our citizens, within the first eight months of 1971, 17,292 cases of robbery, battery and assault and duress alone, openly committed, were reported. The citizen's passivity, being, in turn, a consequence of the fact that he no longer feels satisfactorily protected by the state, allows violent criminals to enlarge their area of action."

Legal and penological improvements in the fight against violent crime will be imperfect if they are not supported by adequate political and social measures. As has already been mentioned, criminal law can only indirectly influence the concept of life in modern times, which involves to a significant degree the resort to violence as a simple means of solving one's own personal conflicts. Penal law and the law of criminal procedure are not isolated parts of social life but are elements among other complementary elements in the common effort of men to achieve a social life.

CHAPTER 9

PROPORTIONALITY AND THE PSYCHOTIC AGGRESSOR: A VIGNETTE IN COMPARATIVE CRIMINAL THEORY*

GEORGE P. FLETCHER

Professor of Law, University of California at Los Angeles

WESTERN LEGAL SYSTEMS diverge radically in their approaches to setting limits on the privilege of self-defense.[1] Some systems incline to the view that a person defending his or another's life or property may use all the force necessary to stifle an aggressive attack. Taken to the extreme this means if there is no other way to apprehend a thief escaping with a petty bounty one may shoot him, if necessary, shoot to kill. In contrast to this approach, which is adverse to limits on the use of necessary force, another set of Western jurisdictions insists that the degree of force meet two desiderata: it must be both necessary and proportional to the interest protected. The requirement of proportionality or reasonableness means that there are some cases like petty thievery where the cost of protecting a threatened interest may

---

* This paper has also appeared in the *Israel Law Review* for July 1973. I should like to thank Ms. Margaret Spencer for her expert research assistance; Ms. Sharon Byrd, for helping me to conceptualize Self-Defense III; Professor Dr. H. H. Jescheck, Director of the Max Planck Institute for International and Foreign Criminal Law, Freiburg, West Germany, for reading the manuscript and making several valuable suggestions.

1. Narrowly construed, the term "self-defense" refers only to the defense of one's person. In the absence of more suitable terminology in English, the term is used in the text to include the defense of others and the defense of property, thus parallel to the German and Russian concept of "necessary defense." See *Strafgesetzbuch* (hereinafter cited as *StGB*) sec. 53; *Ugolovnyj Kodeks RSFSR* (hereinafter cited as *Ugol. Kod.*) sec. 13.

be so great that one must surrender the interest rather than inflict grievous harm on the aggressor.

As examples of the tendency to reject the rule of proportionality[2] I shall focus in this paper on the German Federal Republic and the Soviet Union; and as examples of systems adopting the rule of proportionality I shall take England and the United States. The breakdown among Western systems is not so simple as any neat cleavage between Continental and common law jurisdictions. It turns out that France numbers among the countries unhesitatingly adopting the rule of proportionality and thus is closer in this respect to the position taken in the common law tradition.[3] Of course there are important differences between the Federal Republic of Germany and the Soviet Union; in both countries there have been marked efforts in recent years to move closer to the principle of proportionality. It would be difficult to say that today either jurisdiction flatly rejects all limits on the use of necessary force. Yet in both countries the weight of au-

---

2. The same term appears in French, *proportionnalité*, in German, *Proportionalitaet*, and in Russian, *proportsional'nost'*; unhappily, it is ambiguous in all these languages. The claim that harm is disproportionate may mean either (1) that it unduly exceeds the interest spared, or (2) that it is simply greater than the interest spared. In most contexts, it is clear that the first meaning is intended. See, e.g., H. H. Jescheck, *Lehrbuch des Strafrechts* 231 (1969); Stratenwerth, "Prinzipien der Rechtfertigung," 68 *Zeitschrift für die gesamte Strafrechtswissenschaft* 41, 60-61 (1961). But the Russian literature must be read with caution. Some authors seem to intend the second meaning; accordingly, their rejection of proportionality means merely that they regard defensive force as justified even if it causes more harm than it spares. See *Soviet Criminal Law: The General Part* 373 (M. Shargorodskij & N. Belaev eds. 1960, in Russian) (identifying the issue of *proportsional'nost'* with the rule in necessity cases that the harm caused must not be greater than the harm spared). This ambiguity also explains the unfortunate translation of the word "proportionality" in the Hebrew text of Israel's Criminal Code Ordinance sec. 18. The translators opted for the second meaning above and held that neither self defense nor necessity applies as a defense if the harm caused is greater than the interest spared. This makes the section unsuitable for cases of self defense. See Feller, "Necessity *Stricto Sensu* as a Situation Negating the Criminality of Conduct" (1972) 4 *Mishpatim* 5 at 14.

3. There is little controversy on the point today, 1 P. Bouzat & J. Pinatel, *Traité de Droit Pénal et de Criminologie* 363 (1970) ("everyone agrees that the defense must be proportionate to the attack"); C. Degois, *Traité Elémentaire de Droit Criminel* 168-170 (1912). A few nineteenth century writers followed the German pattern and rejected the rule of proportionality; see, e.g., P. Garraud, *Précis de Droit Criminel* 184 (3rd ed. 1888); J. Ortolan, *Eléments de Droit Pénal* 179 (5th ed., 1886).

thority opposes articulating a formal test for limiting the right of self-defense. This is the position of the 1960 RSFSR Code,[4] as it is presently interpreted,[5] and it is the view reflected in the failure of the new West German Criminal Code to modify the traditional sweeping formula for self-defense.[6]

This position of German and Soviet jurisprudence may come as a surprise to common law jurists, for at least since Blackstone[7] everyone in the common law tradition has assumed, almost without discussion, that use of force in self-defense must be both necessary and reasonable.[8] The rule of reasonableness demands a constant weighing of competing interests. On the basis of detailed balancing, common law courts have worked out rules specifying the amount of force permissible to defend particular interests; such as life, habitation and chattels.[9] In the common law tradition there is no overarching conception of self-defense but rather a number of distinct defenses, each hewn to protect a particular interest. The scope of each defense depends on the importance of the interest protected; the right to defend one's

---

4. *Ugol. Kod.* sec. 13.

5. See *infra* notes 53 and 60.

6. *Zweites Gesetz zur Reform des Strafrechts* sec. 13, enacted July 4, 1969, (1969 (I) *Bundesgesetzblatt* 717). The new code will hereinafter be cited as *StGB* 1975.

7. See text *infra* at note 32.

8. See, e.g. R. Perkins, *Criminal Law* 995 (1969); Comment, "Justification for the Use of Force in the Criminal Law," 13 *Stan. L. Rev.* 566, 566-567 (1961). For present English law, see Criminal Law Act, 1967, ch. 58, sec. 3(1): "A person may use such force as is reasonable in the circumstances in the prevention of crime. . . ." This rule is assumed to control cases of self-defense, J. Smith & B. Hogan, *Criminal Law* 258 (2nd ed., 1969). The word "reasonable" emerged in this context within approximately the last century and a half; it appeared in Bishop's discussion, I J. Bishop, *Criminal Law* 518-519 (7th ed. 1882), but not in Blackstone, see 4 W. Blackstone, *Commentaries** 178-189, and apparently not in earlier texts. It was not used in California's 1872 legislative formulation of the defense and its limits; Calif. Penal Code sec. 197.

9. See generally Comment, *supra* note 8, 573-581; Model Penal Code, sec. 3.04 (self-protection); sec. 3.05 (protection of others); sec. 3.06 (protection of property) (Proposed Official Draft 1962). In addition, one finds references, particularly in the United States, to a privilege to prevent the commission of crime, e.g. Calif. Penal Code sec. 693. This privilege is expressed in absolutist language. The defending party may exert "sufficient resistance" to prevent an offense against his person, family or property. *Id.* In practice, however, this privilege seems to merge with those of self defense and defense of property and is subject to the same rule of reasonable force. *People v. Heisse*, 217 Cal. 671, 20 P.2d 317 (1933); *Commonwealth v. Emmons*, 157 Pa. Super 495, 43 A.2d 568 (1945).

life obviously permits a greater degree of force than the distinct
privilege applicable to the defense of chattels.

In Germany and the Soviet Union all defendable interests,
from life to property and personal honor, receive the same degree of protection. There is but one privilege of necessary defense *(Notwehr, neobxodimaja oborona);* the only question is
whether there is or is not a right to defend a particular interest.
If there is, the cost of protecting that interest is, in principle, irrelevant. German and Soviet jurists do balance competing interests in analyzing the defense of necessity or lesser evils[10] but not
in construing the privilege of self-defense.

One cannot help but be puzzled. Are German and Soviet jurists
inhumane? Why do they resist a rule so eminently "reasonable"
as that requiring a balancing of competing interests? If the rule
is appropriate in cases of necessity, why should it not apply in
the related case of self-defense? This difference between the two
sets of legal systems is profound and in this essay I can only
hope to give a partial account of the problem. The thesis that I
shall develop is that differing attitudes toward the principle of
proportionality derive from fundamentally different conceptions
of self-defense and that these different concepts relate in an intriguing way to the demands placed on the overall theory of self-
defense. I shall focus on a specific theoretical issue—the problem
of the psychotic aggressor—and attempt to show that confronting or not confronting this problem generates different theories
of self-defense and these different conceptions, in turn, lead to
the divergence we have noted on the rule of proportionality.

The problem of the psychotic aggressor raises the question of
whether one may as a matter of right, kill a faultless, insane assailant to save oneself or another from death, rape, or serious
bodily harm. The problem is far more subtle than first meets the
eye. It has traditionally been one of the central theoretical quandaries of the German and Soviet literature.[11] Yet apart from

---

10. *StGB* 1975, sec. 34; *Ugol Kod.* sec. 14.

11. For early systematic discussions, see Loeffler, "Unrecht & Notwehr," 21
Zeitschrift für die gesamte Strafrechtswissenschaft 537, 539 (1901); *Criminal Law
RSFSR* 11 (A. Piontovskij ed., 1924, in Russian). For references to Tsarist discus-
sions of the same problem, see T. Shavgulidze, *Necessary Defense* 101, note 200,

Jerome Hall's treatment of the issue,[12] it has hardly received notice in the common law literature. The fact that a legal system attempts to solve this problem has a bearing on its general theory of self-defense; indeed, the most satisfactory solution to the problem is, as I shall argue, one that leads to the rejection of the rule of proportionality.

The argument proceeds in several stages. First, we examine competing approaches to the problem of the psychotic aggressor, rejecting four theories and finally endorsing the approach accepted in the German and Soviet literature. We then examine this general theory of self-defense and its implications for the rule of proportionality. I will present one model of the possible historical development; namely that confronting or ignoring the problem of the psychotic aggressor caused, respectively, the rejection or the acceptance of the rule of proportionality. Whether it actually happened that way is a more subtle problem. In the final section I shall amplify the thesis and assess the alleged historical nexus in the light of some more general features of common law, German and Soviet legal theory.

It is important to be clear about the form of the thesis. I shall argue that a particular style of theoretical inquiry (whether scholars confront or ignore the problem of the psychotic aggressor) bears a relationship to a concrete legal practice (whether a legal system rejects or accepts the rule of proportionality). This is a novel form of argument in comparative legal analysis. If the argument proves to be satisfactory, it may point the way to similar studies of systematic variations among legal systems.

THE PROBLEM OF THE PSYCHOTIC AGGRESSOR

Imagine your companion in an elevator goes berserk and attacks you with a knife. There is no escape: the only way to avoid serious bodily harm or even death is to kill him. The assailant

---

110 (1966 in Russian). The subject has been a popular one for dissertations in Germany, see e.g., K. Christman, *Der rechtswidrige Angriff bei der Notwehr* (1931); M. Schlaeger, *Die Rechtswidrigkeit des Angriffs bei der Notwehr* (1897). See also the authorities cited *infra* notes 18 and 35.

12. J. Hall, *General Principles of Criminal Law* 233-234, 436 note 85 (2d. ed., 1960).

acts purposively in the sense that he rationally relies on means that further his aggressive end.[13] He does not act in a frenzy or in a fit, yet it is clear his conduct is nonresponsible. If he were brought to trial for his attack, he would have a valid defense of insanity.

This is the problem of the psychotic aggressor as it has appeared in the European literature. In more general form, the problem is whether self-defense applies against excused but unjustified aggression. If the aggressive conduct is itself justified, say in the case of a policeman effecting a valid arrest by appropriate means, it is clear there is no right to resist.[14] Yet if the aggression is merely excused by necessity, duress, insanity or mistake, the aggressor is not acting as matter of right or privilege and there may indeed be a right to resist. In this paper I focus on the case of aggression excused by reason of insanity, for this is the only defense clearly thought of as an excuse rather than a privilege in all the legal systems under discussion. When the issue is one of mistake,[15] necessity,[16] or duress,[17] Soviet and common

---

13. I have defined the problem narrowly. There is ongoing controversy in the German literature whether self-defense is applicable against non-purposive human threats. Compare Jescheck, *supra* note 2, at 229, with E. Schmidhaeuser, *Strafrecht* 271 (1970).

14. This point seems beyond dispute, Jescheck, *supra* note 2, 229; 2 *Course in Soviet Criminal Law*, A. Piontovskij, P. Romashkin and V. Chkhikvadze eds., 357 (1970, in Russian) (herinafter cited as *Kurs* (1970)), but it is curiously omitted from many common law codes, see, e.g., Calif. Penal Code, sec. 197 (deadly force permissible whenever anyone is threatening "great bodily injury to any person"); Israel C.C.O. sec. 18 (defensive force permissible whenever necessary to avoid a greater harm). Neither the California nor the Israeli provision distinguishes between resisting legal and resisting illegal force.

15. Both the common law and Soviet law regard putative self-defense (a reasonable mistake that one is being attacked) as a case of privilege. Model Penal Code sec. 3.04 (Proposed Official Draft 1962); Perkins, *supra* note 8, at 993-94; *Kurs* (1970) at 363-65. German law regards it as a case of excused but wrongful *(rechtswidrig)* conduct. Schmidhaeuser, *supra* note 13, at 281; Jescheck, *supra* note 2, at 233.

16. So far as necessity is recognized legislatively in common law jurisdictions, it is an instance of justification (lesser evils); Model Penal Code, sec. 3.02 (Proposed Official Draft 1962); S. Kadish & M. Paulsen, *Criminal and Its Processes* 544-45 (2d. ed. 1969) (pointing out the gap in the Model Penal Code's coverage). Soviet

law scholars are inclined either to reject the defense or to view it as a matter of privilege, but no one contends that the insane assailant has a privilege to kill. He may not be responsible but neither is his conduct justified or privileged. Thus the case of the psychotic aggressor is one that is problematic in all the systems under study.

There are two basic quandaries posed by the case of the psychotic aggressor. First, if the victim of the attack defends himself and kills the aggressor, should he be acquitted? Secondly, if a third party, a stranger, intervenes on behalf of the victim and kills the aggressor, should he be acquitted? The first question is relatively easy: it is hard to see either the justice or the efficacy of punishing someone who kills for sake of self-preservation. The more difficult issue is whether third persons should be allowed to intervene without risking criminal conviction. If one party to the affray must die, either the insane aggressor or his victim, why should an outsider be encouraged to choose sides? Neither is morally at fault; neither deserves to die. Yet it is hard to deny the pull in the direction of favoring the victim of the attack and permitting intervention to restrain and disable the aggressor.

German and Soviet writers have typically favored acquittals for both the victim and for the third party stranger who inter-

---

law similarily ignores necessity as an excuse. *Ugol Kods.* sec. 14; *Kurs* (1970), at 380-93. German law, on the other hand, recognizes necessity as an excuse, *StGB* sec. 54, *StGB* 1975, sec. 35, and as a justification, *StGB* 1975, sec. 34, A. Schoenke & H. Schroeder, *Strafgesetzbuch* 435-440 (16th ed., 1972). For the difference between necessity as an excuse and as a justification, see text *infra* at notes 20 and 23.

17. Duress has an ambiguous status in the common law. It is based partially on balancing interests, as evidenced by the tendency to limit the defense to compliance with threats of death or serious bodily harm and exempting cases of homicide from the scope of the defense, Israel C.C.O. sec. 17; Calif. Penal Code sec. 26. It is also based partially on the view that submitting to the threats is involuntary, nonculpable, and thus excusable. See, e.g., *Kawakita v. United States*, 343 U.S. 717 (1952). Soviet law holds that cases of acting under duress are to be analyzed as instances of alleged necessity under *Ugol Kod.* sec. 14. *Course in Soviet Criminal Law* 320 (N. Bediav & M. Shargoredskij eds. 1968, in Russian). In German law, on the other hand, duress is clearly an excuse parallel to insanity. *StGB* sec. 52; Schoenke-Schroeder, *supra* note 16 at 464. Cf. *Code Pénal* sec. 64 (treating duress as parallel to insanity).

venes on his behalf.[18] The problem in the literature has been to devise a theory that would account for both of these results. The search for a solution has focused on the areas of self-defense and necessity. Thus we turn to a comparative study of these defenses as they apply to the problem of the psychotic aggressor. As we shall see, there are not merely two rationalia for acquittal expressed in the terms "necessity" and "self-defense." There are no less than five distinct theories and one of our tasks will be to sort out these different rationalia and show how they manifest themselves differentially in common law, German and Soviet legal theory.

TWO DIMENSIONS OF NECESSITY

So far as common law commentators have broached this classic conundrum, they have argued in the language of necessity.[19] Yet the plausability of these claims of necessity may well turn on an internal tension in the theory of the defense. When common lawyers speak of acting under necessity, it is never clear whether they are invoking a theory of justification or of excuse. As has been clear in German theory since Goldschmidt's insightful article in 1913,[20] the rubric of necessity *(Notstand)* encompasses both theories of acquittal. When used as justification, the theory of necessity requires a balancing of competing interests and a judgment that it is right, proper and lawful to favor one interest over another. When used as an excuse, the defense focuses

18. If the problem is analyzed as one of self-defense, the privilege extends, by the language of the code, to attacks against third parties. *StGB* sec. 53; *Ugol. Kod.* sec. 13. There is general agreement today that self defense applies against the psychotic aggressor, e.g. Schoenke-Schroeder, *supra* note 16, at 469; Jescheck, *supra* note 2, at 229; L. Enneccerus & H. Nipperdey, *Allgemeiner Teil des Bürgerlichen Rechts* 1450 (15th ed., 1959) (same conclusion as to tort law); Loeffler, *supra* note 11, 539-40; *Kurs* (1970), *supra* note 14, at 356-57; A. Piontovskij, *Theory of The Offense in Soviet Criminal Law* 426 (1961, in Russian); *Criminal Law: The General Part,* 369 (Text of the Ministry of Higher Education, 1948, in Russian). But note the dissenting view, *infra* note 31.

19. J. Hall, *supra* note 12, at 436 note 85; G. Williams, *Criminal Law: The General Part* 733 (2d. ed., 1961); see also the parallel treatment in the French literature, Bouzat & Pinatel, *supra* note 3, at 363; H. Donnedieu de Vabres, *Traité de Droit Criminel et de Législation Pénale Comparée* 232 (3d ed. 1947). But cf. the dissent by Merle & Vitu, *Traité de Droit Criminel* 318 (1967).

20. Goldschmidt, "Der Notstand: ein Schuldproblem," *Oesterreichische Zeitschrift für Strafrecht* 129, 224 (1913).

not on the propriety of the act but on pressures compelling the defendant to violate the law. If the classic case of *Dudley and Stevens*[21] had been tried in a German court, the shipwrecked sailors might well have been acquitted on grounds of necessity. One might find that they killed the lad Parker and fed on his flesh in order, in the language of the German Code, "to avoid an imminent, otherwise unavoidable risk"[22] of starvation. Yet the theory of this defense is one of excuse, not of justification. The killing was not right—at least not right from the point of view of an ethical system that rejects killing an innocent person for one's own benefit. But the pressures of hunger and the imminence of death might excuse their doing the wrong thing. The two facets of the defense correspond to radically different inferences about the defendant's character. When we justify a choice between evils, we applaud the defendant's judgment in choosing the superior value. His decision reflects well on his character. In contrast, when we excuse conduct as necessitated by overwhelming pressure, we reject the suggestion that the defendant's decision tells us what kind of person he is. We attribute his decision not to his character but to circumstances in which the human thing to do is to succumb to pressure.[23]

Now can one *justify* killing the psychotic aggressor under a theory of necessity? We would have to find that sacrificing the life of the assailant yields a greater expected value. Yet the most that can be gained from the killing is the saving of one's life. If it is life against life, it is hard to see why we should say that it is right and proper for one person to live and the other to die.

The fact is that in the case of psychotic aggressor, we are inclined to favor an acquittal even if the loss to the aggressor is greater than the gain to the defendant. Indeed, as the problem

---

21. *Regina v. Dudley and Stevens* (1884) 14 Q.B. 273.

22. *StGB* sec. 54. The conditions of the defense are that (1) there be an imminent risk or death or serious bodily harm, (2) the risk threatens the actor or his dependent, (3) the situation is not the actor's fault, (4) there is no other way to avoid the risk but to inflict the harm in question. Compare the substantially similar defense in *StGB* 1975, sec. 35.

23. For a fuller discussion of the difference between the concepts of excuse and justification, particularly as applied to tort theory, see Fletcher, "Fairness and Utility in Tort Theory" 85 Harv. L.R. 537, 558-59 (1972) .

is stated, that is the case. For all the defending party knows is that there is a possibility of death if he does not resist. To fend off this possibility, he chooses certain death for the aggressor. When probability factors are included in assessing the competing interests, it is clear the defendant engages in conduct with a higher expected loss (certain death) than expected gain (a probability of death). We could decrease the threat to the defendant without altering our intuitive judgment about the desirability of an acquittal. Would it make any difference if the defendant were threatened with loss of limb, rape or castration? One would think not. As the problem is treated in the literature, it is assumed that justice would require acquittal in these cases as well.

It is possible that those commentators who have looked at the problem as one of necessity have thought that the life of the insane aggressor is worth less than the life of the defendant who is standing his ground. One finds analogies between psychotic aggressors and attacks by wild animals.[24] If one thinks of the psychotic aggressor as subhuman, one might be able to justify the defensive killing as an act preserving the greater value. This is an intriguing if startling approach, but one that is apparently inadequate. Among its other defects it fails to account for the case of temporary psychosis. If the aggressor is a brilliant but temporarily deranged scientist, it would seem rather odd to say that his life is worth less than that of his victim, who for all we know might be a social pariah.[25]

More fundamentally, this approach violates the premise of the criminal law that individuals ought to be judged by what they do, not by their social status or general moral worth. It is true that in assessing culpability we make a judgment about the defendant's character, but that judgment is limited to his character as manifested in commission of the proscribed act. For purposes of sentencing one might wish to engage in a free ranging inquiry about the defendant's background and dangerousness, but those issues have traditionally never borne on the analysis of liability.

---

24. Most strikingly in Bouzat & Pinatel, *supra* note 3, at 362; cf. J. Hall, *supra* note 12, at 436, note 85 (analogy to natural force).

25. The same point was made by Loeffler, *supra* note 11, at 541 note 7, in criticizing those "who regard it as modern to depreciate the life of the insane."

Those who solve the problem of the psychotic aggressor by depreciating the life of the insane depart from the basic premise of equality before the law; they forsake the principle that it is conduct rather than status that determines criminal liability.

If the theory of necessity does not apply as a justification, it might well apply as theory of excuse. There would be little problem in thinking of resisting the attack as a response required to "avert an imminent, otherwise unavoidable, risk to one's life." The claim would be that even though killing the insane aggressor is wrong, it is the natural expression of the human instinct for survival. The claim seems sound; no one can be blamed for killing to save his own life. But reducing one's claim to the level of an excuse is to concede that killing the aggressor is wrong (*rechtswidrig* in the German system) and that has several serious consequences under German and Soviet legal theory. First it would follow that third persons unrelated to the defendant would incur criminal liability if they intervened on his behalf. And why shouldn't they? If he is in the wrong, why should anyone have a right voluntarily to intervene on his behalf.[26] According to the German and Soviet theory of self-defense the implication would be that the aggressor would acquire a right of defense against the defendant's wrongful (*rechtswidrig*) resistance.[27] Third parties would have a derivative right to intervene on his behalf. All of these implications conflict with our sense of justice in the situation. If there is anyone who should be assisted it is the party struggling to save his life against the psychotic aggressor, not *vice versa*. These counterintuitive results derive from conceding that resisting the psychotic aggressor is wrongful though excus-

---

26. In the realm of excuses, intervention is permitted only on behalf of relatives or dependents. See e.g., StBG sec. 54 *(Angehoerige)*, StBG 1973, sec. 35. The reason is that excuses are based on the judgment that intervention is sufficiently involuntary so the actor cannot be fairly blamed for his conduct; this presumably would not be the case if the actor intervened on behalf of a stranger. Many common law formulations of self defense retain this limitation on third party intervention and thus reflect the influence of theories of excuse; see, e.g., Calif. Penal Code sec. 197 (3) (intervention only on behalf of wife, husband, parent, child, master, mistress or servant) ; Israel C.C.O. sec. 18 (intervention only on behalf of persons the actor "is bound to protect") .

27. *StGB* sec. 53; *Ugol. Kods.* sec. 13.

able. An adequate theory, one that would permit third parties to intervene against (and not for) the psychotic aggressor, would have to hold that resistance was not merely excusable but indeed right and proper under the circumstances.

It appears that neither dimension of necessity is adequate to solve the problem of the psychotic aggressor. A theory of justification requires the dubious assumption that the life of a psychotic is worth less than the life of the defendant. A theory of excuse yields unacceptable results with respect to the position of third parties who might intervene. The reason that neither dimension of necessity provides an adequate rationale for acquittal might be that the theory of necessity ignores one important feature of the case: the fact that one of the parties is an aggressor and the other is holding his ground. That is precisely the feature that one would expect to be critical in the theory of self-defense, and therefore we turn to that cluster of theories in our search for an adequate rationale for acquitting the slayer of a psychotic aggressor.

THREE THEORIES OF SELF-DEFENSE

The theory of self-defense is a skein of conflicting theories of acquittal. In the common law world in particular, these conflicting theories generate tensions in analyzing the degree of permissible force, the duty to retreat, the rights of third parties to intervene and the difference between defending oneself in one's home and in public. Similar tensions are brewing in German theory. In this intricate situation one can point to at least three coherent models of the defense that interact in different ways in different legal systems. In the analysis that follows I shall first present the three models as abstract theories, disengaged from particular systems, and then apply the models to the problem of the psychotic aggressor and the rule of proportionality. In the course of the discussion we shall see how these conflicting models of the defense account for disputes over issues beyond our immediate concern, such as the duty to retreat and third party intervention.

The first model, which we may call Self-defense I, represents a theory of excuse. It is limited to those interests like life and bodily security, that individuals feel compelled to protect. It typically requires the defendant to "retreat to the wall" before resorting to deadly force. For it is only when he is against the wall that he has no choice but to kill his adversary. The theory of the defense runs parallel to the excuse of necessity. The critical feature of both defenses is that circumstances "compel" the defendant to resort to deadly force.

This rationale is well expressed in the common defense of *se defendendo* upon a chance medley.[28] According to Coke, Hawkins and Foster,[29] the essence of *se defendendo* was the "inevitable necessity" of killing to save one's own life. This strain in the theory of self-defense provides a rationale for acquitting the party who defends himself against the psychotic aggressor but it suffers from the same shortcoming as the theory of necessity as an excuse.[30] It fails to generate a defense for third persons who choose freely to intervene on his behalf.

The other two models of self-defense are both theories of justification and thus they potentially provide rationalia for acquitting both the victim of the psychotic aggressor and the stranger who comes to his rescue. Self-defense II is a variation on the justification of necessity. Its point of departure is the need to balance the interests of the aggressor against the interests of the victim. Yet it permits one to kill in the name of an interest less valuable than life by adding another factor to the balancing process. In the typical case of self-defense the additional factor is the culpability of the aggressor. The culpability of the aggressor is used as a rationale for diminishing the interests of the aggressor relative to those of the victim. The argument would be that one simply cannot balance the life of a culpable aggressor

---

28. E. Coke, *Third Institute* 55; 1 M. Hale, *Pleas of the Crown* 481-487 (1680); M. Foster, *Crown Law* 275; 1 W. Hawkins, *Pleas of the Crown* 113 (1716); 4 W. Blackstone, *Commentaries** 184; a similarly limited defense emerged in sixteenth and seventeenth century ordinances in German and France. See *Constitutio Criminalis Carolina*, secs. 139 and 140 (1532) ; De Vabres, *supra* note 19, at 227-28 (discussing the Ordinance of 1670) ; G. Vidal, *Cours de Droit Criminel* 312 (9th ed., J. Magnol, 1949) .

29. Coke, *supra* note 28, at 55; Hawkins, *supra* note 28, at 186; Foster, *supra* note 28, at 278.

30. Indeed, *se defendendo* was thought to be part of the theory of necessity. See Blackstone, *supra* note 28, at 186.

against the life of an innocent victim on the assumption that the two combatants are equally situated. The man who chooses to start the fight is held to be entitled to lesser protection than the innocent victim. The problem is how significant the factor of culpability ought to be in diminishing the interests of the aggressor. This is the critical factor in deciding whether self-defense ought to be available against rape, castration, maiming and theft as well as against homicide. The more significantly one regards the culpability of the aggressor, the less significant the victim's interest has to be for the victim to have the right to use deadly force if necessary to repel the attack. Self-defense II is essentially a theory of partial waiver of the aggressor's interests; the waiver is a function of culpability. The underlying premise is that if someone culpably endangers the interest of another, his interests are less worthy of protection than those of the innocent victim.

Self-defense II has found support on both sides of the Rhine River, in Germany,[31] as well as in England and the United States. But it has become dominant only in the common law tradition. Blackstone made it clear that the criterion that determined punishment (namely the gravity of the criminal attack) also prescribed the contours of self-defense. No act "may be *prevented* by death," he wrote, "unless the same, if committed, would also be *punished* by death."[32] Less serious attacks like petty thefts, were not capital offenses and thus they could not be resisted by deadly force. Balancing competing interests is of the essence of Self-defense II; thus the rule of reasonableness or proportionality naturally adheres to any system, like the common law, that is committed to the theory of Self-defense II.

The pinion of the balancing process is the aggressor's culpability. The aggressor's culpability depreciates his interests in the

---

31. Some noteworthy German writers maintain that self-defense is based on a theory of balancing interests. Lenckner, "Gebotensein und Erforderlichkeit der Notwehr," 1968 *Goldtdammers Archiv für Strafrecht* 1; Schaffstein, "Notwehr und Guterabwaegungsprinzip," *Monatschrift für Deutsches Recht* 132 (1952). See also the writers supporting the theory of *Rechtsmissbrauch* as a limitation on defensive force, *infra* note 68.

32. Blackstone, *supra* note 28, at 182. This seems to be the first account of why there are limits to the common law privilege of deadly force.

balancing process and thus distinguishes Self-defense II from the justification of necessity. Yet with culpability as its pinion Self-defense II cannot be geared to solve the problem of the psychotic aggressor. By definition the psychotic aggressor is not culpable and thus Self-defense II fails to explain why his interests should be worth less than those of the victim. One might try to argue that the mere aggression, whether culpable or not, provides a basis for diminishing the interests of the aggressor in the balancing process. Yet this argument does not survive critical examination. Why should someone's interest be diminished by virtue of aggressive propensities for which he is not morally to blame? One can understand diminishing an aggressor's interests if he is to blame for the encounter but it is hard to see why he should be worth less merely because his body is the *locus* of dangerous propensities. It seems that Self-defense II may provide a perfectly sound rationale of self-defense in the typical case, but it fails to give an account of our intuition in the case in which the aggressor's conduct is excused by reason of insanity or by other acknowledged excusing conditions.

What is it about the aggression that prompts us to think the victim and the third person ought to be able to kill the psychotic aggressor? The underlying judgment must be that the victim has a right to the integrity and autonomy of his body and that he has a right to prevent encroachments upon his living space. The notion of individual autonomy and the right to protect autonomy underlies the radically different theory of Self-defense III. All that is required to invoke Self-defense III is a particular kind of aggression against an innocent agent. Not all forms of aggression would trigger this kind of self-defense. If the aggression is justified, say by reason of a right to arrest, then the innocent agent would not have the right to resist. The criterion that is used in German and Soviet law to define the appropriate kind of aggression is the notion of *rechtswidrig* conduct. The concept of *Rechtswidrigkeit* is liberally translated as unlawfulness or illegality, but those definitions fail to capture an important point. The standard for self-defense in German and Soviet law is carefully defined so as to permit self-defense against excused aggressors. The conduct of the psychotic aggressor is *rechtswidrig*. It is not clear that we would call that conduct unlawful in the idiom of Anglo-American law, although the Model Penal Code sought to define the concept of unlawfulness so as to render the conduct of the excused aggressor unlawful.[33] Thus the central requirement for Self-defense III is that the victim be endangered by unjustified, unlawful, but possibly excused conduct. The focus is not upon the culpability of the aggressor, but rather on the autonomy of the innocent agent. The assumption is that the innocent agent has a right to prevent encroachments upon his autonomy. As German scholars put it: Right should never give way to Wrong.[34]

Self-defense III is the dominant theory of self-defense in German[35] and Soviet criminal theory.[36] It also found expression in early common law theory. Sir Edward Coke insisted that no

33. Model Penal Code sec. 3.11 (1) (Proposed Official Draft 1962). The effort was not understood by legislators who adopted the code. See Fletcher, "The Theory of Criminal Negligence: A Comparative Analysis" 119 *U. Pa. L. R.* 401, 428, note 74 (1971).

34. It is generally held that Berner coined the phrase in Berner, "Die Notwehrtheorie" 1843 *Archiv des Criminalrechts* 547, 557, 562. Since then the maxim has appeared in virtually every German analysis of self-defense.

35. There are two features of Self-defense III, as it is defined in the text: (1) applicability of the defense against excused aggression. On this point, see Jescheck, *supra* note 2, at 229; Schoenke-Schroeder, *supra* note 16, 469; R. Maurach, *Deutsches Strafrecht* 264 (3rd. ed., 1968); older authorities, cited *supra* note 11; but cf. Schaffstein, *supra* note 30, at 135-136 (scepticism about self-defense against psychotic aggressors); Schmidhaeuser, "Uber die Wertstruktur der Notwehr," *Festschrift für Honig* 194 (1970) (rejecting self-defense against the excused aggressor). (2) The second feature is rejection of the rule of proportionality. On this point see K. Himmelreich, *Notwehr und bewusste Fahrlaessigkeit* 76-86 (1971); D. Kratsch, *Grenzen der Strafbarkeit in Notwehr* 52 (1968); D. Heinsius, *Moderne Entwicklung des Notwehrrechts* 32 (1965); Stratenwerth, *supra* note 2, at 60-61; Oetker, "Notwehr und Notstand," *Festgabe für R. Frank* 283 (1930); R. Frank, *Strafgesetz für das Deutsche Reich,* 118-19 (1908). But cf. authorities recognizing the limitation imposed by the doctrine of *Rechtsmissbrauch, infra* note 68.

36. See authorities cited *supra* notes 18 and 35. The only dissent in the Soviet literature was voiced by Slutskij who argued that if the defender knew that the aggressor was insane, the case should be analyzed as one of necessity; if the defender did not know, it should be a case of self-defense. I. Slutskij, *Conditions for Negating Criminal Responsibility,* 48-9 (1956, in Russian). This view is routinely castigated in the literature, e.g., Piontovskij, *supra* note 18, at 426-27; *Kurs* (1970) at 357-57; but it received sympathetic treatment in I. Tishkevich, *Conditions and Limits to Self-Defense,* 22-4 (1969, in Russian).

"man shall (ever) give way to a thief, etc., neither shall he forfeit anything."[37] And John Locke supported the same theory of an absolute right to protect one's liberty and rights from encroachment by aggressors.[38] Among the various accounts of Self-defense III one finds the common theme that the act of aggression puts the aggressor outside the protection of the law. Locke, for example, speaks of the aggressor's being in a "state of war" with the defender.[39] The argument is that the aggression breaches an implicit contract among autonomous agents, according to which each person or country is bound to respect the living space of all others. The intrusion upon someone's living space itself triggers a justified response.[40]

The same doctrine finds expression in the rhetoric of the American revolution. The slogan "Don't tread on me" expresses the claim that "treading" upon someone else in itself entails a justified response. It is irrelevant whether the country or person so "treading" is culpable for his deeds. When at war, one is concerned only about the enemy's aggression, not about its possible excuses. The roots of the right of defense are not in the culpability of the aggressor, but in the autonomy of the defender.

Self-defense III generates a paradoxical view of aggression. It treats the aggressor as a participant in the legal system yet it views the aggression as a breakdown of the framework for compassion and solicitude. The aggressor is protected by the legal conditions for exercising defensive force and simultaneously treated as though his interests were irrelevant. He is at once inside and outside the legal community, simultaneously a colleague and an outlaw.

This paradoxical status is generated by a characteristic set of legal expressions. In the German idiom each case of self-defense represents a conflict between *Recht* (Right) and *Unrecht*

---

37. E. Coke, *Third Institute* 55.

38. J. Locke, *Two Treatises on Civil Government* 120-7 (1690).

39. *Ibid* at 126.

40. This is a theory of self-defense developed in the Kantian tradition. For survey of other theories, including some that might be more difficult to comprehend today, see Himmelreich, *supra* note 35, at 70-72.

(Wrong); the victim stands for the Right; the aggressor for the Wrong—as though each instance of self-defense were an Everyman drama. Another central concept is that of the Legal Order *(die Rechtsordnung),* which in the German view is threatened by every breach of the law.[41] Thus the autonomy of the defender is identified with the idea of Law itself and every act of self-defense is a defense of the basic structure of legal relationships. This conceptual framework, much of which appears as well in the Soviet literature,[42] thrusts the aggressor to the fringes of the legal system.[43] Though he may be psychotic and morally innocent he becomes an enemy of the Law itself.

SELF DEFENSE AND PROPORTIONALITY

As one may imagine, the doctrinal lens of Self-defense III filters out shades and nuances and transforms all situations into black and white relief. The only question is whether the aggressor has intruded upon the defender's sphere of autonomy; questions of degree are suppressed. This absolutist perspective proves to be hostile to the rule of proportionality, as confirmed by the German Supreme Court in 1920 in a classic case.[44] An orchard owner shot a couple of thieves running away with fruit from his trees. He claimed that he shot in self-defense, namely in defense of his property. He was acquitted, the prosecutor appealed and the Supreme Court affirmed, adding that if necessary the de-

41. E. G. Schoenke-Schroeder, *supra* note 16, at 471 *(Die Notwehr dient der Bewahrung der Rechtsordung im ganzen:* Self-defense serves to maintain the Legal Order in its entirey); Schmidhauser, *supra* note 35, at 93-94 *(Der Angriff stellt die Rechtsordnung in Frage:* The aggressor's attack put the Legal Order into question).

42. There is no concept in the Soviet literature corresponding to *Unrecht* (the Wrong), but Soviet writers do dely heavily on the notions of *protivopravnost' (Rechtswidrigkeit)* and social dangerousness to make even excused aggression appear to be a threat to the Soviet social order. For a general treatment of these concepts, see *Kurs* (1970) at 131-34 and 342-46.

43. In contrast to the German and Soviet emphasis on the connection between self-defense and protecting the Right and the Legal Order, it is interesting to note Joseph Beale's effort to banish a similar analysis from the common law of self-defence; he went so far as to say: "The law does not ordinarily secure the enjoyment of rights. . . . Still less frequently the law permits one to protect his own rights. . . ." Beale, "Retreat from a Murderous Assault" 16 *Harv. L. R.* 567, 581 (1903).

44. Decision of September 20, 1920, 55 *Entscheidungen des Reichsgerichts in Strafsachen* 82.

fendant could have shot with the intent to kill. The court recalled the basic premise of Self-defense III: Right need never yield to Wrong. Thus any intrusion upon a protected interest generates a right to use whatever force is necessary to restore the victim's autonomy.

German and Soviet scholars have been anxious for generations about the problem of shooting petty thieves.[45] Yet there are powerful pressures against recognizing the principle of proportionality. Both autonomy and proportionality are jealous standards. It seems neither can accommodate the other without surrendering its primacy. If autonomy is protected only to the extent compatible with the rule of proportionality, then it is in fact the latter and not autonomy that determines the boundaries of the defense.[46] Thus one must choose between the standards of autonomy and balancing interests. It is clear German and Russian theorists still adhere to centrality of autonomy in the theory of self-defense.

Many Soviet and German writers object to an imprecise boundary to self-defense, for one cannot fairly expect someone in danger to reflect on the merits of competing interests.[47] Thus the

45. There was strong opposition in nineteenth century Germany to an unlimited right of self-defense. See, e.g. A. Geyer, *Die Lehre von der Notwehr*, 39-42 (1857) (favoring use of deadly force only to save life; citing other writers in accord). Dissent continued after the 1920 decision, cited, *supra* note 44. Coenders, "Zur Lehre vom Notrecht," *Juristische Wochenschrift* 891 (1925). Several factors in post-war Germany stimulated academicians to rethink the established view. One was a 1949 decision by the Higher State Court in Stuttgart, which held that acquitting a guard who intentionally killed a petty thief in flight was "a gross violation of natural law"; OLG Stuttgart, 1949 *Deutsche Richterzeitung* 42, another stimulating factor was the 1952 German ratification of the European Convention on Human Rights, which provides in Article II (2) that deadly force is justifiable only to avert threats to life. See Woesner, "Die Menschenrechtskonvention in der deutschen Strafrechtspraxis" 1961 *Neue Juristische Wochenschrift* 1381. Though this provision is legally binding as law in German Federal Republic, its impact has been nullified by a variety of interpretative maneuvers; Heinsius, *supra* note 35, at 18-30; Schoenke-Schroeder, *supra* note 16, at 467.
46. But note that there is one strain in the German literature which regards proportionality as an exception, rather than as a rationale for the defense. E.g. Schoenke-Schroeder, *supra* note 16, at 472.
47. E.g., Kratsch, *supra* note 35, at 43-44; Berner, *supra* note 33, at 584-85. The argument recalls the classic formulation of Justice Holmes: "Detached reflection cannot be demanded in the presence of an uplifted knife," *Brown v. United States* 256 U.S. 335, 343 (1921).

rule of proportionality invites excessive caution in order to avoid the risk of conviction. This caution results in undue deference to aggressors and encourages criminal conduct.[48]

Whatever the force of these arguments, the consensus of German and Soviet writers supports some limitation at the extreme edges of the right to use deadly force. The basic problem is whether there is some way to acknowledge this limitation in the formal definition of the right of self-defense. Since 1925 German draftsmen have been proposing formal limitations on the right to use whatever force is necessary to repel an aggressive attack. The 1925 draft code demanded defensive force be used only "in an appropriate way";[49] the 1927 draft, that the harm caused not be out of proportion to the harm threatened;[50] the 1939 National Socialist draft, that the use of force not violate the "sound sensibilities of the people."[51] All of these proposals approximate the common law rule of reasonableness, but none of these drafts was ever enacted. The 1962 draft which finally succeeded in generating a new West German criminal code, retains the traditional formula for self-defense: the defender may use all the force "necessary" to thwart a wrongful *(rechtswidrig)* attack.[52]

The Soviet government, on the other hand, introduced a new phrase in the 1958 Fundamental Principles of Criminal Legislation which at first glance seems to refer to the principle of proportionality. The Principles and the new Codes they inspired provide explicitly that there are limits to self-defense and these lim-

---

48. The Soviet literature routinely stresses the importance of individual self-defense in combatting crime, e.g., *Kurs* (1970) 347-349; M. Jakubovich, *Theory of Self-Defense in Soviet Criminal Law,* 17-20 (1967 in Russian).

49. Draft 1925 sec. 21 (II) (" . . . *in einer den Umständen nach angemessenen Weise . . .")* as quoted in Heinius, *supra* note 35, at 5; Cf. the Swiss Criminal Code sec. 33, which also relies on the word *angemessen* (appropriate) to define the limits of self-defense. V. Schwander, *Das Schweizerische Strafgesetzbuch* 83-84 (2d ed., 1952).

50. Draft 1927 sec. 21 (". . . *nicht ausser Verhaeltnis . . . steht")* as quoted in Heinsius, *supra* note 35, at 6. Cf. the German Civil Code *(BGB)* sec. 228, which used the same formula to regulate the justification of necessity against risks emanating from objects.

51. Draft 1939 sec. 24 (II) *(. . . dem gesunden Volksempfinden nicht widerspricht),* as quoted in Heinsius, *supra* note 35, at 6.

52. *StGB* 1975, sec. 32.

its are exceeded when the defense is "clearly out of conformity to the character and the dangerousness of the attack."[53] There is no independent reference to the requirement that the force used be necessary to stifle the aggressive attack.[54] Thus the Soviet drafts contain a built-in ambiguity; it is not clear whether the proviso refers to the requirement of proportionality or to the requirement that the force be no more than necessary. A number of writers have addressed themselves to the problem in recent years and the weight of the literature is clearly hostile to the rule of proportionality.[55] The writers devote a great deal of space to criticizing lower courts that impose limitations on the right of self-defense either by imposing a duty to retreat or by finding that the defendant used excessive force.[56] This pattern of the lower courts was apparently so disquieting to the Federal Supreme Court that it intervened with a special decree in 1969;[57] the Supreme Court chastised trial judges for "mechanically" concluding that defensive force was excessive without giving due attention to factors, like the age and condition of the defender, that might yield a more flexible right of defense.[58] On the basis of this decree and the tradition in the literature, the 1970 textbook on criminal law published by the Academy of Sciences concludes that "the character of the defended interest" is irrelevant to the scope of self-defense.[59] It is obvious that despite the new legislative language, the Soviet higher courts remain opposed to

---

53. *Fundamental Principles of Criminal Legislation* sec. 13, (1958). The identical language appears in *Ugol. Kods.* sec. 13.

54. Note that one could relate the issue of proportionality to the word "character" and the issue of necessity to the word "dangerousness." There were some early signs that this interpretation might emerge; see the 1960 text on criminal law, cited *supra* note 2, at 346, which held that the word "character" referred to the quality of the interest protected. But this view is not to be found in the subsequent Soviet works canvassed in this paper.

55. E.g., *Kurs* (1970) at 369 and 371; Tishkevich, *supra* note 36, at 97; Shavgulidze, *supra* note 11, at 111.

56. E.g., Tishkevich, *supra* note 36, at 93, 98; see also the criticism of lower courts in the 1969 decree of the Supreme Soviet, *infra* note 57.

57. Decree No. 11 of the Plenum of the Supreme Court of the USSR, December 4, 1969 (On the Practice of Courts in Applying Legislation on Self-defense), *1970 Bulletin of the Supreme Court of the USSR* No. 1, p. 15 (in Russian).

58. *Id.* at 18 (point 3).

59. *Kurs* (1970), at 371.

the rule of proportionality. Paradoxically, most writers agree there should be an exception in the case of the apple thief.[60] The logic is not at all clear; and, as I suggest below, there may be a systematic effort to obfuscate the issue in order to permit a solution to the extreme cases without introducing a rule expressly recognizing the balancing of competing interests.

It is characteristic of law reform in West Germany in particular that theories are not given a firm cast in legislation until they are first resolved in the scholarly literature.[61] Thus it is in the literature and in the case law not in the new Code that one should hope to find progress toward an acceptable doctrinal technique denying the right of self-defense for the sake of disproportionately petty interests.

The theorists have struck out in two basic directions. One approach is to develop categorical distinctions between grievous and minor attacks with a differentiated right of response in each category. This indeed seems to be the way the common law developed. The common law progressively revised the categories for using defensive force by distinguishing first between felonies and misdemeanors;[62] and thereafter between atrocious felonies and less serious felonies.[63] A few German writers have tried the same approach. Oetker argued in 1930 that attacks on minor interests should be regarded as mischief *(Unfug)* rather than *Unrecht* and that they should not trigger the full response permitted in a case of self-defense.[64] Recently Schmidhauser revived

---

60. *Id.* at 371; Shavgulidze, *supra* note 11, at 109; Piontovskij, *supra* note 18, at 442.

61. A good example is the development of the new defense of mistake of law: the issue was first debated in the literature; the Supreme Court endorsed one of the competing schools in its decision of March 18, 1952, 2 *Entscheidungen des Bundesgerichtshofs in Strafsachen* 194; and that position was then incorporated in the new code, *StGB* 1975, sec. 17.

62. Hale, *supra* note 28 at 485-86 (distinguishing between trespass and felonies); Calif. Penal Code sec. 197 (1), permitting deadly force "when resisting any attempt . . . to commit a felony. . . ." This sweeping language has been narrowed in the case law, e.g., *People v. Jones,* 191 Cal. App. 2d 478, 481; 12 Cal. Rptr. 777 (1961) (privilege limited to felonies involving danger of serious bodily harm).

63. Blackstone, *supra* note 28, at 180 (deadly force limited to "forcible and atrocious crimes"); *Storey v. State,* 71 Ala. 329 (1882) (limited to "atrocious crime(s) committed by force").

64. Oetker, *supra* note 35, at 359.

this effort by claiming that petty attacks, those usually tolerated by the society at large, do not represent violations of the Legal Order.[65] His example is the violation of an anti-noise regulation by a group of motorcyclists. The only way to suppress the noise might be to shoot them—a patently absurd result, but one suggested by Self-defense III. These kinds of violations would not generate a right of self-defense for they are implicitly tolerated by the community as a whole. This is an intriguing suggestion, if only because it reveals the sophistication required to accomplish that which is assumed as a matter of course in the common law tradition.

Most German writers focus on a basically different approach to the problem. A basic principle of French and German private law is that private rights may not be abused to the detriment of others. Thus Continental jurists speak of *abus de droit* and *Rechtsmissbrauch*[66] instead of relying, as do common law jurists, on the pervasiveness of reasonableness in specifying the contours of private rights. German courts and theorists have invoked this private law doctrine as a device for limiting the right of self-defense. One of the leading cases is a 1963 Bavarian decision,[67] in which the defendant was convicted of attempted extortion for driving toward a lady pedestrian and threatening to run her down. The lady was standing in the single parking space available in a lot where the defendant wanted to park. The victim maintained that she was holding the spot for someone else, whereupon the defendant drove toward her. His argument was that the victim's behavior was illegal and that he was exercising self-defense. One fascinating point of the case is that the Bavarian appellate court agreed; this was a case of self-defense. But, the court added, in this situation the defendant abused his right of defense for "the harm inflicted was disproportionate to that threatened by the attack" (i.e. standing in the parking space). There would seem to be many reasons not to take this case as a

---

65. Schmidhaeuser, *supra* note 35, at 196 (in the author's words, these attacks do not put "the empirical validity of the Legal Order in question").

66. See generally, Ennecerus—Nipperdey, *supra* note 18, at 1442-48.

67. Decision of the Bavarian Higher State Court, January 22, 1963, 1963 *Neue Juristische Wochenschrift* 824.

precedent requiring tolerance of thefts or of petty physical injuries when the only alternative is death to the assailant. First, this is a case on the fringes of self-defense; it is dubious whether one should regard sequestering a parking space as an attack akin to physical assault. Secondly, it seems obvious that the defendant could have used lesser means to remove the lady from the space; the force was excessive even apart from the issue of proportionality.

This case is widely cited to support the growing scholarly consensus in favor of applying the doctrine of *Rechtsmissbrauch* to impose limits on the right of self-defense.[68] Though this doctrine is gaining ground, it poses a significant difficulty. As argued recently by Dietrich Kratsch,[69] judicial qualification of the legislated right of self-defense may violate the rule of *nulla poena sine lege* which has the status of a constitutional rule in West Germany.[70] Applying the principle of *Rechtsmissbrauch* to cases of self-defense creates a new class of punishable acts, namely those that would be covered by the traditional right but not covered by the qualified right of self-defense. According to Kratsch, these acts are rendered punishable by judicial decree and thus imposing liability violates the rule of *nulla poena sine lege*.[71] This argument does not inhibit legislative reform but it does suggest that circumscribing a defense by judicial decree is a dubious practice.

If legislative reform is the preferable technique, one is puz-

---

68. Jescheck, *supra* note 2, at 230-31; Schoenke-Schroeder, *supra* note 16, at 472-473; H. Welzel, *Das Deutsche Strafrecht* 87 (11th ed., 1969) ; J. Wessels, *Strafrecht* 50 (1970) ; W. Sauer, *Allgemeine Strafrechtslehre*, 120-22 (3rd ed., 1955) ; Baumann, "Rechtsmissbrauch bei Notwehr" 1962 *Monatschrift für Deutsches Recht* 349 (discussing earlier references) . The phrase *Rechtsmissbrauch* appears regularly in judicial opinions, even though the context rarely requires it. See, Decision of the Supreme Court, June 6, 1968, 1969 *Goltdammers Archiv für Strafrecht* 1 *(dicta;* issue was excessive force) ; Decision of the Supreme Court, January 8, 1961, 1962 *Neue Juristische Wochenschrift* 308 (confusing the issue of necessary force with the problem of proportionality) . See the comment by Guttman, "Die Berufung auf das Notwehrrecht als Rechtsmissbrauch" 1962, *id.* at 286.

69. Kratsch, *supra* note 35, at 30; Cf. Schaffstein, *supra* note 31, at 135.

70. *Grundgesetz* sec. 103 (II) .

71. One reply to this argument is that imposing limits on the defense only makes explicit the underlying theory of the defense; see Lenckner, *supra* note 31, at 8-9. This argument assumes, without support, that the German theory of self-defense reflects the balancing of interests and is thus based on the model of Self-defense II.

zled by the failure of the German draftsmen to write the rule of *Rechtsmissbrauch* into law. Eberhard Schmidt's commentary to the 1962 draft suggests that the problem could well be handled within the framework of the traditional rule of "necessary force."[72] This move is intriguing for it intimates an uncharacteristic trend in German theory toward muddling a basic distinction. It has always been fundamental in the analysis of self-defense that necessary force is one issue and reasonable force another. The requirement of necessary force may be suited to introducing a duty to retreat in some situations or by requiring resort to public assistance instead of private force. These are alternative means of frustrating the aggressor's design. But the rule of proportionality raises the fundamentally different question whether one should be required to let the aggressor succeed because the cost of stopping him is too great. If the new German code purports to conflate these distinct issues, one cannot but sense a trend toward obscurity in the analysis of self-defense.[73]

If there is a trend toward purposeful muddling of the German theory of self-defense, it runs parallel to similar developments in the Soviet literature. Contemporary Soviet writers agree on concrete cases (deadly force is permissible to prevent rape but not an apple theft).[74] Yet they abjure all formal standards and remain hostile to the systematic balancing of interests.[75] The 1970 text even concedes that Soviet law has not yet worked out a test for excessive self-defense.[76] Instead of formulating a formal criterion Soviet jurists are content to list the factors relevant to the questions both of necessary and of reasonable force.[77] Thus they merge these distinct issues and muddle through without articulating the principle that makes the distinct factors rele-

---

72. Schmidt, "Notwehr," 11 *Niederschriften Über die Sitzungen der Grossen Strafrechtskommission* 54 (1958).

73. See also Schmidt, *id.* at 58, suggesting that one should wait until the "hypothetical" problems arise in cases and then trust in the capacity of judges to solve with "creative judicial legislation."

74. E.g., *Kurs* (1970) at 371; Jakubovich, *supra* note 48 at 85.

75. E.g., *Kurs* (1970), at 369; Piontovskij, *supra* note 18 at 441.

76. *Kurs* (1970) at 369.

77. Tishkevich, *supra* note 36, at 100-1; Yakubovich, *supra* note 48, at 43-44; see also Decree of the Supreme Court, *supra* note 57, at 16.

vant. This is a technique of low-visibility problem-solving that stresses concrete solutions rather than the working out of basic principles. It is an approach long favored by the common law and now finding favor among some German and Soviet jurists who may have despaired of finding a principled solution within their theory of self-defense.

COMPARATIVE LEGAL THEORY AND
THE PROBLEM OF PROPORTIONALITY

The intriguing question of comparative legal theory is why German and Soviet jurists have been as anguished as they have about the problem of proportionality, while common law (and French) jurists unhesitatingly accepted the rule of reasonable force. In the course of this essay I have attempted to elucidate the link between the problem of the psychotic aggressor and the German-Soviet hostility to the rule of proportionality. The argument has been that in contrast to the common law literature, German and Soviet theorists have seriously confronted the problem of using deadly force against a psychotic or otherwise excused aggressor and they have thus adhered to the only theory, which in their opinion as well as mine, generates a right to use a deadly force against the psychotic aggressor. I have referred to this theory as Self-defense III to distinguish it both from theories of self-defense based on balancing competing interests and from theories that generate only an excuse and not a justification. Self-defense III is based on a concept of individual autonomy analogous to the concept of sovereignty in the relations between states. In Germany and the Soviet Union this central concept has proved to be absolutist and thus resistant to intrusions by the rule of proportionality.

There seems to be a causal connection between solving the problem of the psychotic aggressor and generating another problem in defining the limits of self-defense. Yet the nature of that causal tie requires some clarification. From the time of Blackstone, the common law has never had cause to question the implicit limitation of reasonableness in the contours of self-defense. It seems fairly clear that one reason for this confidence is that commentators never considered whether there might be something defective about a system of self-defense based on balancing interests. One reason they never questioned their system is that they never seriously confronted the one type of case in which their approach to self-defense is inadequate, namely the case of excused, nonculpable aggression.

This half of the thesis is negative; it holds that one thing never happened (questioning the rule of proportionality) because something else never happened (analyzing the problem of the psychotic aggressor). The positive side of the thesis is more problematic. It would be difficult to maintain that curiosity about the psychotic aggressor in itself generated Self-defense III and its relatively inflexible commitment to the value of individual autonomy.[78] There must have been other features of the German and Soviet legal systems that make them receptive to an absolutist conception of self-defense. I shall point out some of these features here, but I fear the account will be more superficial than the subject deserves.

If one is to build a theory of self-defense around the defender's autonomy rather than the aggressor's culpability, one has to have a conceptual filter for identifying those cases of aggression, both culpable and nonculpable, that generate a right of defense. The Germans and Russians rely on a standard that is unique to their systems of jurisprudence and which is not found in systems committed to Self-defense II. The cornerstone of the German and Russian approach is the concept of *rechtswidrige (protivopravnye)* attacks. As we have seen, attacks need not be culpable to meet this test. They are attacks that, as the Germans put it, are incompatible with *Recht,* with the Legal Order, with the Right.

These definitions elude the common lawyer for there is no concept of Right in the modern common law; nor is there a notion of a Legal Order that transcends particular laws and precedents. The common law concept of self-defense is tied to the more concrete concept of physical assault and thus it befuddles the common law mind to think of preventing someone from blocking a parking space as a case of self-defense. The best way to

---

78. One source of scepticism is that in his classic article coining the maxim "Right should never yield to Wrong," Berner does not even mention the problem of the psychotic aggressor. See Berner, *supra* note 33.

grasp what the Germans have in mind is to turn to the Soviet version of the same concept. Soviet theorists have lent clear substantive content to the concept of *rechtswidrig* conduct by identifying it with the principle that all criminal conduct in the Soviet system must be socially dangerous. If conduct is *protivopravnye* (*rechtswidrig*) it is also socially dangerous. Yet social dangerousness is not a test for liability; it is a concept that underlies the legal system and invests it with coherence and purpose. The notions of *Recht* and Legal Order function the same way in legal systems like the contemporary German system that stresses structural criteria such as individual rights. The Right is the set of individual rights writ large. It is a construct onto which individual rights are projected.

The concepts of social dangerousness and of the Right are essential in formulating a theory of Self-defense III. They provide a medium for viewing attacks against individuals as attacks against the entire society and its legal system. If aggression is socially dangerous or if it violates the Legal Order, the aggressor is seen as an enemy of the system; he has ruptured the bonds of social concern and put himself outside the realm of normal human solicitude. Thus his attack, whether culpable or not, can and should be stopped at all costs. This is but a more sophisticated way of speaking, as did John Locke, of a state of war between the aggressor and his victim.[79] Yet the difference in sophistication is important. It is difficult to integrate a theory of warfare into a legal system. An outlaw, someone at war with society, is not a participant in the legal system. He has no rights; he can be shot at will. But this is not true of the psychotic aggressor; he can be shot only if it is necessary to prevent an imminent attack on a legally protected interest. He is protected by the law, yet considered an enemy of the legal order.

The conceptual structure of the common law makes it much harder to think of the psychotic aggressor as both a fellow citizen and an outlaw. There is no standard in the common law that runs parallel to social dangerousness in the Soviet system or *Rechtswidrigkeit* in German theory. It may be that the notions of

---

79. See text *supra* at notes 35 and 43.

"felon" and "felony" once approached this function but felony has long since become merely one form of crime. The rise of legal positivism in the last hundred years makes theorists skeptical of transcendental notions like social dangerousness and the Legal Order, for these are constructs of the legal system that are neither defined by case law nor proclaimed by the legislature. The modern common law is unreceptive to abstractions of this sort and thus the system lacks the conceptual lens necessary to focus on the aggressor now as friend, now as foe.

The common law is inclined to view the problem of self-defense as a conflict between individual interests, analogous to problems of necessity and therefore to insist upon balancing interests in the one case as in the other. However inadequate the concept of necessity may be for coping with the psychotic aggressor, the common law writers fail to transcend this perspective. They lack the conceptual framework for thinking of self-defense as a vindication of the Legal Order.

Another reason the German and Soviet systems have been more receptive to Self-defense III is that these systems are generally more amenable to justifications based on individual rights rather than the public interest. German and Soviet jurists think of self-defense as an undeniable, even natural right of the individual. In contrast, the common law takes self-defense to be a derivative of the state's function to keep the peace.[80] Where the state fails the individual may intervene—but only so far as his conduct furthers the good of the community. It is clear that the good of the community includes the aggressor's interests and self-defense detracts from the common welfare where the use of force inflicts undue hardship on the aggressor.

Soviet writers are particularly hostile to the view that self-defense is a derivative institution. They castigate the "bourgeois" tendency to dethrone self-defense from its status as an individual private right.[81] Soviet writers insist that the capacity of the po-

---

80. See W. Blackstone, *supra* note 25 at 185 (referring to the King and his court as *"vindices injuriarum,"* and the primary role of the state in responding to aggression) ; accord, Hale, *supra* note 4 at 481.

81. *Kurs* (1970) , at 349; Piontovskij, *supra* note 18 at 425; see also Decree of the Supreme Court, *supra* note 57, at 17 (referring to self-defense as "inalienable right") .

lice to keep the peace is irrelevant to self-defense; if one's interests are attacked one may respond without determining first whether official help is at hand.[82] Even though Soviet jurists start from different social premises they concur with their German colleagues that self-defense is a basic private right.

The analogy of self-defense to private rights accounts for the tendency toward absolutism of Self-defense III. It is in the nature of recognizing private rights that one concedes that others may be affected and even harmed by their exercise.[83] Whether one fails to exercise one's rights is a matter of private judgment, not of state policy. Yet even contract rights may not be "abused" according to Continental legal theory and thus one understands the reliance on a private law doctrine, namely abuse-of-rights or *Rechtsmissbrauch,* in drawing the limits to the right of self-defense.

The conceptual background of German and Soviet law and the tendency to think of self-defense as a private right provides the background for the emergence of Self-defense III. Against this background German and Soviet theorists accepted the one theory of self-defense that solved a recurrent theoretical problem in the literature, the problem of the psychotic aggressor. Yet solving one quandary generated another and today German and Soviet jurists are still wrestling with the unruly issue of proportionality in trying to set limits to self-defense. The common law has been spared the latter problem only because it never faced the former. It would be difficult to say the common law's avoidance of the entire thicket was purposeful but one cannot but feel there was some method in the common law's minding issues more practical than that of the psychotic aggressor. There is no doubt the common law is still in Plato's cave and that it barely perceives the shadows of criminal theory. Yet as this study has shown onerous burdens befall jurists who emerge from the cave and try to work out a coherent and comprehensive theory of self-defense.

---

82. *Kurs* (1970) at 349 (criticizing a Tsarist rule conditioning the right of self-defense on the unavailability of official help) : Tishkevich, *supra* note 36 at 62.

83. See generally, Enneccerus—Nipperdey, *supra* note 18 at 1440.

CHAPTER 10

SENTENCING THE PSYCHOPATH: A STUDY OF CONFLICT IN CORRECTIONAL THEORY

H. H. A. Cooper

Deputy Director, Criminal Law Education and Research Center, New York University

INTRODUCTION

Sentencing a man may be and often is decisive as to his fate. Therefore it seems to be a fair demand on society that its organs, the courts of justice, should not use their enormous power on the citizens lightheartedly, but be fully aware of the consequences of their decisions.

Olof Kinberg[1]

THE PRIMARY OBJECTIVE of criminal justice administration is the control of human behavior in the interest of the better protection of society. The techniques and ulterior goals of penology have varied widely over the years but the broad, underlying purposes of the criminal sanction are well-defined and their manifestations clear-cut, if not always expressly avowed.[2] The judici-

---

1. "Forensic Psychiatry without Metaphysics," 40 *J. Crim. L. & Crim.* 555, at 557 (1950).

2. One article among many is worthy of special mention in the present context: De Grazia, "Crime Without Punishment: A Psychiatric Conundrum," 52 *Colum. L. Rev.* 746 (1952). Worth repeating too, are Jerome Hall's words: "If an adequate theory of punishment is to be established, the imperious need is to understand the complexity of the criminal law and its administration, where norms of justice coalesce with the objective of deterrence and an unremitting search for rehabilitation." "Mental Disease and Criminal Responsibility," 45 *Colum. L. Rev.* 677 at 716 (1945). See, too, the excellent article by Mueller "Punishment, Corrections and the Law," 45 *Neb. L. Rev.* 58 (1966).

ary is, in the main,[3] the organ through which society expresses its correctional predilections, its choice of aims and the purposes of its penal policy. The sentencing of the offender is not an end in itself but rather the initiation of a meaningful process that others will carry on. It will affect not merely the individual sentenced and those immediately connected with him but also the wider society of which he forms a part. This phase of judicial activity does not take place in a vacuum but rather presupposes a juridical continuum and a sociological context of whose relevance the judge must be constantly and acutely aware in the formulation of his sentence.

The pressures on the judge as he seeks to translate into objective, normative terms these broad, penological purposes are considerable. The aims of society in the correctional field are never truly static nor even stabilized for long.[4] The more dynamic the system the greater will be the confusion, out of which the judge must perforce select the elements of his sentence so as to give effect, subjectively, to what he conceives of as society's aims and purposes[5] in a general sense and thus be able to apply them consistently, in the instant case, to the individual before him. The intellectual component is never consistent nor harmonious as to quality or content,[6] with the result that on a broad, overall view,

---

3. The idea of the sentencing panel has not yet achieved a corresponding popularity. It has been said that, "Sentencing forms such a vital part of a criminal proceeding that much can be said in favor of leaving at least the initial determination of a sentence to the chief organ for the administration of justice, the judge." Edgar Bodenheimer, *Treatise on Justice*, at pages 193-194 (1967). See, however, George, "The Role of the Court in the Determination and Enforcement of Punishment," 15 *Wayne L. Rev.* 655 at 657-658 (1969).

4. See, in particular, the excellent article by Joseph D. Lohman, "Crises of a Society in Ferment," 14 *Crime & Delinquency* 31-41 (Jan. 1968).

5. See, McCall, "Humaneness, Logic and Economy," 13 *Crime & Delinquency* 385 at 387 (July, 1967): " . . . few of us view punishment realistically. Let me paraphrase Judge David Bazelon on the subject: 'Whether applied to criminals or our own flesh and blood, we are profoundly confused about punishment. We waver between feeling 'he deserves it' and that 'it will do him good.' The first reaction is our immediate emotional response and is unprovable: the second is our rationalization after the fact and can be proved or disproved.' "

6. See, for example, Downs, "Wanted: A Balanced System of Justice," 15 *Crime & Delinquency* 193 (April, 1969). See, too, Dressler, "Which Public Do You Read," 9 *Crime & Delinquency* 129 at 131 (April, 1963): "Consequently, when the penologist undertakes to interpret the will of the people he must specify which people he has in mind—the entire body politic or a specific segment."

it seems society as a whole is quite uncertain of its purposes and objectives in the correctional field. Different parts of society (any given society) are quite sure of what they want but these goals are often so disparate as to create antagonisms and contradictions[7] which the judge must try to reconcile if he is to implement anything like a homogeneous, purposeful, penal policy. At times of crisis or of change the judge and in particular the judge of a common law jurisdiction finds himself caught in a maelstrom of ideas through which he must pragmatically pick his way—often without legislative guidance—towards a correctional goal which is broadly acceptable not merely to the most informed, technically-minded class of the community but rather to that massive, conservatively-oriented majority which is somewhat less cerebrally directed.[8] The judge, while exercising his art[9] or craft[10] in accordance with those principles he has chosen for guidance must be ever mindful of these pressures and the modificatory effects they have upon correctional aims.

In depriving an offender of his liberty the judge ought to have a clear idea of the consequences of his action. If this is to be more than simply a vengeful, impulsive reaction against some harm which the offender has inflicted upon society, the judge must take into consideration what is going to happen to the transgressor as a result of his decision and on a long term basis, what is going to happen to society as a further consequence of that determination. There is a tendency, especially in the lay mind, to conceptualize these consequences in dualistic terms: one thing is good for society as a whole and another is "good" for the individual offender, the two being diametrically opposed. This is not merely unsound penological practice, it is hopelessly

---

7. See, Stuart, "A Citizen's View of the Impact of Crime," 15 *Crime & Delinquency* 323 at 324 (July, 1969): "The awareness of violence creates dangerous and divisive reactions in an already troubled country."

8. Koestler remarks on the motives of those anxious for the execution of Ruth Ellis: see, *Reflections on Hanging*, cited in *Perspectives on Correction* 274 (D. MacNamara & E. Sagarin eds., 1971).

9. See, Sir Henry Slesser, *The Art of Judgment* (1962).

10. "The interpretation of statutes is a craft as much as a science and the judges, as craftsmen, select and apply the appropriate rules as the tools of their trade." Per Donaldson, J. in *Corocraft v. Pan American World Airways, Inc.,* [1964] 3 W.L.R. 714, at 732.

illogical due to the offender's irrevocable involvement in society. Even his permanent removal through the death penalty, whether motivated by vengeance, general deterrence or social hygiene, has unsatisfactory consequences that society cannot escape.[11] The purpose of the criminal sanction is to influence present and future human behavior. It cannot, in the nature of things, affect past behavior[12] and insofar as its imposition is related to past conduct it is a purely retributive act and can, of itself, have no corrective effect. The consequence of the perpetuation of the dualistic attitude towards correctional aims is social warfare[13] and, moreover, a war which society cannot logically hope to win. It has been well said by a modern criminologist[14] that, "Imprisonment is more than a punishment; it involves the creation of a new society—the society of the captive. In prison, the persistent offender really comes to believe that society is his enemy." If the proper correctional goal is the promotion of social harmony with a satisfactory equilibrium of interests, the administration of criminal justice must attune itself to a monistic policy designed to procure that for the future, the offender live at peace with and within society. Neither repression nor even elimination of the transgressor can achieve this end, for the delicate balance of society is upset thereby and the Kantian categorical imperative[15] is not a redress

---

11. Sometimes there are international repercussions, as in the case of Caryl Chessman. Most observers would regard this case, unreservedly, as a blot on American jurisprudence. Few have considered the facts so painstakingly analyzed at 44 *Minn. L. Rev.* 941-97 (1960).

12. "Moreover, in conformity to this characteristic of punishment it is retrospective in principle whereas the measures of a constructive criminal policy ought to be always and decidedly forward-looking." Kinberg, supra note 1, at 561.

13. This is well brought out in the perceptive article by Max Radin, "Enemies of Society," 27 *J. Crim. L. & Crim.* 328 (1936).

14. Cormier, "Violence—Individual and Collective Aspects," 9 *Criminology* 99, at 103, (May, 1971).

15. This philosophical precept translates, penologically, into the "revenge" aspect of the retributive theory of punishment. This is excellently expressed by Herbert Packer in *The Limits of the Criminal Sanction* 38 (1968): "The criminal is to be punished simply because he has committed a crime. It makes little difference whether we do this because we think we owe it to him or because we think he owes it to us. Each theory rests on a figure of speech. Revenge means that the criminal is paid back; expiation means that he pays back."

of the balance upset by the offender, but rather a further, point-less aggravation of the discord produced by his transgression of the social norm. If social harmony is the aim then what is good for society must also be good for the offender. He must not be vengefully excluded from society at one moment only to be rein-corporated after this treatment with the glib, unscientific hope that he will have so profited by the experience that, even in this disadvantaged state, he will conform to society's dictates in the future. This latter is indeed a difficult reaction to overcome, for all our instincts run counter to the counsels of logic and com-monsense. The difficulties to which this attitude gives rise in the correctional field have been pointed out by Timasheff:[16] ". . . the connection between crime and punishment, within the basic structure, is so narrow, that social repulsion is often transferred from the offender to the punished: it is well known how difficult it is for a punished individual to join again his social group which is inclined to treat him as an outsider; the rehabilitation of offenders is one of the most difficult problems of practical criminology." The basic conflict in penological thinking is not between deterrence—which at least pretends a scientific basis—and rehabilitation or reform but between retribution, which is purely instinctual, and the more purposeful policies designed to prepare the way for the offender's reintegration into society. Ret-ribution is exceedingly simplistic: it is not designed to do more than assuage the feelings of the injured party. Lord Gardiner[17] has characterized it as, "revenge for an injury done. You hurt me and I will hurt you. Indeed that is its literal meaning."

Retribution does nothing to restore the disturbed societal equilibrium: it may cause a further, chain-reaction response in the criminal, which only exacerbates the situation.[18] But the idea

16. Timasheff, "The Retributive Structure of Punishment," 28 *J. Crim. L. & Crim.* 396 at 402-403 (1938).

17. "The Purposes of Criminal Punishment," 21 *Mod. L. Rev.* 117 at 119 (1958).

18. The philosophical idea of retribution in some way "freeing" the offender, who has paid society's price for his crime, is struck down by the harsh realities of a conviction. The offender is never *free,* under even the most benign of systems and the consequences of his conviction, particularly if he is a member of a certain class of society, will almost invariably drive him back to crime.

of retribution is so primal that it is exceedingly difficult to eradicate. Timasheff has opined that,[19] "The very possibility of overcoming the retributive structure of punishment is doubtful." The notion of punishment is essentially retributive: it is intended to hurt.[20] As retribution is society's own reaction to hurt, it is logically to be supposed that the individual punished will also react with further harm to society's interests insofar as it lies within his power to do so. Were society's sanctions wholly retributive it is clear that they would have no other value than that of prolonging the war with the errant members to whom they were applied: something more is needed to convert punishment into a corrective. It is here that society, in the interests of its correctional objectives, begins to annex other purposes to the basic retributive structure of punishment, so as to constructively modify both the harm done by the offender and the harm done by society itself through its initial, instinctual reaction. So far as the individual offender is concerned, the suffering which imprisonment represents both to society and that individual can only be constructive when it is purposefully oriented towards rehabilitation: the deliberate reordering of the offender's future behavior to conform to society's requirements.[21] It is clear that imprisonment, on this view, is only purposeful where the individual offender is deprived of his liberty in order to influence his future behavior after the desired fashion and when having regard to his personal qualities it is possible to influence him in this way. Where the penalty imposed by the court depriving the offender of his liberty is thus directed exclusively to these ends, the inevitable, consequential suffering takes on the nature of a treatment[22] directed towards the betterment of the individual and his relationship with society. The proper attainment of this ideal minimizes

---

19. Supra note 16, at 400.

20. "The essential trait of punishment is to inflict suffering." Kinberg, supra note 1, at 561.

21. Speaking of another class of "special" offender, Morris Ploscowe has said, "The only value of prison or jail incarceration is in diminishing the dose of heroin or morphine necessary to keep the addict comfortable." Methods of Treatment of Drug Addiction," in *Essays in Criminal Science* 369 (G. O. W. Mueller ed., 1961).

22. But, see, Rubin, "Illusions of Treatment in Sentences and Civil Commitments," 16 *Crime & Delinquency* 79 (Jan. 1970).

the harm done by society's reaction and the balance of advantage in the process far outweighs such initial harm by reason of the redress of the societal inbalance and the return and reintegration of a rehabilitated individual to the ranks of free society.

These relatively simplistic criteria cannot suffice for judicial guidance and so confusion creeps in to ruin the neat, correctional logic of those who would order society on these somewhat utopian lines. We have seen that while we cannot dispense with pure retribution, we can to a certain extent neutralize its malignancy. Incarceration is not wholly motivated by the desire to punish, the primal response to the harm caused by the transgressor. In such a determination, there is a more defensive, practical purpose in the desire to protect the community from future harm either by that individual—the "prevention" principle,[23] or by others like-minded—the principle of "general deterrence."[24] If retribution is the product of righteous anger, preventive and deterrent measures are most properly to be seen as the outcome of fear. It is hardly surprising that some of this underlying emotion is transmitted to the correctional apparatus[25] that the system has erected for handling the offender. Yet it is important to emphasize that prevention and deterrence are, in themselves, by no means incompatible with the idea of rehabilitation; the latter may even be perceived from the start as a useful auxiliary. The real problem is that the primary sentencing considerations tend to become confusingly equated, by association, with rehabilitation which in this context can only be secondary and as a practical matter may not even be possible. This is the result of justificatory rationalizations deriving from an attitude which cannot, on philosophical grounds, accept the inevitability of punishment

23. See, on this generally, the classic work of Johannes Andenaes, "The General Preventive Effects of Punishment," 114 *U. Penna. L. Rev.* 949 (1966) .

24. See, for example, Andenaes, "General Prevention—Illusion or Reality," 43 *J. Crim. L., Crim. & P. S.* 176 (1952) .

25. See, for example, Wertham, "Psychiatry and the Prevention of Sex Crimes," 28 *J. Crim. L. & Crim.* 847 at 848 (1938) : "Those who advocate more drastic measures of punishment remind me of a judge years ago who was faced in court with the case of a sex delinquent. He gave this man the most severe sentence he was able to pronounce on him, and said strongly: 'I did not know such things could exist! I shall stamp them out!!' "

for its own sake: it must be seen to have some other purpose, however unrealistic. Rehabilitation in relation to either retribution or deterrence is really a secondary modifier, a "taking advantage" as it were of a situation produced by a more immediate appreciation of what is needed for the protection of society. In the long run rehabilitation of the offender represents the ideal protection of society. Anything less, whether by elimination, perpetual exclusion or lengthy incarceration of the offender, is a disturbance of the very equilibrium which the punishment on Kantian principles is supposed to restore. A rehabilitative sentence can be seen as being in the nature of an armistice between society and the offender: its proper execution is like the signing of the treaty which allows both parties finally to live at peace.

A modern authority has asserted that[26] "The leading tendency in the development of judicial sentencing policy in recent years has been the growing recognition by the courts of the principle of individualisation of sentence." With such a theory the remedial, therapeutic character of the sentence can be stressed so as to push into the background any less comfortable and comforting philosophies that might have been its primary motivation. Lord Gardiner has observed that[27] "The sentence of the court is gradually beginning to reflect, not so much the indignation and anger of society (though this still happens frequently enough), but an attempt at diagnosis so that the punishment may be made to fit the criminal as well as the crime." Despite the attractiveness and apparent logic of rehabilitation as a correctional theory the vulture of retribution is always perched ominously above and behind the Seat of Judgment. What has been so aptly called the "urge to punish"[28] all too often takes over and shapes the judicial response to the transgression. The true and the chimerical value of the therapeutic sentence lie in it being possible and needful, both by reason of the resources available to society and by reason of the personal qualities of the offender, to rehabilitate him. Very often it is self-evident that because of the condi-

---

26. Thomas, "Sentencing—The Basic Principles," [1967] *Crim. L. Rev.* 455, at 455.
27. *Supra* note 17, at 129.
28. See the work of that name by Henry Weihofen, included in *Perspectives in Correction* 62-97 (D. E. J. MacNamara and E. Sagarin eds., 1971).

tion of the offender[29] and the nature of his transgression,[30] rehabilitation is otiose. This brings the latent correctional conflict to the fore, thrusting impetuously aside the thin veneer of noble purpose pasted over the more primitive urge to punish. As Norval Morris correctly points out,[31] ". . . many murderers could safely be released from the court without further punishment on the day that they are convicted of their murder. Deterrence[32] will, however, be a primary and usually controlling consideration precluding such a decision." What D. A. Thomas has called[33] "the tariff system" is the remnant of retributive justice which obliges in such cases the imposition of a wholly inappropriate sentence judged by rehabilitative considerations. In the case of the "normal" offender—one whose personality and social characteristics are such that the available rehabilitative resources might so work upon him, at least in theory, during his incarceration so the judge in all conscience is able to satisfy himself as to the therapeutic value of his sentence—no problems arise with the philosophical bases of the disposition. It is in connection with the "special" offender that the inherent, theoretical conflicts come surging once more to the surface and the practical inadequacies of criminal justice administration only serve to aggravate them. Henry Weihofen has said,[34] "The public is willing to recognize the mentally irresponsible as a class that should be exempted from punishment, since it is futile to threaten and punish people who cannot be 'cured or taught a lesson' by such sanctions. But the exception must be narrowly restricted."

The problem of the control, containment and disposal of the psychopathic individual throws into critical relief the fundamen-

---

29. See, for example, Cooper, "A Sentencing Problem: How Far Is a Fall From Grace?," 15 *Cleveland-Marshall L. Rev.* 587 (1966).

30. A good example of a sentence which could have no therapeutic value is provided by the English case of *Regina v. Morris*, [1961] 2 All E.R. 672. There the judge (at 673) expressed the view that the defendant's mental state was probably even worse than alleged by the defense, yet he felt obligated to impose a prison sentence because he would not take the responsibility of setting the defendant "anywhere near liberty."

31. "Impediments to Penal Reform," 33 *U. Chi. L. Rev.*, 627, 646 (1966).

32. What is meant here is, of course, general deterrence.

33. Supra note 26, at 460.

34. Supra note 28, at 69.

tal antinomies of penal policy and correctional theory. On the one hand society finds itself faced with an offender who is hopelessly refractory yet seemingly in the majority of cases in full possession of his faculties. He cannot be "taught a lesson" by punishment nor is treatment apparently of any avail for his condition. Yet something must be done about him when he transgresses for, as one writer has observed,[35] "It is easy to see how one would rebel at the thought that this person, who is apparently just 'bad' and refuses to make an honest attempt to change himself, should escape atonement for his criminal actions." Society's feelings are often exacerbated by the repugnant quality of the offender's personality[36] and the abhorrent nature of his crime.[37] There is the further complication[38] of the limited range of alternatives for the control and containment of this type of offender.[39] The fear of the psychopath, particularly the violent psychopath, is very strong and society's natural anxiety to protect itself is often translated into the extreme measures of extermination or perpetual exclusion. It has even been opined that,[40] "From the purely practical point of view, there would seem more rather than less reason to hang the severely psychopathic, for their disorder is more deeply rooted and the danger to the public greater than with other offenders." On the other hand there is the desire to maintain

35. Hayden, "The Psychopathic Personality: Treatment and Punishment—Alternatives Under Current and Proposed Criminal Responsibility Criteria," 10 *Rutgers L. Rev.* 425, at 435 (1955).

36. See, for example, the jury's reaction in the case of Matheson, [1958] All E.R. 87 and Lord Goddard's observations at id. 89-90.

37. For example, the notorious New York case of Albert Fish graphically commented upon by Henry A. Davidson in "The Psychiatrist's Role in the Administration of Criminal Justice," 4 *Rutgers L. Rev.* 578, at 587-589 (1950).

38. This is particularly noticeable where the offenses are of a sexual nature. See the example given by Nathan Roth, "Factors in the Motivation of Sexual Offenders," 42 *J. Crim. L., Crim. & P. S.* 631, at 632 (1952).

39. There is, strictly, only death or detention, be it in prison or in hospital. The problem is particularly acute in the case of the sexual psychopath. See Guttmacher & Weihofen, "Sex Offenses," 43 *J. Crim. L., Crim. & P. S.* 153 at 172 (1952): "The Sexual psychopath laws typically make no provision for treatment. The public demand that the legislature do something about 'sex fiends' spends itself with the enactment of a law providing for commitment, and the problem of providing a place to which to commit is not faced."

40. Fox, "Sin, Crime and the Psychopath," 27 *Mod. L. Rev.* 190 at 196 (1964).

a proper consistency in the administration of criminal justice. Fear and anger are natural enough reactions but neither of these emotions has any correctional value when expressed in terms of a judicial sentence and there is a very real need to dispose of the psychopathic offender in a manner harmonious with the general aims of a particular society's penal policy. The judicial dilemma is well illustrated by what has been written of Soviet experience in this matter[41] "... between 1921 and 1924 'psychopaths' were frequently adjudged 'not accountable.' As late as 1928 official Soviet psychiatry tended to regard the 'psychopaths' as 'too well for hospital and too sick for prison' and their adequate disposition was still thought of in terms of their accommodation in special institutions with a modicum of psychiatric supervision. The earlier trend has been completely reversed for the last decade. Current theory rejects all thought of 'pampering' and maintains that 'criminal psychopaths' would be encouraged to persist in socially harmful activities by receiving a special status under the Code which would provide them with an excuse of an illness and an incentive of a degree of immunity from punishment." The judicial choice lies between leniency on account of the defective personality of the offender regardless of the nature and circumstances of his crime or increased severity regardless of the inefficacy of the sanction on deterrent or rehabilitative grounds. As society veers between punishment of the deed or the doer,[42] all that is left is an unsatisfactory and unsatisfying retribution. It falls to the judge to reflect, as accurately as possible in this confusing state, the prevalent penal philosophy of society. To do this with any prospect of success he ought not only to understand and appreciate the nature of the underlying conflict but also be able to answer the question, "what is a psychopath?" and to know what he might in practical terms be able to do about such an offender consistently with contemporary correctional aims and societal resources.

The judge has a very special responsibility in relation to the

41. Killian & Arens, "Use of Psychiatry in Soviet Criminal Proceedings," 41 *J. Crim. L. & Crim.* 136 at 148 (1950/51).

42. See, for example, Beaver, "The 'Mentally Ill' and the Law: Sisyphus and Zeus," *Utah L. Rev.* 1 at 13 (1968).

sentencing of the psychopathic offender. It would be all too easy to abdicate this responsible role for a more comfortable, more popular one, emotionally attuned to the immaturity of uninformed society: no judge can hope for popularity by appearing to "pamper" the psychopath and it is both human and tempting to incline in the opposite direction. In the long run, the wise judge will heed the words of Lord Gardiner,[43] "The purposes of criminal punishment are all intended for the protection and benefit of the community. It is easy to turn away from what happens to those convicted of crime. I suspect that by and large the public get the penal system which their interest in the subject deserves."

THE PSYCHOPATH: A MEDICO-LEGAL ENIGMA

Psychopathy is, at best, an imperspicuous term.
John P. Reid[44]

The terms "psychopath" and "psychopathic" are extraordinarily imprecise.[45] The vagueness of the medical label has been little improved by the endeavors of lawyers and legislators to give some definite form and content to the notions implicit in it as it is used forensically.[46] Koch[47] is usually credited with the first technical use of the words "psychopath" and "psychopathic in-

---

43. Supra note 17, at 235.

44. "The Companion of the New Hampshire Doctrine of Criminal Insanity," 15 *Vand. L. Rev.* 721, at 761 (1962).

45. See, for example, Arieff & Rotman, "Psychopathic Personality: Some Social and Psychiatric Aspects," 39 *J. Crim. L. & Crim.* 158 at 158 (1948): "There is no category in the entire array of psychiatric classifications that is being misused more than 'psychopathic personality.' It has indeed become the waste basket of psychiatry, displacing even dementia praecox from its position of primacy."

46. See, for example, Section 4 of the English Mental Health Act, 1959, or the various definitions offered by the sexual psychopath statutes in United States jurisdictions. On this latter, see Slovenko & Phillips, "Psychosexuality and the Criminal Law," 15 *Vand. L. Rev.* 797 at 821-826 (1962). The definitional problem has other implications by reason of the fact that the United States Immigration and Nationality Act, 1952, excludes from admission into the United States "aliens afflicted with psychopathic personality." See, on this, the note in 40 *Temple L. Q.* 328-347; " 'Psychopathic personality' and 'sexual deviation': medical terms or legal catch-alls—analysis of the status of the homosexual alien."

47. See, for example, Scott, "The Psychopath," 10 *Howard Journal* 6, at 6 (1958).

ferior" in 1891 and although Pritchard[48] is said to have described the condition in reasonably accurate terms in 1835, it seems that clinical precursors (Pinel in 1806[49] and Rush in 1812[50]) had already considered these manifestations as aberrant behavior worthy of inclusion in a scheme of classification. Despite the prodigious efforts of clinicians and nosologists since that time, one British psychiatrist has observed,[51] "The concept of psychopathy is as confusing and confused in this century as in the last." He goes on to say that[52] "We are left then as Pritchard began with a cluster of descriptive aspects of behavioural abnormality, which, subject to their degree, to their concentration in one individual and to his actual situation in time and place, may amount to pathological social behaviour." The clinical identification of the psychopath in any particular case is essentially a very subjective matter[53] upon which many specialists would disagree fundamentally. The prominent British forensic psychiatrist, Scott, has warned that[54] "Even the best descriptions such as that of Cheyne (1934) are not very helpful. 'Psychopathic personalities are characterised largely by emotional immaturity or childishness with marked defects of judgment and without evidence of learning by experience. They are prone to impulsive reactions without consideration for others, and to emotional instability with rapid swings from elation to depression, often apparently for trivial causes.' " Psychiatrists are faced with a bewildering collection of manifestations in an incredible number of unclassifiable pat-

---

48. See, for example, J. Stuart Whitely, "Concepts of Psychopath and its Treatment," 35 *Medico-Legal Journal* 154, at 154 (1967).

49. See, Annesley, "Psychopathic Personality," 31 *Medico-Legal Journal* 137, at 137 (1963).

50. Ibid.

51. J. Stuart Whitely, supra note 48, at 154.

52. Supra, note 48, at 155.

53. See, for example, the interesting admission of Dr. Sturup: "I have a built-in temptation to diagnose psychopathy in prisoners who started a life of crime early and have had many prison admissions. I do not know to what extent I base this diagnosis on psychiatric observations at the time of the examination and to what extent on the previous history." "Psychopathic and Neurotic Offenders in Mental Hospitals," in *The Mentally Abnormal Offender: a CIBA Symposium*, at 150 (1968).

54. Supra note 47, at 7.

terns and permutations. Dr. Scott himself concludes that[55] "All we really have to go on is oft-repeated misbehaviour." It is small wonder then that a leading criminology textbook contains the statement,[56] "Because it is difficult to define or identify a psychopath, the label 'psychopathic personality' can be applied to almost anyone."

These diagnostic difficulties have not diminished the forensic popularity of the term nor deterred its application to particular individuals.[57] The proliferation of these descriptive terms has been remarked by a stern critic of the psychiatric approach to crime and correction. Hakeem writes,[58] "Probably the mental condition most often discussed in connection with delinquency and crime is 'psychopathic personality' or 'psychopathy.' One investigator (Cason) has listed 202 terms as equivalents of these but even this list does not exhaust the number. In 1952 the American Psychiatric Association adopted the new term 'sociopathic personality'[59] for this condition. Since then the old term continues to be the more widely used one." Hakeem adds that,[60] "Discussions on 'sociopathic personality' are identical to discussions on 'psychopathic personality.' " The same writer poses the question[61] "Is psychopathic personality a clinical entity?" On this point there is a considerable area of disagreement and much inconsistency among the authorities. There is some broad agreement among psychiatrists as to certain descriptive symptomology, but as Annesley points out,[62] ". . . this clinical description is often equally applicable to cases of schizophrenia or hypomania and is of little help in diagnosis." How one sees any particular pattern of behav-

---

55. Supra note 47, at 14.

56. E. H. Sutherland & D. R. Cressey, *Principles of Criminology*, at 159 (8th ed. 1970).

57. Ibid: " . . . under the administration of one psychiatrist 98 per cent of the inmates admitted to the state prison of Illinois were diagnosed as psychopathic personalities. . . . "

58. Hakeem, "A Critique of the Psychiatric Approach to Crime and Correction," 23 *Law & Contemp. Prob.* 650, at 668 (1958).

59. This term would appear to have been coined by Partridge in 1930: see Annesley, supra note 49, at 138.

60. Supra note 58, at 668.

61. Supra note 58, at 670.

62. Supra note 49 at 137.

ior, whether as a clinician, social scientist, legal practitioner or judge depends upon the social standards against which it is set.[63] The matter is, however, complicated for the psychiatrist by reason of his own professional standards and techniques. Psychoanalysis in particular depends very much upon the establishment of a special, empathic relationship with the patient. As has been well observed,[64] "The difficulty is that assessment of, say, impulsiveness, remorse, insight or capacity to form a relationship depends very much upon how well the psychiatrist knows the patient and what he feels about psychopaths." The accuracy of psychiatric diagnosis is to a large extent dependent upon the cooperation of the patient and to the fullness and veracity of the information he is prepared to relay. The psychopath is often peculiarly uncooperative or if cooperative, his willingness to assist must in the nature of things always be suspect.[65] A distinguished psychiatrist has said,[66] "It is a most difficult task to obtain any true information of value in the case history of a psychopath." Despite these evident diagnostic obstacles, psychopathic personality continues to be both medically and legally recognized as such. Perhaps the most that can be said is[67] "Even though there is no consensus amongst doctors about the exact description of the so-called 'psychopaths' experienced Prison Medical Officers, and for that matter, Prison Governors, are agreed that there is a type of prisoner who is quite incapable of foresight, who cannot learn even from the experience of punishment, much less from the threat of it."

Of prime importance from a legal as well as a medical point of view is whether the condition of the psychopath constitutes

---

63. See, for example R. M. Lindner, *Rebel Without a Cause: The Story of a Criminal Psychopath* 2 (1944) : "In short, psychopathy is a disorder of behavior which affects the relationship of an individual to the social setting."

64. Fox, supra note 40, at 194-95.

65. This is often remarked by clinicians. See, for example, Karpman, "Felonious Assault Revealed as a Symptom of Abnormal Sexuality," 37 *J. Crim. L. & Crim.* 193, at 212 (1946) : "No psychopath would have furnished the cooperation which this patient did or have engaged in the self-examination which he did in an effort to discover the source of his 'trouble.' "

66. Karpman, " 'Lying' " A Minor Inquiry into the Ethics of Neurotic and Psychopathic Behavior," 40 *J. Crim. L. & Crim.* 134, at 153 (1950) .

67. Lord Gardiner, supra note 17, at 123.

a true mental illness or some sort of mental impairment which ought to govern or modify questions of criminal responsibility and affect his consequent disposal.[68] This is central to any consideration of psychopathy and it is around this vital question that most of the discussion of the condition turns. The hesitancy of psychiatry in this matter is reflected not merely in the caution of professional utterances on the subject but also in the very terminology that is used. There is agreement that the psychopath is emotionally abnormal and suffers from a serious character defect but there is, in the absence of any collateral, recognized mental illness, no manifestation of the break with reality that characterizes the psychotic state.[69] The great difficulty is that the principal, objective indication of the medical condition is some sort of antisocial behavior.[70] The psychopath is a decided nonconformist who has manifested in his conduct some observable degree of asocialization which leads the clinician to label him in this way.[71] The essential circularity of this is pertinently pointed out by Hakeem, who critically observes that[72] "To be able to diagnose psychopathy, the psychiatrist needs to have evidence that the subject shows a history of psychopathy." This question of the true nature of the psychopathic condition is of the utmost importance for the administration of criminal justice. In many

68. See, for example, Coon, "Psychiatry for the Lawyer: Common Psychiatric States not Due to Psychosis," 31 *Corn. L. Q.* 466, at 475-76 (1946) : "Under the law it is customary to make no allowance for his special mental state." But see the comment on *H. M. Advocate* v. *Gordon* (1967) , unreported, in 31 *J. Crim. L.* 270-72 (1967) .

69. A prominent forensic psychiatrist has said: "A psychopath may be anything else, but he is *not* insane." Davidson, supra note 37.

70. Melitta Schmideberg has said: "The psychopath's failure to socialize is no accidental omission, but a concerted and successful effort to ward off the levers of society." "The Psychopath's Strange Concern with Social Values," 6 *J. Offender Therapy* 25 (Sept., 1962) .

71. See, for example, "The Relation Between Crime and Psychopathic Personality," 42 *J. Crim. L. & Crim.* 199, at 200 (1951) : "In the ultimate analysis, however, perhaps the chief distinguishing feature in psychopathic personality is nothing but a conspicuously defective or else almost completely undeveloped super-ego (Freud) which results in the psychopath being to all intents and purposes, quite unmoved by any sense of the difference between socially desirable and socially undesirable behavior."

72. Supra note 58, at 674.

cases the determination is literally a matter of life and death for the individual whose condition is being pronounced upon.[73] On perhaps no question does the psychiatrist find himself under greater pressure from the courts, whether the matter comes before them under the M'Naghten Rules, the Durham Rule or the principles governing diminished responsibility. Dr. Neustatter has said[74] "The psychiatrist was put in an invidious position with regard to psychopaths. (Like Sir David Henderson he felt that) a psychopath was basically ill, but his illness took a most unpleasant and antisocial form and, he could be responsible[75] for loathsome murders. Nevertheless, one would be bound to say that there was abnormality of mind, however distasteful this might be." The absence of those symptoms which characterize the psychotic state can give the psychopath an appearance of "normality" that even to the trained eye is inconsistent with the presence of mental illness. A distinguished British criminologist,[76] Edward Glover, has said of psychopathy that "The seriousness of the condition can be suggested by saying that it is graver than a neurosis and not so grave as a psychosis (insanity). The reason that psychopathy is not generally recognized is that even advanced psychopaths are sometimes able to maintain an apparently normal facade and are often regarded as normal persons not only by those who come in superficial contact with them but by most judicial authorities who see them in the dock." The forensic implications of this are well exemplified by the English case of Wilkinson (1953),[77] a 24-year-old psychopath sentenced to death for the murder of a 5-year-old girl. Dr. Desmond Curran,[78] a leading British forensic psychiatrist said "I have no doubt this man is a psycho-

73. This is the case in those jurisdictions where the death penalty has not been abolished and the court requires a determination under the M'Naghten, Durham or like rules in relation to the defendant's condition.

74. Lord Keith of Avonholm, "Some Observations on Diminished Responsibility," 27 *Medico-Legal Journal* 4, at 12 (1959) (debate following Lord Keith's address).

75. The word responsible is used loosely here in a non-legal sense despite the context.

76. "Psychiatric Aspects of the Report on Capital Punishment," 17 *Mod. L. Rev.* 329, at 331 (1954).

77. See, Walton & Docherty, "The Psychopath and the McNaghten Rules," [1954] *Crim. L. Rev.* 22.

78. Walton & Docherty, supra note 77, at 25.

pathic personality, but I do not consider he is suffering from any mental disease." He added,[79] "I have no doubt Wilkinson would be classified as a psychopathic character by any psychiatrist." The learned judge, after canvassing a number of opinions to clarify the matter in his own mind, held that there was no evidence on which the issue of the accused's sanity might go to the jury. He was upheld on appeal.

Although the uncertainties to which these classification difficulties have given rise are far from being satisfactorily resolved in the English courts, the English Parliament has in another field made a notable essay into the solution of the problem. The Mental Health Act of 1959,[80] passed after a very full public enquiry into all the aspects legislated, provides at Section 4 (4): "In this Act 'psychopathic disorder' means a persistent disorder or disability of the mind (whether or not including subnormality of intelligence) which results in abnormally aggressive or seriously irresponsible conduct on the part of the patient or is susceptible to medical treatment." One commentator has observed,[81] "It may be regarded as extremely courageous of Parliament to attempt to define psychopathic disorder in the light of the controversial nature of the condition. Indeed the Royal Commission advised strongly against any statutory definition being attempted." The Act is a notable step forward as a disposal measure for it is premised upon the availability of and commitment to special facilities of those adjudged to be suffering from the type of disorder to which Section 4 (4) refers. The Act is intended to provide treatment of the psychopath as an alternative to imprisonment and is a positive measure designed to relieve some of the judicial perplexities in dealing with and disposing of this class of offender.[82] It has been said that[83] "It is a legal definition and leaves the medical profession free to continue to argue at length

---

79. Walton & Docherty, supra note 77, at 26.

80. On all the sentencing aspects of this statute, see Thomas, "Sentencing the Mentally Disturbed Offender," [1965] *Crim. Law Rev.* 688.

81. Havard, "The Mental Health Act and the Criminal Offender," [1961] *Crim. L. Rev.* 296, at 302.

82. See, for example, Hermann Mannhaim, "The Criminal Law and Mentally Abnormal Offenders," 1 *Brit. J. Crim.* 203 (1961).

83. Maclay, "Psychopathic Disorder," 4 Crim. L. Q. 296, at 298 (1961-2).

the question of what is a psychopath in clinical terms and does he in fact exist at all? It may be unfortunate that the word psychopath was retained with all its medical vagueness, but legally the definition means something that is sufficiently clear to be workable." Ten years after this legislation was passed a forensic psychiatrist was impelled to comment,[84] "The law has taken cognisance of 'psychopathic disorder' as defined in Section 4 of the Mental Health Act, but its definition is so hazy that taken together with the equally vague term of 'mental illness' it is possible to bring almost anybody with any abnormality within the scope of the Act. Even today most psychiatrists have still not faced up to the challenge." Dr. Westbury adds the significant statistic that[85] "Only few cases are dealt with under the Mental Health Act or under Section 4 of the Criminal Justice Act, 1948; only 0.65 percent of all adult male offenders (excluding traffic offenders) and only 21 percent of those found guilty of manslaughter through diminished responsibility are disposed of medically." This "workable definition" notwithstanding, psychiatry has yet to give a clear and consistent answer to the lawyer's question of what is a psychopath.

These problems are enormously augmented in the United States by reason of what are known as the "sexual psychopath laws."[86] The association of an already vague term with an emotionally charged adjective[87] has done little to help the objective administration of criminal justice in this field. Sutherland

---

84. Westbury, "Forensic Psychiatry in Britain: Its Potentials," 13 *Int. J. Offender Therapy* 165, at 165 (1969).

85. Supra note 84, at 169.

86. "During the years immediately following World War II, several states became panic-stricken because of a small number of sexual attacks, and their legislatures hurriedly enacted "sexual psychopath" laws, which spread through certain sections of the United States. Because no one has been able to identify a sexual psychopath any more than any other psychopath, the laws have been absurd in principle and futile in operation." Sutherland & Cressey, supra note 56, at 161. Some of these statutes antedate World War II. The pioneer Michigan Act of 1937 was declared unconstitutional, but was quickly followed by others.

87. See, for example, Loehner, "The Sexual Psychopath," *Lex et Scientia* 266, at 266 (1965): "A discussion of the matter of the sexual psychopath is usually marked by emotional reactions in the participants of the discussion so that it may become very difficult for them to give an opinion on the subject which is not colored by emotion and which is not based upon prejudice."

opined that[88] "The conclusion from this analysis of the concept of the sexual psychopath is that it is too vague for judicial or administrative use either as to commitment to institutions or as to release as 'completely and permanently cured.'" These statutes are predicated upon the notion that there is a certain type of offender—who can be positively identified—with a marked propensity for serious sexual crime and that such offenders can be classified, segregated and treated so as to protect the community and correct their defect. Such abnormal offenders seem unsuitable for sentencing on ordinary penological principles by reference to the nature of their crimes and seem to require "treatment" by reference to the deficiencies of their personality.[89] It has been rightly pointed out that[90] "A label of sexual psychopathy carries with it an immediate penalty which may take freedom from the individual for periods varying from months to lifetime and in addition place a social stigma that possibly may never be removed. It is a process that is easy to impose, but very difficult to erase." Perhaps the main objection to these statutes is that they attempt some form of prediction based upon the typical indices of observed psychopathic behavior, namely a pattern of previous antisocial conduct.[91] Some sociologists, in the early days, became particularly enthusiastic[92] about the possibilities of crime control offered by these statutes. A more careful appraisal and greater experience of the working of this legislation has led to

---

88. Sutherland, "The Sexual Psychopath Laws," 40 *J. Crim. L. & Crim.* 543, at 551 (1958).

89. See, for example, "Sexual Psychopathy—A Legal Labyrinth of Medicine, Morals and Mythology," 36 *Nebraska L. Rev.* 320, at 320 (1957): "Such legislation is predicated on the theory that the sex offender can be recognized and treated and that therefore he should be in a mental hospital rather than a prison."

90. Meyers, "Psychiatric Examination of the Sexual Psychopath," 56 *J. Crim. L., Crim. & P. S.* 27, at 27 (1965).

91. The statutes are basically preventive and, as has been aptly pointed out, "All forms of preventive justice suffer from one critical defect—an inability to know whom to prevent." Anthony & Susan Jamart Granucci, "Indiana's Sexual Psychopath Act in Operation," 44 *Ind. L. J.* 555, at 564 (1969). Meyers, supra note 90, at 27, says: "The hard fact is that there are no pathognomonic signs of sexual deviation other than the behavioral background."

92. See, for example, Reinhardt & Fisher, "The Sexual Psychopath and the Law," 39 *J. Crim. L. & Crim.* 734 (1949).

other conclusions.[93] The statutes themselves have given rise to much abuse and have done little to eradicate the mischief against which they were erected. Many nebulous criteria of dangerousness[94] have grown out of the application of these statutes with the result that individuals are incarcerated as psychopaths on an assessment of their proclivities, often on the flimsiest of evidence. Psychopathy by reason of the factors involved in its clinical diagnosis is peculiarly prone to give rise to injustices.[95] Careful researchers have stated,[96] "As we have tried to demonstrate, the presence of mental illness is of limited use in determining potentially dangerous individuals. Even when it is of evidentiary value, it serves to isolate too many harmless people." Another writer has said[97] ". . . it is clear that many innocent victims, who because of their illness are unable to legally contest their own rights, are being indiscriminately trampled upon. It must be borne in mind that this legislation has a most sweeping impact and a judicial willingness to conclude that constitutional requirements have been satisfied has far-reaching consequences—a gloomy and hopeless confinement for an extremely long period of time." Tappan exploded many of the myths upon which these sexual psychopath laws are based.[98] Karpman, whose experience in the field is considerable, has said[99] "The terms 'sexual psychopath' and 'sexual psychopathy' have no legitimate place in psychiatric nosology or dynamic classification." It has been well con-

93. For a sociological view, see Sutherland, supra note 88.

94. The literature on dangerousness is now very extensive. In the present context it is only necessary to remark the introduction of the concept into the Model Sentencing Act and to refer to the useful and somewhat overlooked article by Manfred S. Guttmacher, "Dangerous Offenders," 9 *Crime & Delinquency*, 381 (Oct, 1963).

95. See, in particular *Rouse v. Cameron*, 373 F.2d 45 (1966).

96. Livermore, Malmquist & Meehl, "On the Justifications for Civil Commitment," 117 *U. Penna L. Rev.* 75, at 85 (1968).

97. Roche, "The Plight of the Sexual Psychopath: A Legislative Blunder and Judicial Acquiescence," 41 *Notre Dame Law.* 527, at 550 (1966).

98. See Paul W. Tappan, *The Habitual Sex Offender, Report to the New Jersey Legislature* (1950). See, also, the same author's "Sentences for Sex Criminals," 42 *J. Crim L. & Crim.* 332 (1951).

99. Karpman, "The Sexual Psychopath," 42 *J. Crim. L. & Crim.* 184, at 185 (1951).

cluded by another writer that[100] "Knowledge of the nature and development of sex psychopathy is imperfect; its meaning is shrouded with ambiguities. As such the term has no place in dynamic, medical or legal classification."

The psychopath remains a medical and legal enigma. His identity is uncertain and his forensic classification even more so. Neither law nor medicine has produced a satisfactory definition[101] of "psychopath" or "psychopathic personality" although both claim to recognize the psychopathic offender when they see one. A great deal is now known about this ill-defined condition but there is much argument as to its etiology and criminological significance. It is about as difficult to determine how many criminals are psychopaths as it is to establish how many psychopaths are criminals, for psychopathy and criminality are far from being coterminous.[102] As Melitta Schmideberg has observed,[103] "Psychopathy is essentially a failure in socialization, but not necessarily identical with criminality." There exists the real danger of psychopathy becoming a "residual category," as Howard Jones puts it,[104] ". . . a waste paper basket into which one can toss all the cases one does not understand with which one has been unsuccessful. And as it has always been assumed that the psychopath is incurable, one's guilt about failure is allayed." There is no single category of psychopaths all of whom might be susceptible of recognition and disposal on a common ground. There is a world of difference between Henderson's three descriptive categories[105] of predominantly aggressive, predominantly inadequate

100. Mihm, "A Re-Examination of the Validity of Our Sex Psychopath Statutes in the Light of the Recent Appeal Cases and Experience," 44 *J. Crim. L., Crim. & P. S.* 716, at 734 (1954).

101. See, for example, Scott, supra note 47, at 14: "Like all their witnesses the Commission has, of course, been unable to find an adequate clinical or legal definition of psychopathy."

102. Hakeem, supra note 58, at 670 observes: "The proportion of criminals who are psychopaths and the proportions of psychopaths who are criminals vary from 0 to 100 per cent."

103. "Psychopathy: Diagnostic Considerations," 5 *J. Offender Therapy* 13, at 13 (1961).

104. *Crime in a Changing Society*, at 54 (1967).

105. See, for example, J. Stuart Whitely, supra note 48, at 159.

and predominantly creative. Bromberg and Thompson[106] have pointed up the important differences even within these categories themselves: "The differentiation between the explosive psychopath and the aggressive (antisocial) type is that the latter are consciously so. They are cool, callous, choosing the aggressive way of life by preference, whereas the explosive psychopaths are uncontrolled only during the attack and are often mild in temperament and tending to avoid violence." The most that can usefully be said in our present state of knowledge is perhaps that the psychopath is an individual who will not or who cannot accept the responsibility that society seeks to impose upon him. Or, as Stuart Whitely has put it,[107] "The total picture is of an adult *unwilling* or *unable* to function in a socially adaptable or acceptable way." The strength of the psychopath's response to the pressures which society brings to bear upon him in order to obtain his conformity is the measure of his social dangerousness and the principal factor that society must take into account in determining his disposal.

SENTENCES FOR PSYCHOPATHS
"PUNISHMENT" v. "TREATMENT" OR "BAD" v. "MAD"

> There is no more reason for turning over to the psychiatrist the complete supervision of a criminal who is found to be psychopathic than for turning over to the dentist the complete supervision of a criminal who is found to have dental cavities.
>
> *Edwin H. Sutherland*[108]

On the hypothesis that both law and medicine coincide in recognizing a particular offender as a psychopath or as having a psychopathic personality, the question arises at law, as to the effect this identification should have upon his disposal. Laws are made for the protection of society and judges are entrusted with the task of seeing that they are upheld and respected; that is, that they serve their dynamic purpose in molding the conduct of those to whom they apply, to the model or pattern that society

---

106. Bromberg & Thompson, "The Relation of Psychosis, Mental Defect and Personality Types to Crime," 28 *J. Crim. L. & Crim.* 70, at 81 (1937).

107. Supra note 48, at 155.

108. Supra note 88, at 554.

has prescribed. When there is some transgression, it falls to the judge to decide what to do about the revindication of society's interests—the reestablishment of the social equilibrium upon which the law is posited. The judicial dilemma in sentencing the psychopath is not difficult to appreciate. Many psychopaths are highly dangerous individuals, often ranking among the most dangerous criminals with whom our criminal justice administration has to deal.[109] Their crimes are often peculiarly obnoxious or by reason of their nature give rise to extreme public concern. The urge to punish in the purely retributive sense becomes very strong indeed when one is confronted with such fiends[110] or such deeds. Coincident with such sentiments is the seeming impossibility in the present state of our knowledge of taking satisfactory steps towards reclaiming the psychopath so he might pay a proper price for his crime and yet return rehabilitated to the ranks of open society.[111] Everything would seem to point to the inevitability of heavy, individually deterrent or preventive sentences being applied to psychopaths on the footing that the gravity of their conduct merits condign punishment and their condition is such that they must be presumed to be fully responsible for their actions. On a purely retributive view of punishment, there is a lot of logic to such a course. Viewed from the standpoint of other penological considerations however, there are obvious contradictions to disturb judicial equanimity.

Deterrence is a controversial and little investigated matter un-

---

109. See, for example, the Glueck's introduction to *Rebel Without a Cause,* supra note 63.

110. The use of this pejorative in connection with the psychopath, particularly the so-called sexual psychopath is very common. See, for example, Fahr, "Iowa's New Sexual Psychopath Law—An Experiment Noble in Purpose?" 41 *Iowa L. Rev.* 523, at 529 (1956) : "But popular fallacies regarding 'sex fiends' are legion."

111. The reason for these difficulties was cogently pointed out by Karpman in 1947 and is still true today. See, "An Attempt at a Re-Evaluation of Some Concepts of Law and Psychiatry," 38 *J. Crim. L. & Crim.* 206, at 215 (1947) : "The psychogenic cases should be treated for they can be cured, as many have been. The psychopathic cases, however, at least in the present state of our knowledge, are not approachable by psychotherapy or some other form of dealing or treatment; these must be devised."

der even the best of circumstances.[112] It is probably true to say that while we know a great deal about why some people were not deterred by the system's regulators, we cannot say precisely why the majority of ordinary people do not commit crimes.[113] There are difficult problems both of individual and general deterrence in connection with the psychopath. Punishment as such, seems to have no remedial effect upon the psychopathic personality. It has been said of the psychopath,[114] "He forgets the punishment of yesterday in the desires of tomorrow." Manfred Guttmacher has stressed that,[115] "Sociopaths seemingly do not learn by experience, since despite admonitions and punishments, they continue their same pattern of objectionable conduct." It would be very wrong to assume from this that the psychopath is intractably opposed to all learning. The case may be stated that the psychopath is deaf to the lessons that society urges upon him. This is well put by Melitta Schmideberg, who says,[116] "He does not anticipate being caught, yet he spends much time thinking of the future— scheming. He does learn from experience; he perfects his methods of safecracking, but fails to socialize. He is not unaffected by punishment, but does his best to wipe out such unpleasant memories." This also points up another important aspect of individual deterrence in relation to the psychopath. Deterrence is largely postulated upon the effectiveness of detection and apprehension;[117] punishment is worse than useless if it is seen to be but irregularly or half-heartedly applied. This factor can make but little impression upon the psychopath who is confident in his

---

112. Wolf Middendorff, states: "There are few empirical studies concerning the operation of general deterrence." *The Effectiveness of Punishment* 57-58 (1968).

113. See, for example, one of the works of a leading authority—Johannes Andenaes, *The General Part of the Criminal Law of Norway* 70 (1965).

114. Lipton, "The Psychopath," 40 *J. Crim. L. & Crim.* 584, at 585 (1950).

115. "The Psychiatric Approach to Crime and Correction," 23 *Law & Contemp. Prob.* 633, at 638 (1958).

116. Supra note 103, at 14.

117. See, for example, J. Edgar Hoover in *The Death Penalty in America*, (H. A. Bedau, ed. 1967), at 134-135: "For the law enforcement officer the time-proven deterrents to crime are sure detection, swift apprehension and proper punishment. Each is a necessary ingredient."

own abilities to avoid detection and arrest. General deterrence on the other hand has as its prime purpose the reinforcement of respect for the law.[118] In theory, the punishment of the bad is educative of the good, who avoid thereby the misdeeds of the delinquent punished as a horrible example. The really dangerous psychopath is so abnormal that the ordinary, decent citizen would have no desire whatever to emulate him or his behavior which is repugnant to the normal, average individual in society. However much the punishment of the psychopath might be welcomed by the citizenry at large, this cannot be on the grounds that it is necessary or desirable for reasons of general deterrence. The normal need no such warning and the abnormal (other psychopaths among them) are, for the reasons we have already considered, unlikely to heed it.

Treatment or rehabilitation poses similar problems. Having regard to the present state of our correctional facilities sentencing the psychopath to a lengthy term of imprisonment in the hope of improving his condition is quite unrealistic.[119] Prison has no therapeutic value for the psychopath and is likely simply to aggravate his criminal tendencies and perfect his capacity for mischief.[120] The psychopath can pose a serious disciplinary problem in the ordinary prison and there are regrettably few facilities equipped to handle this type of offender.[121] Dr. Scott has put

---

118. See, for example, Ball, "The Deterrence Concept in Criminology and Law," 46 *J. Crim. L., Crim. & P. S.* 347, at 348 (1955): "Most jurists take the position that deterrence is necessary for the maintenance of the legal system and the preservation of society."

119. In 1935 it was said, "He usually begins his career through various small delinquencies, is institutionalized, and here learns from previous offenders the more desperate and involved criminal methods. Our institutions for punishment in these cases merely become advanced schools for the psychopath." Henry Hadley Dixon, "Psychiatric Angles of Criminal Behavior," 14 *Ore. L. Rev.* 352, at 335. The same is tragically true today.

120. See, for example, Train, "Unrest in the Penitentiary," 44 *J. Crim. L., Crim. & P. S.* 277, at 294 (1953): "Of particular significance to the custodial officer is the intractable, unstable, explosive, aggressive reactions to frustrations of the psychopathic personality. Although few in number, they demoralize the penitentiary and are responsible for a plethora of prison rules and close supervision."

121. Dr. Stuart Whitely, supra note 48, at 159 has opined: "The aggressive type probably requires the authoritarian control of a system such as at Herstedvester."

the position very realistically:[122] "Returning to the three methods of dealing with psychopaths, we may dismiss punishment for the good reason that by the time a person is dubbed 'psychopath,' he will almost invariably have been frequently and unavailingly punished, so that it would be unreasonable to repeat the process. We have to rely on a combination of control and treatment. Control is a euphemism for locking-up and the essential and very difficult point is to ensure that it should only be applied when really necessary." The matter is further complicated by the lack of meaningful collaboration on the part of the psychopath in the treatment which might be prescribed for his case.[123] The psychopath prefers his own way to that of society and sees no reason to change. He may present a false front of seeming conformity for the sake of some temporary advantage[124] but he is in no way cured of his vicious tendencies. The condition of some is undoubtedly aggravated by the opportunities that incarceration offers for extending the conflict with society. The judge must realistically take into account these facts in estimating the possibilities of treating or rehabilitating the psychopath but he is further pressed by the knowledge that even an indeterminate sentence will have the effect of one day turning such an offender loose upon the community once more. The point has been well put that,[125] "To enforce criminal sanctions consisting of temporary prison confinement on this type of person will do little good and society will be the only loser, for the majority of these per-

---

122. "Current British Attitudes Toward Treating Psychopathy," 5 *J. Offender Therapy* 1, at 2 (Sept., 1961).

123. See, for example, Sharkey, "Four Stages in the Treatment of the Psychopathic Delinquent," *J. Offender Therapy* 7 (Sept., 1961): "Motivating a psychopath is an extremely difficult job since he invariably feels that there is nothing wrong with him; it is society, 'bad luck' that contributed to his apprehension, or the other fellow who should bear the brunt of the blame while he is guiltless."

124. See, for example, Karpman, "Criminality, Insanity and the Law," 39 *J. Crim. L. & Crim.* 584, at 604 (1949): "To the psychiatrist, they (psychopaths) have always presented a problem, for they are a difficult lot to handle, although they are very easy to get along with once they make up their minds that it would be to their benefit to get along and not to create a disturbance."

125. Hayden, *supra* note 35, at 436-37.

sons will not be discouraged either by the threat of, or the imposition of, temporary confinement, and are bound to repeat their
criminal acts as soon as they are released." If confinement is
known from the start to have no remedial properties, the conscientious judge must seriously question his motives in imposing
a long prison sentence in such cases. Whatever these motives
might be, they clearly cannot be said to have any real relation to
the rehabilitation of the offender.

The judge is thus left with the twin props of retribution and
social defense with which to support his sentence. Allusion has
been repeatedly made to the force of the former and Professor
Gibbens has said,[126] "The psychiatrist is also well aware of the
existence of strong retributive forces within society's attitude to
the offender and that the courts are obliged to take these forces
into account." The latter objective, that of social defense[127]
raises quite different considerations since it is more positive in
character but the problem is how to translate the concept into
concrete terms. Hence the matter turns into a question of who
is to be responsible for the execution of the chosen policy. The
conflict becomes one between those who regard the psychopath
as bad and responsible and those who regard him as seriously disturbed if not actually mad and accordingly, irresponsible or at
least of diminished responsibility. There would seem to be some
agreement that the psychopath is not suitable for confinement in
prison as it is presently conceived but the main problem is that
there are no special medical treatment facilities for one in his
condition either. The psychopath is not ordinarily considered to
be mentally ill so that he might appropriately be placed in an institution for the treatment of the psychotic. This is a problem
which has been encountered in many systems.[128] It has been said

---

126. Gibbens, "Psychiatry and the Abnormal Offender," 24 *Medico-Legal Journal*
142 (1956).

127. On this, see in particular, Edwards, "Social Defence and the Control of the
Dangerous Offender," 21 *Current Legal Problems* 23 (1968).

128. See, for example, Kinberg, "The Swedish Organization of Forensic Psychiatry," 44 *J. Crim. L., Crim. & P. S.* 135 (1953).

of Switzerland,[129] "One often sees a sort of tennis game. The convict is placed in a psychiatric hospital at the request of the penitentiary authorities who consider him mentally ill. Then he is returned to the penitentiary because the psychiatrist considers him to be a psychopath and not a psychotic." Dr. Scott has said,[130] "There are two ways of humanely dealing with these relatively few dangerous criminal psychopaths. Either they are admitted to hospital which will then become something of a prison, or else they are admitted to prison which should become something of a hospital." In either case, institutions capable of handling the special problems posed by the psychopath are required. The English judges cognizant of the deficiencies of the ordinary prison system looked forward optimistically and with some relief to the passing of the Mental Health Act in 1959.[131] It was hoped these special institutes for the containment and treatment of the psychopath would be provided. In all countries save those with a minimal crime problem of this nature, the major difficulty resides not in the quality but rather in the quantity of the special institutions provided. This more than anything has hampered the application of the United States sexual psychopath laws and has given rise to a certain, understandable judicial nervousness in relation to their application.[132] Yet withal, a more fundamental judicial caution remains, for it is not merely a question of choosing between practical alternatives, however inadequate these might be, but rather of overcoming in the first instance that massive disgust which in turn becomes society's retributive mindless reaction against the psychopathic offender. The conscientious judge is understandably reluctant to turn over to the psychiatrist the treatment of an offender whose incorrigible nature and dangerous propensities are presently beyond the capacity and re-

---

129. Remy, "Recent Developments of the Swiss Penal Jurisdiction," 4 *Crim. L. Q.* 305, at 310.

130. Supra note 47, at 15.

131. See, Havard, "R. v. Cowburn," [1959] *Crim. L. Rev.* 554.

132. The real doubts of the thoughtful lawyer regarding the operation of these statutes are expressed by Jerome Hall in "Science, Common Sense and Criminal Law Reform," 49 *Iowa L. Rev.* 1044, at 1058 (1964).

sources of medical science to control or cure.[133] Yet judges are, too, conceivably moved by other more primitive considerations. While judicial aversion to the possibilities of "treatment" are in the nature of a confession of the system's failure to socialize this type of offender the deeper, more significant explanation serves to expose the inherent, inescapable contradictions in our penological thinking.

A TENTATIVE CONCLUSION

"What do they want with you and me? How do I know what they want with you? I know what they want with me. I broke the law, so I have to pay for it." (Silence.)

An asylum dialogue.
(Cited by W. H. Auden)[134]

It is not the present purpose to investigate more exactly the puzzling and penologically disturbing phenomenon of psychopathy. It is enough for the moment to say that we know and have always known there was something wrong with the psychopath; even though we may still be very far from being able to say with certainty what it is or what we ought to do about it. The problem of psychopathy itself is almost incidental to the matter which is under examination here: the unsatisfactory way in which we approach the problem of the psychopath simply points to and sharpens the focus upon that matter. The case argued here is that we are in danger of losing sight of the present, unsatisfactory state of our correctional policies. This is not to say that informed criticism is absent or muted, for the very reverse would

---

133. Although written in 1955, the words of Gerald Flood are equally applicable today: "The fact that we now talk about psychopaths, or about even more refined categories of abnormal and criminal behavior is apt to make us think that we know as much about the psychopathic criminal as we do about the paranoic or schizophrenic. Nothing could be farther from the truth . . . So far as we judges can see, diagnosis is in no better situation. The symptoms that constitute the psychopathic state are so vague that they are of little help to us and as for the various subdivisions of that state we constantly see the psychiatrists disagree as to the category into which any defendant falls." "Sentencing Function of the Judge," 45 *J. Crim. L., Crim. & P. S.* 531, at 535 (1955).

134. This is the concluding part of a psychotic dialogue cited in Auden's commonplace book, *A Certain World* (1970), at 242. It is chilling in its sudden, abrupt departure from madness and the return to hard reality.

be true.[135] What does seem to be the case is that collectively the judges seem unwarrantedly satisfied that there has been developed a modern penological policy which wholly supersedes the earlier, barbaric, unscientific notions of punishment and which makes, almost automatically in theory, for satisfactory disposal of the offender. If there are imperfections they are due to the human element in the execution of the sentence, lack of understanding by legislators, administrators, economic difficulties, etc.[136] This is a very myopic attitude. We tend to be grossly overconfident of our technological progress in the corrections field[137] but worse still, our basic philosophy has remained quite unchanged. Beneath the very thin veneer of rehabilitation with which we now cover the execution of sentences lies all the old, primeval thinking as deep and inerradicable as ever. Far from replacing the older, instinctual themes of punishment, we have barely covered them up and it would be well for us not to be deceived on the point.

Our corrections system regrettably remains tied to the idea of punishment in its pure unadulterated sense. It is only when we

---

135. See, for example, Lohman, supra note 4, at 33-34: "The foremost myth says we handle crime with all the techniques developed by our most advanced knowledge . . . the fact is that when one looks at law enforcement the correctional system in the United States, the most one can say is that it is a massive program of law enforcement and correctional housekeeping. For all practical purposes we are only *warehousing* the problem. . . . We ought not to masquerade the system by reference to a few progressive gestures."

136. That these can be major contributory causes is not denied. See, for example, Schwartz, "The Effect in Philadelphia of Pennsylvania's Increased Penalties for Rape and Attempted Rape," 59 *J. Crim. L., Crim. & P. S.* 509, at 514-15 (1968): "The inefficacy of the new legislation should create much disappointment among those in Philadelphia who had taken for granted the deterrent impact of increased penalties. Of course, the question of deterrence was quite beside the point for those who supported the new legislation for the sake of a more perfect retribution, or with a view to the May primary elections."

137. See, for example, the interview with Professor Herman Schwartz, in 7 *Crim. L. Bull.* 822 (Dec. 1971): "Q. Will Attica set back the cause of reform? Was New York really on the way to reform? A. I am not certain about the answer to the second question. I think the state was on the way to making some changes but the New York prison system has deteriorated so badly that the distance to be traveled is incredibly long. If you say it was on the road, yes, it was on the thousand-mile journey that the Chinese talk about where one or two steps, at most, had been taken."

consider the case of the "special" offender, such as the psychopath, that we see just how markedly retributive our system remains: we do little more than trade hurt for hurt. So distinctive is this feature that however abnormal the offender may be, he knows he will be called upon to "pay" for his crime, even though such payment of a future, anticipated account of some other crime. Deterrence, individual or general, may fail time and again; rehabilitation may be a nonstarter. Yet that primitive spirit of retribution which moved man to respond in kind long before the lex talionis moderated his scale of responses, remains as the real force behind society's official reactions; even though we try out of shame or false pride to dress up our punishments in other, more attractive habits. We retain—whatever our rationalizations—all our old, absolutist, justifications for our penological thinking.[138] This dominates our criminal policy and prevents any meaningful development of a constructive model based on a true theory of corrections rather than simply making the criminal "pay" for his crime. Retribution may well be very necessary for social cohesion and the prevention of anomie;[139] it cannot improve the offender or alter the social attitudes of the like-minded.

It has been said that[140] "In a society that values freedom, the decision to imprison a man is one of the heaviest responsibilities anyone can assume." Such responsibility does not end with the imposition of the sentence, but that act marks the beginning of a new and special responsibility. Glanville Williams has said,[141] "Briefly, the attitude of the courts has always been that there is in gremio judicis a moral scale which enables the judge to pronounce what quantum of punishment is justly appropriate to what offense. This is the punishment that fits the crime." The punishment is also presumed to fit the criminal and for this the judge has his moral scale or tariff of punishment which guides him in his task. But can the conscientious judge rest easy in this

---

138. See, S. Schafer, *Theories in Criminology*, 293 (1969).

139. This would certainly seem to be the opinion of those responsible for the Preliminary Report of the Governor's Special Committee on Criminal Offenders, State of New York (1968), at 73.

140. D. Glaser, *The Effectiveness of a Prison and Parole System*, at 287 (1964).

141. "The Courts and Persistent Offenders," [1963] *Crim. L. Rev.* 730, at 733.

role of tariff collector, even though he plays his part in the setting of the charges? Can he close his eyes to what happens, in fact, as a result of his decisions?[142] If there is to be "justice under science rather than justice under law,"[143] the judge must take a greater share of responsibility for what happens as a result of his sentence. The judge cannot remake society; but by a more concerned, activist attitude he can see that society shapes up to its obligations. All too often, the judge does little more than give voice to society's sense of outrage. In many cases this comes from a degree of involvement in the drama, above which the judicial office ought really to rise.[144] We should perhaps remember judges are human and despite the almost divine nature of their office, we can justly expect from them only human responses. It may be that our theoretical standards are too high and that we must aim for a realistic compromise in this, as in other, fields. Whatever may be decided, the judge will always be left with the difficult task of getting the mixture right.

---

142. See, for example, James V. Bennett, "After Sentence—What?," 45 *J. Crim. L., Crim. & P. S.* 537, at 537 (1955) : "It seems to me altogether proper that judges and lawyers know how the kind of medicine they prescribe is administered."

143. See, Luther W. Youngdahl, "Development and Accomplishments of Sentencing Institutes in the Federal Judicial System," in *The Tasks of Penology*, (H. S. Perlman & T. B. Allington eds. 1969) , at 159.

144. Helen Silving makes the following interesting observation: "It may be worth exploring whether the psychological relationship of appellate judges to the trial judge may not have a stronger impact on their decision than their relationship to the accused. It is important to remember that historically the trial judge was the 'accused' on appeal, for judicial review grew out of a 'trial' of trial judges." "Psychoanalysis and Criminal Law," 51 *J. Crim. L., Crim. & P. S.* 19, at 21-22 (1960) .

PART IV

DEALING WITH DEVIANCE OUTSIDE THE CRIMINAL LAW SYSTEM

CHAPTER 11

THE VICTIM'S CONSENT IN CRIMINAL LAW: AN ESSAY ON THE EXTENT OF THE DECRIMINALIZING ELEMENT OF THE CRIME CONCEPT

AMNON RUBINSTEIN

Dean of the Law School, Tel Aviv University

INTRODUCTION

PROFESSOR JEROME HALL, in his treatise on the *General Principles of Criminal Law,* is one of the few scholars who treats the victim's consent as a general element of justification in criminal law.[1] That consent does "justify" the apparent offense in certain cases is beyond dispute. There is no theft or larceny unless done without the owner's consent, and there can be no such thing as "consensual rape." In these cases absence of consent is an element of the offense. On the other hand, it is also clear that in certain cases consent is immaterial: no person is entitled to take another man's life, even if the victim's consent is clearly and unquestionably established. The question of justification arises in an area lying between these two extremes.

The demarcation line between areas in which consent is valid and those in which it is invalid has never been clearly established. Moreover, the very question of consent has recently acquired a philosophical significance outweighing questions of interpretation and technique. It became part and parcel of the debate concerning society's right to enforce its moral code via the machinery of the criminal law and its purely legal meaning has become inextricably intertwined with the ubiquitous concept of "consent-

---

1. J. Hall, *General Principles of Criminal Law* 232 (2d ed. 1960). See also R. M. Perkins, *Criminal Law* 962 (2d ed. 1969), and for a wholly different view, see Helen Silving, *Constituent Elements of Crime* 418 (1967).

ing adults." The decriminalization of deviate behavior and attempted suicide as well as the relaxation of censorship over ob-
scenity have only a nebulous relation to the question of consent
in criminal law. In the final analysis, criminal sanctions for consensual homosexuality were eliminated because of the growing
recognition that an adult person's sexual behavior in private is
of no concern to the criminal law. The recognition is unrelated
to the question of consent by the victim. By legalizing aberrant
sexual behavior the law in effect determines that there is neither
crime nor victim and the question of consent does not arise. The
same is applicable, *mutatis mutandis*, to similar reforms, urged
or carried out, with regard to use and possession of marijuana
and other offenses where there is no specific individual who can
be described as the victim for whose defense the criminal law intervenes. But because these reforms were drafted in terms of
rights of "consenting adults" the question of consent and its effect on criminal law has attracted public attention.

In the famous debate between Lord Devlin and Professor
Hart on the Report of Lord Wolfenden's Committee on Homosexual Offenses and Prostitution, the question of the victim's consent figured rather prominently.[2] The debate revolved around
the right of society to impose moral norms on its members. Lord
Devlin endeavored to prove that English Law was based from
earliest times on the enforcement of morality:

> The criminal law of England has from the very first concerned itself
> with moral principles. A simple way of testing this point is to consider
> the attitude which the criminal law adopts towards consent. . . . It is
> not a defence to any form of assault that the victim thought his pun-
> ishment well deserved and submitted to it; to make a good defence the
> accused must prove that the law gave him the right to chastise and that
> he exercised it reasonably.

Lord Devlin argued that if law were intended only for the

---

2. Report of the Committee on Homosexual Offenses and Prostitution, Cmnd.
247, para. 355 (i) (1957). See also Model Penal Code at 277 (Tent. Draft No. 4,
1955). In England, the Sexual Offenses Act, 1967, legalized private consensual
homosexuality. A similar step was taken by Illinois in 1961 and Connecticut in
1971.

protection of the individual, his waiver and consent would be a sufficient defense. It therefore follows that

> There is only one explanation of what has hitherto been accepted as the basis of the criminal law and that is that there are certain standards of behavior or moral principles which society requires to be observed; and the breach of them is an offence not merely against the person who is injured but against society as a whole.[3]

These remarks encountered sharp criticism. It was pointed out that Lord Devlin's approach was based on a misunderstanding of applicable legal doctrine,[4] since negation of consent in cases of bodily harm may be explained as legal paternalism[5] and in such cases the very authenticity of the victim's consent is suspect.[6]

All these answers do not detract from the fact that in certain circumstances the law does not recognize the right of an individual to consent to the infliction of damage to himself and this limitation on his free will raises problems of principle as well as the familiar problems of boundary delineation. It is, however, questionable whether this refusal to recognize consent is by definition an enforcement of morality.

Let us take as an example the case of a sick person who does not consent to life-saving medical treatment because of religious objections or superstitions. Can it be said that a law which does not recognize this person's will and which takes into account medical considerations enforces morals? A system which makes medical treatment obligatory in such cases obviously prefers pragmatic social considerations to individual faith, but it would be hard to define this as the enforcement of morals—unless morals are equated with public welfare. For example, the French system in which medical treatment and doctors' responsibility are based not only on consent but also on considerations of public

---

3. Devlin, *The Enforcement of Morals* 6-7 (1965) .
4. Glanville Williams, "Consent and Public Policy," [1962] *Crim. L. Rev.* 74, 154.
5. Cf. H. L. A. Hart, *Law, Liberty and Morality* 31 (1963) : "The rules excluding the victim's consent as a defense the charges of murder or assault may perfectly well be explained as a piece of paternalism designed to protect individuals against themselves."
6. G. Hughes, "Morals and the Criminal Law," 71 *Yale L. J.* 662, 671 (1970) .

welfare[7] is founded on the secular-rational philosophy governing French Law since the Revolution.[8]

There is another reason for distinguishing between the enforcement of morals—in the accepted sense of the phrase—and the question of the victim's consent. Emphasizing "consenting adults" in questions of sex in general, and legal reforms in matters of homosexuality in particular, have endowed our era with an aura of permissiveness. Attention is focused on repeal of the prohibitions and the crucial importance of an adult person's consent. It should be recalled, however, that in this very era a growing body of law rejects individual consent even if freely given. This is the case in social welfare legislation which frequently provides that an employee may not waive rights accorded to him by statute and in laws designed to protect a person from his own negligence. Such legislation can in no way be considered "permissive." The different ways in which consent is treated by law reflect substantive changes in the current social values: the modern legislator is concerned less with man's spirit than with his physical welfare. Legal rules of conduct are drawn not from religious texts or moralistic beliefs but rely on rational and pragmatic considerations. In other words, there is no purely legal answer to the question of consent in criminal law, for what we are really dealing with is political philosophy. A disciple of the rational utilitarian school in its purest form will follow John Stuart Mill's teachings and will view consent as the be-all and end-all of criminal law. Society's power to use force derives, according to this school, from the need to protect the individual from others. Once that individual consents to be injured, there is no longer any utilitarian consideration justifying the use of the criminal law.

Those who view law as a tool for imposition of religious or moral norms—or generally for the "betterment of mankind"—will not hesitate to spurn the victim's consent if their goal can thus be served.

But a middle road also exists, which in certain circumstances

---

7. See G. Hughes, "Two Views on Consent in the Criminal Law," 26 *Modern L. Rev.* 233, 239 (1963).

8. See note 38 infra.

ignores the victim's consent, sacrificing it for a greater public interest if such interest is itself based upon rational considerations. I submit that the rule governing questions of consent in criminal law must be based upon such considerations which can be justified in terms of a modern secular society.

DEFINING THE PROBLEM

Criminal law defines and punishes undesirable acts. A good part of criminal law prohibitions is designed to protect society as a whole. These prohibitions raise no question of consent by the victim, since the victim by its very nature is incapable of giving it.[9] When, however, the criminal prohibition is designed to protect the person, property or reputation of an individual, the question of his consent to the prohibited act does arise.

Yet in English speaking countries one notices the conspicuous absence of a general doctrine regarding consent. Many authors ignore the subject entirely while others couch the applicable legal rule in tautological terms, saying that "consent is not a defense if it is granted for an unlawful purpose, or where the law does not recognize that consent of the injured party is an element of the offense."[10]

The question is what is an "unlawful purpose" and when should consent be justification? In crimes against private property consent is generally regarded as negating the offense.[11] But even in this case the law is not always clear and thus the words "without the owners' consent," long an integral part of the definition of the crime of theft, were deleted from the English Theft Act of 1968.[12] The situation is the same with regard to

9. See G. Hughes, "Consent in Sexual Offenses," 25 *Modern L. Rev.* 672, 673 (1962) ; Note, 33 *Canadian Bar Rev.* 88, 89. Silving, supra note 1, at 418, rejects this distinction and maintains that apart from crimes where consent nullifies the offense, "consent affords no justification, since under present jurisprudential doctrine there are no private crimes, all crimes being deemed a matter of public concern."

10. M. C. Bassiouni, *Criminal Law and Its Processes* 107 (1969) . See also Kadish & Paulsen, *Criminal Law and Its Processes* 15 (2d ed. 1969) .

11. When an employer consents to his employee taking property from him for the purpose of entrapping him, the employee is not guilty of theft. *R. v. Turvey,* [1946] 2 All E. R. 60.

12. Cf. *R. v. Lawrence,* [1970] 3 All E. R. 933, aff'd *Lawrence v. Metropolitan Commissioner,* [1971] 2 All E. R. 1253 (H.L.) .

medical operations: the law does not define the area in which consent of the patient is recognized and we must turn to the judicial decisions whose rules are not sufficiently crystallized.

The law may hold that consent is justification but invalidate its effectiveness by other means. Consent is inherently different from submission and consequently must be a product of an adult and sane person's mind. It presupposes full knowledge of the injurious act and a capacity to intelligently understand the nature of the act and its possible consequences.[13] The rules precluding consent seem to be well-established[14] but it should be noted that the technique of invalidating consent may be used as a substitute for the substantive issue of the need for consent. Even where the law conditions criminal liability on the absence of consent, it can establish legal presumptions which will nullify this condition. For example, every legal system provides that consent may be given only by adults and that consent by a person under a given age, determined arbitrarily, is ineffective. In the converse situation where no consent has been given, the law may imply it (as

---

13. For a dated but still useful discussion of this subject, see Beale, "Consent in the Criminal Law," 8 *Harv. L. Rev.* 317 (1894).

14. English law distinguishes in sexual assaults between two types of fraud affecting the woman's consent. If a woman agrees to sexual intercourse because she believes the man's tale that it is a medical act which will improve her voice, the consent is ineffective: she did not understand the substance of the act itself. *R. v. Williams*, [1923] 1 K.B. 340. As against this, a man whose wife consented to have relations with him without being told by him that he had a venereal disease, was not guilty of assaulting her, for her consent was effective: it was given to the act itself albeit without knowledge of the possible consequences. *Queen v. Clarence,* [1888] 22 Q.B.D. 23. Stating that there is no general rule providing that consent secured by fraud is inoperative, Justice Wills at 27 notes that such consent in contract law does not destroy the contract but only renders it voidable. See also *Hegarty v. Shine,* [1877] 2 Q.B.D. 410. In *Latter v. Bradell* (1881) 50 L.J.Q.B. 448, consent of a maid who initially objected to but under pressure of her employer later submitted to an examination for pregnancy by a physician was held valid because no threats of violence were made towards her. In *Bolam v. Friern Hospital Management Committee* [1957] 2 All E.R. 118, the consent of a mentally ill person to undergo shock treatment without being fully apprised of the possible dangers was held valid in an action for damages. But this case must be understood against the background of its special circumstances in that the treatment of a mentally ill person was at issue. In an ordinary case of assault, consent secured by any form of deception is inoperative. See K. L. Kahn, "Consent and Responsibility in Sexual Offenses," [1968] *Crim. L. Rev.* 81, 150, at 87; Perkins, supra note 1, at 109-110.

in the case of a person brought unconscious to the operating table). The law attributes consent to the unconscious patient in those legal systems such as the United States, England or Israel where consent is a prerequisite.[15] The law may thus rule out consent which was in fact given and create it where it was nonexistent.

By invoking the same technique it is possible to achieve results which alter the substance of the law. For example, it is possible to explain the law's refusal to recognize a person's consent to be killed or injured by another as an exception to the rule requiring nonconsent of the victim. The same result can be obtained by holding this consent ineffective in that it is contrary to human nature and experience and therefore automatically suspect. In the end, it is irrelevant how the law ignores the victim's consent. The determinative fact is that in certain matters the law spreads its protective wing over the acts of men, despite their apparent will and even though there is no injury caused to any other person.[16]

The crucial fact is that the law—statutory as well as judicial—treats consent not in a uniform, analytical way but according to the subject matter and type of behavior in which the question is raised. We shall now deal with the principal subjects in which the question of consent arises.

---

15. See note 36 infra.

16. Another matter which may affect the final decision on the issue of consent relates to the question of whether the offender must know of the victim's consent or whether its existence is sufficient to justify him. In matters of theft there is a tendency to recognize mere existence of consent even without the offender's knowledge of it as sufficient to negate criminal responsibility. See *R. v. Turvey*, [1946] 2 All E.R. 60. In this case the accused did not know and could not have known of the owner's consent. The reason for this is that the law here is directed to protection of the owner of stolen property and his waiver of the protected interest leaves nothing to concern the law. But can the same rule apply to sexual offenses and to assault? In *R. v. Collins*, [1972] All E. R. 1105, the defendant was accused of breaking and entering for the purpose of committing rape. He entered the room of the woman who mistook him for someone else and voluntarily had relations with him. The court held that had the woman extended her arm beyond the window prior to his entry, the defendant might have been entitled to understand this as an invitation and would have been entitled to acquittal. Failure to so instruct the jury vitiated the conviction.

PROTECTION OF HUMAN LIFE

Viewing human life as of supreme value means—in legal terms—that a person is not master of his own life and consequently may not consent to be killed. It is irrelevant how this will is nullified—whether by saying that it cannot be effective or by holding that it is suspect and therefore defective. The crucial issue is that the various legal systems—without a single exception —do not view a person's life as property which may be taken from him at his consent. Ostensibly, this axiom is an expression of a religious faith; in fact, the supremacy of human life accords with anthropocentric views which see man as the center of the universe. Principles of liberty allow consent to be withdrawn, whereas taking life not only eliminates that possibility but also puts an end to the entire voluntary process. Therefore there is no difficulty in principle, from a rational point of view, in coming to terms with the concept of protecting a person's life against his will, although the limits of protection will vary from one system to another.

The protection may take several forms:

1. Protection against self-murder, i.e. against suicide.
2. Protection of a consenting person against the taking of his life by another.
3. Protection against self-killing, i.e. negligently or recklessly risking one's life without the intention of ending it.

The criminal prohibition against suicide has been relaxed in recent years and abolished in many states.[17] This tendency is capable of two interpretations: one recognizes man's right to end his life, the other realizes that a legal prohibition cannot be effective in these matters. As to the person committing suicide, it is of no consequence how we explain the abolition of the offense. If in fact it is an expression of the lack of effectiveness

---

17. In England the offense of attempted suicide was abolished by the Suicide Act, 1961. In Israel, sec. 225 (1) of the Criminal Code Ordinance, making attempted suicide a misdemeanor, was repealed along with other enumerated sections of the Ordinance by the Criminal Code Ordinance (Amendment No. 28) Law, 5726-1966, *Sefer Hahukim* (No. 481) 64, 20 *Laws of Israel* 56.

of the criminal law, criminal responsibility must still be imposed on all those who abet the suicide. In common law jurisdictions which have abolished the offense—such as England and Israel[18]— consent of the person committing suicide will not avail those who assisted him.

This attitude is characteristic of the present policy of the liberal legislator: he is prepared to recognize his own powerlessness to intervene in cases of attempted suicide where no other parties are involved. But he is unwilling to accept the active intervention of another person, even if there is no inherent difference between the two types—aided and unaided—of suicide. This may be seen as taking an illogical position, but the policy of the liberal legislator reflects a consistent approach: when we deal with the offense of attempted suicide we do not deal at all with the question of the victim's consent. The perpetrator and victim are one and the problem of consent is not raised at all in its ordinary significance. The only question is whether the law should prohibit such behavior or not. When, on the other hand, we speak of intervention by another person, we have the ordinary situation of offender and victim with consent of the victim claimed as justification. Therefore the law is able from an analytical viewpoint to distinguish between attempted suicide on the one hand and abetting suicide or euthanasia on the other.

---

18. See sec. 2 of the English Suicide Act, 1961, and sec. 225 (1) of the Israeli Ordinance. The law in France is different and the abettor is also exonerated. See Hughes, supra note 7, at 240-241. Despite this, Hughes maintains that French law is not based on a right to commit suicide but on the ineffectiveness of the criminal sanction. There is, therefore, no contradiction, according to this view, between permitting suicide and prohibiting killing with the victim's consent. By allowing suicide and punishing the abettor, the law creates a certain discrimination: handicapped, chronically ill persons will find it difficult to put an end to their life, although they are more "justified"—if one may use the phrase—than other persons in seeking suicide. The question whether there is a substantive right to commit suicide may, however, have extra-legal ramifications. Thus recently, a public debate has been going on in San Francisco and the Bay area with regard to a proposed suicide-prevention barrier on the Golden Gate Bridge—one of America's most popular suicide spots. The debate revolves mainly around the aesthetical aspect, but it is also argued in terms of the right of every person to put an end to his life. See "Right to Leap Off Golden Gate at Issue on Coast," *New York Times,* October 5, 1973, at 32.

The difference is not merely analytical. The prohibition against taking another person's life even with his consent reflects deep conviction that the 6th commandment, "thou shalt not kill," outweighs all other considerations, including the victim's will. It is not merely a question of whether the victim fully consents (a reason frequently cited in this context) but it is a matter of basic rejection of an act in which man assumes a role not his—a godly role in the religious view and a prohibited and dangerous role by utilitarian-rational principles. It is occasionally claimed that to permit such killing would have dangerous results in that the perpetrator once having killed with the victim's consent, might develop aggressive and murderous tendencies. It seems, however, that the matter is more profound. The law cannot allow an act which is entirely at odds with its basic values: permissible taking of life becomes a symbolic act which completely denies the fundamental concept of a civilized society—the sanctity of life.

This does not mean this principle must always and in all circumstances override other considerations. In extreme cases where the victim's death seems certain and taking his life is not only done with his consent but also for the purpose of easing his suffering and distress, other considerations are involved. The debate on legalization of euthanasia is not within the purview of this article.[19] However it ought to be emphasized that those who seek to legalize euthanasia do not rely solely upon the consent of the patient but mainly upon the existence of objective criteria, including reasonable probability of the patient's imminent death.

---

19. Under the codes of some European nations, consent of the victim reduces the charge from murder to manslaughter. Criminal Code of Holland, sec. 293, 294; Criminal Code of Italy, sec. 579; Criminal Code of Spain, sec. 409; Criminal Code of Switzerland, sec. 114; Criminal Code of West Germany, sec. 216. See Hughes, supra note 7, at 241; Note, supra note 9, at 93. In English law, consent of the victim reduces murder to manslaughter only in two cases: the Suicide Act, 1961, provides that a person who remains living after a suicide pact shall be guilty of manslaughter; and this is also the law when a death has been caused as a result of abortion or unlawful operation. *R. v. Pike*, [1961] *Crim. L. Rep.* 114.

PROTECTION OF THE BODY AND HEALTH
OF AN INDIVIDUAL

The distinction which the law makes between suicide and consensual killing is also the basis of the protection afforded by the law to the person of an individual.

The criminal law does not generally tell a person how to treat his body. Most criminal codes do not recognize the crime of self-inflicted injury unless the injury was caused for the purpose of evading military service or in order to otherwise damage the public as, for example, by displaying physical handicaps for the purpose of begging.[20]

There are a few exceptions to this rule—mainly those relating to drug abuse.[21] But aside from such prohibitions, the health and physical well-being of a person are not a fit subject for intervention of the criminal law. Under law, man is master of his body and health.

The question of consent of the victim does not arise in cases of self-inflicted injury. It arises only when a person consents to have another person injure him. Here again, as with the prohibition against self-killing, injury permitted when self-inflicted becomes prohibited if inflicted by another. A person who deforms himself is generally not criminally responsible, whereas a person

---

20. G. Williams, supra note 4, at 154; see also the case of Wright (1603), Co. Lit. f. 127a-b.

21. The controversy over the criminalization of drug use and possession lies beyond the scope of this article. In this case, too, there is no specific victim and, consequently, the question of consent cannot really arise. However, one of the ways in which criminalization of addictive drugs can be justified deals with the concept of consent. Freedom of will, it may be argued, means freedom to consent and to withdraw consent. The law does not recognize consent whose result is denial of personal freedom. Consequently, the law does not recognize a person's capacity to consent to becoming a slave. A drug which creates physiological dependence impairs the addict's ability to resist the drug in the future. The law may thus ignore the initial consent in the same manner as it does not recognize a person's consent to become a slave. The prohibition against taking drugs which impair one's grasp of reality can be explained specifically as respect for man's free will. There can be no volition and there can be no consent except where there is understanding of those facts upon which a considered decision, free from extraneous influences, is predicated. See Rubinstein, "The Enforcement of Morals," 2 *Israel Yearbook on Human Rights* 57, 92.

who causes a deformity to another will be held guilty even if the victim freely consented to the injury. The law's refusal to recognize consent in such cases can be explained as based on human experience: no sane person will agree to severe physical injury—particularly injury that is untreatable—unless he suffers from some emotional disturbance which impairs his free will. Consent to injury which is beyond treatment damages one's freedom to withdraw consent and to preserve freedom of action by creating an irreversible situation. However, it should be emphasized that the prohibition is not directed against self-inflicted injury; it is designed to prevent public desecration of one of the law's basic rules of behavior. Beyond the concern for the physical well-being of the person, there lies the need to preserve the legal rule which prohibits one man from injuring another.[22]

The prohibition against consensual injury cannot be absolute: to apply it to ordinary cases of assault would create impossible results. It would result, for instance, in the illegality of most sporting events, which involve possible injury to participants. The law must therefore seek a compromise and determine that in certain cases consent will be recognized. This is not a question of absolutes but rather of legal policy attempting to make its way between the Scylla of recognition of free will and the Charybdis of adhering to a sacred rule. In traditional common law and in Anglo-American practice this policy is based on two criteria: one dealing with the extent of the injury, the other dealing with the social value of the act which caused the injury.

SOCIAL VALUE OF THE INJURIOUS ACT

The social value of the injurious act does affect the court's readiness to recognize the victim's consent.[23] The nature of the

22. Hughes, supra note 6, at 670, furnishes an additional utilitarian reason for negation of consent in these cases. In such cases society suffers a double loss—loss of services of the injured party and the economic burden imposed upon society by the victim becoming dependent upon it.

23. Glanville Williams deals with social value in a similar way. For example, he explains the difference in the attitude of the law to a person's voluntary risk-taking as depending on the social value of his act. "These circumstances include not merely the degree of probability of the risk eventuating but the social value of his act by running the risk," G. Williams, *The Mental Element in Crime* 30 (1965); similarly,

act involved seems in these cases to overshadow other circumstances. In other words, in identical situations regarding both *mens rea* and *actus reus,* recognition of consent depends on the type of action concerned. The questions raised by the victim's consent in this sphere were considered by a California court in an action for aggravated assault against a sadomasochist, who by his own admission gave vent to his creativity by producing and actively participating in sadomasochistic films.[24] One of his films, in which he flagellated another person, was turned over to the police by the firm which developed it. The person flagellated was not located but was identified by the accused as a sadomasochist who gladly consented to the acts. The court held that consent of the victim does not diminish the guilt of the person inflicting the beating.[25]

A similar result was reached by an English court in *R. v. Donovan,* a case involving a seventeen-year-old girl who consented to be beaten by the accused.[26] Justice Swift held that consent in such a situation could not render a criminal act lawful for "no person can license another to commit a crime." Furthermore,

. . . as a general rule, although it is a rule to which there are well-established exceptions, it is an unlawful act to beat another person with such a degree of violence that infliction of bodily harm is a probable consequence.[27]

The decision has been criticized as laying down too broad a rule; previously it was held that consent will not be recognized only when grievous bodily harm is involved and not in every case

---

id. at 94; G. Williams, *Criminal Law: The General Part* 60-61 (2d ed. 1961). As an example of social utility which would in his opinion justify the risk-taking involved, he cites the entertainer-sharpshooter who injures his assistant when attempting to shoot ashes from a cigarette held in the assistant's mouth, as an act which serves some useful social purpose. But see *R. v. McLeod,* 34 N.Z.L.R. 430 (1915), in which the Court of Appeals of New Zealand refused to give effect to the consent of a spectator to hold the cigarette in decidedly similar circumstances. The use of a deadly weapon, in the court's opinion, was decisive and because of it, the "game" could not be considered a sporting event.

24. *People v. Samuels,* 58 Cal. Rptr. 439 (1967).
25. See also Williams, supra note 4, at 75.
26. *R. v. Donovan,* [1934] All E. R. 207.
27. Id. at 210.

of assault likely to cause physical injury.[28] The rule in *Donovan,* would appear to be unnecessarily broad, in that it ought to have been limited to cases of serious physical harm.[29]

But the main point lies in the very distinction made by the courts between "legitimate" consent—such as in dangerous sports and "illegitimate" consent which, although involving similar harm, is unrecognized in cases of sexual assault. We shall deal now with two such spheres in which consent is "legitimate"— sports and medical treatment.

Dangerous Sports

Even within the realm of sport, the law is not prepared to recognize every dangerous game. The Common Law has traditionally distinguished between permissible and prohibited games. Prize fights[30] were in the latter category and the English courts refused

28. G. Williams, "Authoritarian Morals and the Criminal Law," [1966] *Crim. L. Rev.* 133, 146. Were the law to refuse to recognize consent in every case of "sexual assault" difficult situations would arise: various degrees of force and pain are involved in sexual contact and were it not for consent of the parties, it would, of course, be possible to classify them within the framework of assault and other offenses designed to protect the person. Cf. "Consent as Defense to Charge of Mayhem," 86 A.L.R.2d 268-270.

29. The Criminal Code Ordinance, 1936, legislated by the British in Palestine, embodies these principles of the Common Law and defines them with precision and clarity. Sections 235, 238 and 241 deal with unlawfully causing grievous harm or wounding and do not mention consent as an element of the offense. On the other hand, sec. 248 defines assault by referring to a act done "without the consent" of the person assaulted. This distinction is interesting because the Ordinance defines "grievous harm" as any harm which endangers life or which seriously or permanently injures health or comfort or which tends to cause permanent disfigurement or any permanent or serious injury to any external or internal organ. The emphasis is on injuries which create permanent damage and which consequently cannot be undone by withdrawal of consent by the victim.

30. One of the landmark decisions in this area is *Queen v. Coney* [1882] 8 Q.B.D. 534, in which the court dealt with a fist fight held in an improvised arena and which was observed by a large number of persons. The participants were held punishable because, as opposed to other games of sport, this contest was both dangerous to the life and health of the participants and to the public order. During the nineteenth century the English courts often dealt with this subject, but it is doubtful whether any rules can be culled from the plethora of decisions which will allow one to determine in advance what the likely approach of the court will be to a particular match. See *Reg. v. Orton,* 14 Cox C. C. 225 (1878) ; *Reg. v. Perkins,* 4

to give effect to the participants' consent to injury in such games. On the other hand, according to Anglo-American usage, dangerous sports—such as car racing, ice-hockey, football and boxing—are permissible and consent of the participants is effective.[31]

Distinctions made between desirable and undesirable games and between permissible and prohibited sports are apparently based on the law's revulsion toward physical injury for its own sake. No court of law would recognize consent in a revival of Roman gladiator tradition, even if the casualty rate can be shown to be lower than that involved in permissible sports. The court in *Donovan* cites Foster's *Crown Cases* as an authority for the proposition that a person who maliciously beats another is criminally responsible because the act is *malum in se*. Exceptions to this rule which relate to contests likely to cause physical injury are explained in two ways: causing physical injury is not the motive of either side, and the sporting contests are beneficial—"manly diversions, they tend to give strength, skill and activity, and may fit people for defense, public as well as personal in time of need."[32] This rather naive view will not be shared by many—the distinction between *malum in se* and commercially organized

---

C. & P. 537, 172 E. R. 814 (1831); *Reg. v. Knock*, 14 Cox C. C. 1 (1877); *Reg. v. Young*, 10 Cox C. C. 371 (1866). Consent in sports, as well as in medical treatment, is recognized even where consent is no justification. Cf. Williams, supra note 1. "The violent tackle which wins applause on the football field would be a battery if practiced on an unwilling citizen on the street." Perkins, supra note 1, at 109. Thus, in the Puerto Rican draft Penal Code, consent in such cases is covered by the general provisions regarding exemption of "Persons Acting Pursuant to Legal Authority or Leave." See Silving, supra note 1, at 402.

31. But even within permissible games, an intentional physical blow which causes the death of a player may be manslaughter. This was shown to be true in soccer: *Reg. v. Moore*, 14 T. L. R. 229 (1898). And the rule applies even though the attacker acted within the rules of the game, for "no rule of a game can sanction behavior likely to cause the death of another person." *Reg. v. Bradshaw*, 14 Cox C. C. 83 (1878). Cf. Beale, supra note 13, at 323. But observance of the rules of the game is evidence of the absence of intention to injure; and where there is no intent to injure, the promoters of the games are immune from civil responsibility for foreseeable injuries, so long as "rules of the game" are observed, because of attributed consent of the spectators to the risk. *Murray v. Harringay Arena Ltd.*, [1951] 2 K. B. D. 529.

32. [1934] All E. R. at 211.

fights is tenuous but a distinction of principle does exist between sports causing injury and injury itself being sported.

Consent in cases of deviant sexual behavior will be rejected because the primary objective is the infliction of physical harm. As opposed to this, in a football game the primary purpose is sport and entertainment and the extent that physical injury is caused is a necessary result but not an inherent purpose.[33]

It is, however, doubtful whether the legality of dangerous or cruel sports should at all be determined by the validity of consent. Two questions arise in this context. First, is it proper for the distinction to be made by the court, *ex post facto?*[34] The disadvantage of such judicial determination lies in the fact that it arises by coincidence, after the injury has been caused and after the disputed sport has already taken root. It seems matters such as these should properly be determined by the legislature which can systematically and logically deal with the entire subject of dangerous sports. The second question relates to the drawing of the line between permissible and prohibited games. The emphasis which English courts put upon intentional causation of injury is still serviceable, but it is doubtful whether it can be the sole criterion. Questions of actual harm caused—such as in professional boxing—as well as harmful educational effects ought to be taken into account.[35]

---

33. It is possible, of course, to maintain that the primary objective in sado-masochistic relations is not inflicting pain and injury, but rather gratification of the sexual impulse. However, it may be argued that, when serious physical injury is involved the law must intervene expressly because of this impulse in order to counteract it. It is significant to note that in the cases mentioned an additional negative element was involved: in *Donovan*, consent was given by a young and inexperienced girl, while *Samuels* involved the filming of a sadistic movie.

34. See the comment on *People v. Samuels* in 81 *Harv. L. Rev.* 1340 (1968).

35. The distinction between prize fights and other boxing matches is nowadays unclear. See Williams, supra note 4. Russell, *Crime* 597 (12th ed. 1964) agrees that the distinction is not easy and depends primarily upon public opinion. See also the comparative analysis of W. T. S. Stallybrass in *The Modern Approach to Criminal Law* 390 at 435 (Radzinowicz & Turner eds. 1945), expressing amazement at the fact that, despite the importance of sport in English life, there is no proper definition of the applicable legal rule. The Abridged Oxford Dictionary defines a prize fight as "a boxing match for money" but the cases indicate that the reference is to contests for money which end only when one of the participants is knocked out. *Reg. v. Young*, 10 Cox C. C. 371 (1866).

Medical Treatment

Consent of the patient is at the core of Anglo-American law on medical treatment. Anglo-American law views medical treatment, *prima facie*, as an assault upon a person which would appear to be a civil wrong and criminal offense but which, because of the patient's consent, is justifiable.[36] As a result of this view the patient under Anglo-American law has, as a matter of principle, the right to refuse medical treatment.[37] In other systems, such as that existing in France, this subject is viewed as a matter of legal policy which considers consent of the patient as a relevant but not exclusive consideration.[38]

36. Compulsory medical treatment can be justified by the utilitarian view only when it is intended to prevent harm to others, such as in cases of inoculation against contagious disease. See *e.g., Sadlock v. Board of Education,* 58 A.2d 218 (1948), in which the State's power to condition entry into school upon proof of vaccination was upheld. But not every intervention will be considered compulsory medical treatment. Introduction of fluoride into drinking water was upheld in *Dowel v. City of Tulsa,* 273 P.2d 859 (1954) because it was not considered medical treatment. As to minors, the court may act as guardian in the place of the parents when the latter deny consent to necessary medical treatment and their behavior is liable to injure the child's welfare. "In a case . . . in which the choice is between abandoning a child to a fate of death and saving his life by an operation which will leave him crippled, refusal of the parents to agree to an operation amounts to a breach of their duty . . . and it is within the authority of the court to give . . . the permission denied by the parents." *Garshy v. State of Israel,* C.A. 372/63, 18 (2) P.D. 449, at 457. See also *Application of President and Directors of Georgetown College,* 331 F.2d 1000 (1964); Note, 113 *U. Pa. L. Rev.* 290, 294 (1964); R. L. Trescher & T. N. O'Neil Jr., "Medical Care for Dependent Children: Manslaughter Liability of the Christian Scientist," 109 U. Pa. L. Rev. 203 (1961). As to the English law on the matter, see D. Foulkes, "Consent to Medical Treatment," [1970] *New Law Journal* 194.

37. For a survey of American law on the subject, see "Compulsory Medical Treatment: The State's Interest Reevaluated," 51 *Minn. L. Rev.* 293. An extreme example of the freedom not to receive medical treatment even when life or death is at issue is the case of *Erickson v. Dilgard,* 252 N. Y. S.2d 705 (1962). As to tort liability for an operation not consented to, see *Yale v. Parmley* [1945] S.C.R. 635 (Can.).

38. See Hughes, supra note 7, at 239 et seq. Hughes, at 236, urges acceptance of the French view according to which the doctrine of consent should be replaced by one of necessity because the principle of necessity includes recognition of consent, whereas emphasis on consent alone ignores necessity. The principle of necessity seems justified only in situations in which operations on children, unconscious or mentally ill persons are at issue, and in these cases, the doctrine of consent is, in any event, not serviceable. However, it would be difficult to apply the doctrine of necessity against the express wishes of an adult and sane person.

The emphasis on the patient's consent creates certain legal problems. If everything depends upon consent there can be no difference between treatment given by a medically qualified person and that given by a layman.[39] The patient who is the master of his consent may give it to whomever he wishes. Secondly, there are situations in which the patient is incapable of actual consent, whether because of unconsciousness or because of mental illness. To such patients constructive consent may be attributed.[40] It may be noted, however, that it is precisely in the ordinary case of a conscious and sane patient (dependent upon his doctor or surgeon) that doubts may arise concerning the quality of his consent.[41] Rules of medical ethics recognize this difficulty and lay down rules which are designed to ensure that the patient's consent is given without pressure or undue influence, particularly in cases of medical experiments[42] or organ transplants.[43]

---

39. English rules which recognize operations by laymen are outdated, and the reasoning behind them—the shortage of physicians in outlying areas—is usually inapplicable today. See Hughes, supra note 7, at 234. However, medical treatment or even simply operations will have to be legally recognized where the lightness of the wound or difficulty in obtaining qualified medical help justify the act. The relevant legal distinction, it is submitted, depends not exclusively on the patient's consent but also on the competence of the person performing the operation as well as on other circumstances relevant in questions of civil or criminal negligence.

40. See *Yackovach v. Yocom*, 237 N.W. 444, 76 A.L.R. 551 (1931); *Kennedy v. Panott*, 90 S.E.2d 754, 56 A.L.R.2d 686 (1956).

41. Consent given without an explanation as to all risks involved is not valid. *Woods v. Brumlogs*, 377 P.2d 520, 524. But as to the nature of the explanation required there is a difference of opinion. See J. Fletcher, "Human Experimentation: Ethics in the Consent Situation," 32 *Law & Contemporary Problems* 620, 629.

42. See Fletcher, supra note 41, at 623 et seq., in which shocking testimony is furnished on procuring consent for medical experiments from the severely ill.

43. Donation of organs from living persons also raises questions of medical ethics, because the physician's responsibility is toward the patient on whom the operations are being performed. See "Legal Problems in Donation of Human Tissues to Medical Service," 21 *Vand. L. Rev.* 352, 368. In Canada the question of donation of organs from a living person becomes complicated because the criminal law of Canada protects the surgeon only when he is acting for the benefit of the patient upon whom the transplant operation is being performed. J. G. Castel, "Some Legal Aspects of Human Organ Transplantation in Canada," 46 *Canadian Bar Rev.* 345, 365. As a matter of legal policy, however, the sole consideration is one of general social welfare and from this viewpoint there can be no doubt of the value of the transplant. For the legal provisions of other systems concerning transplants, see Dukeminier, "Supplying Organs for Transplantation," 68 *Mich. L. Rev.* 811, 849; G. Dworkin, "The Law Relating to Organ Transplantation in England," 33 *Modern L. Rev.* 383 (1970).

Beyond problems of medical ethics there is the question of the law's attitude to the patient's consent. Will such consent to *every* operation by a qualified surgeon be sufficient to protect the surgeon in an action against him? Do operations of sterilization or castration, for example, or operations for sex alteration fall within the category in which the law recognizes consent? Is consent of a sick person—assuming it is genuine and freely given—to donate organs or to undergo medical experimentation valid? In other words, is the patient's consent sufficient in every case of treatment by a qualified medical person or are there some considerations of public policy which limit the scope of consent?

One would have expected these questions to have been dealt with on many occasions because of the frequency of such operations. However, there are only a small number of decisions because in the ordinary situation there is no aggrieved person to institute criminal proceedings against the physician. The matter comes before the courts only where there is some additional defect, relating either to the doctors' professional standard or to the validity of the patient's consent.

One extreme approach was expressed by Lord Denning on operations for sterilization. In a petition for divorce a woman claimed that her husband had, without her consent, undergone such an operation. On the question of her consent to the operation, Lord Denning said:

> even if we assume that the wife did consent at the time of the operation I do not think that her consent then precludes her from complaining of its ill effects in later years when it does in fact injure her health.[44]

On the general subject of sterilization operations he continues:

> When it is done with the man's consent for a just cause, it is quite lawful, as, for instance, when it is done to prevent the transmission of an hereditary disease, but when it is done without just cause or excuse, it is unlawful, even though the man consents to it.

As an example of the latter situation, Lord Denning cites a sterilization operation performed merely to enable a man to have the pleasure of sexual intercourse without the responsibil-

---

44. *Bravery v. Bravery* [1967] 3 All E. R. 59, 67.

ities. Such a reason according to Lord Denning is contrary to the public interest, degrades the man, harms his wife or any woman he may marry and opens the way to licentiousness. Finally, the learned judge mentions that sterilization is distinguishable from the use of contraceptives because the operation is in most cases irreversible and does not permit change of mind after it is performed.[45]

The opinion has been criticized by Hughes:

> Assuming that sterilization might be irreversible, it can still be forcibly argued that it ought to be regarded as a proper and lawful operation when done at the request of an adult patient. If it is considered from the point of view of the patient, then it is of course true that he may later bitterly regret what he has done, but life continually presents us with opportunities for storing up regret. The question is whether protecting him from the possibility of a future unhelpful change of mind outbalances depriving him of liberty of action in this respect and it is submitted that it does not. If the matter is considered from the point of view of the community, then it is doubtful whether present population trends in England necessitate the intervention of the criminal law to compel fertility by threat of sanction. The great majority of people will probably acknowledge that they may at some time want to have a child and will therefore not contemplate such an operation. If, contrary to this expectation, the public knowledge of the legality of a sterilization operation produced a host of candidates for the knife then the state of the law might have to be reviewed. At the moment it is submitted that public policy would be best expressed by acknowledging the legality of the operation and perhaps surrounding it by mild discouragements such as a complicated procedure for the expression of consent and the exclusion of the operation from the facilities of the National Health Service.[46]

It seems to the present author that intervention of the law in this area, though permitted as a matter of principle, must be minimal. It is not the function of the courts or the legislature to involve themselves in an operation that at least *prima facie* is

---

45. Id. at 65. This reason, based on the inability to alter the consequences of consent, is controversial, for, as Lord Denning himself points out, in certain cases it is possible, apparently, to reinstate male potency. This is not the case in actual castrations. Cf. Meyers, *Human Body and the Law* 1, 18 (Edinburgh, 1970).

46. Hughes, supra note 7, at 239.

performed for the benefit of the patient, so long as it is performed by qualified medical personnel: the fact that the operation or other medical treatment is carried out by professionals is
strong evidence that it was done for the patient's benefit. To
distinguish nowadays between operations designed to improve the
physiological condition of a patient and those which deal with
his emotional well-being seems highly improper. Plastic surgery
belongs in many cases to the latter category and it would be
strange if surgeons performing such operations were not legally
protected so long as they maintained a proper degree of professional skill. Sex change operations—which in the past were rare
and exceptional and were allowed only in a few countries—have
become acceptable and the emotional need which drives people
to seek them is certainly no less significant than physiological
needs.[47]

It is therefore submitted that the law's right to intervene in
such cases must be limited to the extreme cases mentioned in
Lord Denning's opinion,[48] such as severing a limb to evade military service and other such esoteric cases. The law's function is
mainly to determine whether consent was in fact given with
aforethought and whether the operation will be injurious to persons dependent upon the patient.

47. The French approach does not view consent as determinative either with
respect to an operation with consent or one without it. Under this approach it must
be proved that a general interest of society is served by the operation. Thus, for
example, sterilization is prohibited in France, apparently because of the traditional
desire to encourage a higher birth rate. Some doubt exists as to plastic surgery as
well. See Hughes, supra note 7, at 242-243. With regard to voluntary sterilization,
see G. Williams, *The Sanctity of Life and the Criminal Law* 74 (1957) ; Barthole-
mew, "Legal Implications of Voluntary Sterilization Operations," 2 *Melbourne L.
Rev.* 77 (1959) . As to sex change operations, the law is likely to be called upon
to act more frequently than usual because of requests for change of registrations.
Nevertheless it seems that legislatures in many countries prefer not to deal with
this subject. See Meyers, supra note 45, at 52. Courts, too, have rarely dealt with
the problem. For such a case, see *Anonymous v. Weiner*, 270 N.Y.S.2d 319 (1966) .
Certain American states do recognize sex alteration for the purpose of registration.
Illinois Statute 73-17 provides that "For a person born in the State, the State
Registrar of Vital Records shall establish a new certificate of birth when he receives . . . an affidavit by a physician that he has performed an operation on a
person, and that by reason of the operation the sex designation on such person's
birth record should be changed. . . ."
48. Supra note 44.

CONCLUSION

To claim that the victim's consent is operative only where so-cially acceptable is merely to replace one ambiguity by another. The law's attitude must essentially be one of compromise: it can-not disregard the wishes of the person for whose benefit the criminal law has intervened, nor can it regard such wishes as the sole and exclusive consideration. In extreme cases the law may disregard the victim's express wish and punish the offender. We submit that such extreme cases arise where the enormity of physi-cal harm done outweighs considerations of personal autonomy and free will or where the physical harm was done in the course of an act wholly repugnant to current views.

CHAPTER 12

CIVIL LAW AS A CRIMINAL SANCTION
The Use of the Jury in the Coming of the American Revolution*

JOHN P. REID

Professor of Law, New York University

A MONG THE MANY CONTRIBUTIONS made to comparative criminal law by Jerome Hall have been his historical studies—
scholarly reminders that when we seek to test our legal institutions by the comparative method we are not limited to searches
in foreign climes.[1] It is sometimes claimed, though without much
accuracy, that comparative law is vertical legal history while legal
history is comparative law from a horizontal perspective. We
need not press the argument to accept the point that Jerome Hall
has made for us: legal history may tell us more about comparative criminal law than traditional-minded comparativists might
think.

Studies arising out of the bicentennial celebration of the
American Revolution should teach us much about our early law
but it may be doubted if any will reveal a more interesting cross
between traditional legal categories than that which occurred
during the stamp-act crisis—the Whigs of Massachusetts Bay employed the civil law of tort damages to impose sanctions or crimi-
nal-type punishments upon the officials of the imperial customs
service. Their legal strategy may prove to have been unique yet
it holds a story that is worth retelling. It is well to be reminded
that traditional categories are occasionally expanded and that to-

---

* In the preparation of this paper thanks are extended to William E. Nelson
for an afternoon spent on Massachusetts writs and Pennsylvania battlefields.

1. J. Hall, *Theft, Law and Society* 3-36 (1935).

day's definitions should confine scholars less than they confine courts.

The common law as applied in Boston and Massachusetts Bay may not have been typical of all British North America, but it was that common law—civil as well as criminal—that gave the authorities of the Crown their greatest trouble for it was the common law of the most troublesome of the Whigs. The British honored Boston's leadership, in a backhanded way, by calling all American rebels "Bostonians." In 1775, Guy Johnson spoke the sentiment of many a Tory when, using the symbolism of Indian oratory he invited the Six Nations of the Iroquois League "to feast on a Bostonian and drink his Blood."[2] As an historian of the British army in eighteenth-century America has recently written:

> It would be difficult to overstate the importance of Boston in the few years before the clash at Lexington. Opposition to British policy and legislation was widespread, but resistance—the readiness to push opposition to any necessary length—centered in the capital of Massachusetts. Elsewhere even the hardiest Whigs refused until late 1774 to contemplate rebellion as a deliberate act that might soon present itself as the lesser evil among several alternatives, but in Boston there were many who saw the likelihood of something more than accidental violence, and they began to prepare for it, psychologically as well as physically.[3]

One of the ways they began to prepare for it was to bend the law and mold the courts to serve their cause.

Whatever might eventually go wrong for the British in Massachusetts, they could not blame the organization or the quality of the courts. Like the Massachusetts bar,[4] the Massachusetts judiciary during the 1760s and 1770s was sophisticated and professionally competent.[5] While there were more laymen than lawyers on all levels of the system—from the Superior Court of Judica-

2. Barbara Graymont, *The Iroquois in the American Revolution* 68 (1972).

3. John Shy, *Toward Lexington: The Role of the British Army in the Coming of the American Revolution* 398 (1965).

4. 1 *Legal Papers of John Adams* lxxvii-lxxviii (L. Kinvin Wroth & Hiller B. Zobel, editors, 1965).

5. Hiller B. Zobel, "Law Under Pressure: Boston 1769-1771," in *Law and Authority in Colonial America* 187-88 (George Athan Billias, editor, 1965).

ture[6] at the top to the justices of the peace[7] on the local level—no one was heard to complain of justice, at least not in cases that lacked political overtones. Perhaps that fact is one explanation why the issue of judicial tenure was not as troublesome in Massachusetts as in some of the other colonies to the south, although it is not the only explanation. More significant was that while Massachusetts judges as well as those elsewhere in North America, were appointed at the King's pleasure rather than for good behavior, in practice the Crown could not remove them at will. The governor of the province might nominate the members of the judiciary but they had to be confirmed by the popularly-oriented council.[8] The governor could not remove any magistrate, not even for neglect of duty, without the consent of the council.[9] It was this constitutional fact-of-life more than anything else which would shape the role of the judiciary of Massachusetts Bay during the two decades before the Declaration of Independence. While the judges of the Superior Court might be Tory, the justices of the peace would, in the main, be Whigs and there was nothing the governor or the colonial secretary back in London could do to alter the situation.[10]

Another reason why the Massachusetts judiciary was less controversial than in some other colonies—at least until 1773 when the Crown sought to bypass the General Court and pay directly

6. For the superior court see John D. Cushing, "The Judiciary and Public Opinion in Revolutionary Massachusetts," in *Law and Authority* . . . , supra note 5, at 168.

7. For the justices see 1 *Legal Papers* . . . , supra note 4, at 289.

8. Thomas Hutchinson cited this fact to counter Whig propaganda: "The Commissions of the Judges of this Court are, it is true, during Pleasure; . . . but when we consider by whom our Judicatories are appointed, we shall find that we approach very near the Privilege enjoyed by our Brethren, in England: At least, we are in a Middle between them, and some of our Brethren in America, whose Judicatories are erected at Home, their Judges appointed from thence, and are removable at Pleasure." Therefore, Hutchinson contended: "This, I think, amounts to near the Privilege of y People in England:—*There*, the judges hold *quamdiu*, &c;* and *here*, they are displaced by the Governour, *with the Consent of Council* . . . this People are as secure, and as firmly established in their *Liberties*, as they are in Great Britain. I know of no Difference." Chief Justice Thomas Hutchinson's Charge to the Grand Jury, *Quincy Reports* 302-03 (1768) .

9. Hiller B. Zobel, *The Boston Massacre* 177 (1970) .

10. That is, until the intolerable acts when it would be too late.

the judges' salaries—was that the province did not receive many of the English, Scottish, or Irish placemen sent over to staff American courts.[11] The judges, the attorney general, the advocate general and most other law officers in Massachusetts were native sons. The Massachusetts judiciary, however, did suffer from two of the other defects of British rule that helped to bring about American independence: plural officeholding as symbolized by the career of Thomas Hutchinson[12] and the current British tradition that a government post was a sinecure owned by the occupant to be held for personal profit not public service. The last abuse was not too great in regard to Massachusetts' own legal system for salaries were low. There was not enough money available to allow a judge to hire a deputy to do the work while he stayed at home enjoying part of the income. All of the Massachusetts common-law judgeships and legal offices were filled by the men appointed to them. The imperial positions independent of the Massachusetts charter were sometimes the subject of private bargains, a situation which might possibly weaken their efficiency and prestige. Should that happen the damage could have consequences in Massachusetts whenever the court involved was one created by the home government either to correct or to supplement some shortcoming in the Massachusetts judicial system.

A case in point would be the admiralty court located in Halifax, Nova Scotia. It had been created to avoid hostile juries in the old colonies and located in Halifax, a garrison and naval town, to be free of local political pressure. The judgeship was "one of the fattest political jobs open to the legal fraternity in America." It paid a permanent salary of £600 a year in return for duties that did not interfere with the incumbent's private law practice.[13] In 1769 the appointment went to Jonathan Sewall, who at that time was both attorney general of Massachusetts

---

11. For example, South Carolina. See Robert M. Calhoon & Robert M. Weir, "The Scandalous History of Sir Egerton Leigh," 26 *Will. & Mary Q.* 47 (1969).

12. Thomas Hutchinson, while he was chief justice of the superior court was also lieutenant governor, a member of the council, and held other minor offices as well. See generally, Ellen E. Brennan, *Plural Office-Holding in Massachusetts 1760-1780* (1945).

13. Oliver M. Dickerson, "Opinion of Attorney General Jonathan Sewall of Massachusetts in the Case of the *Lydia*," 4 *Will. & Mary Q.* 499, 500 (1947).

and advocate general of the vice-admiralty court sitting at Boston. Sewall surrendered the advocate generalship but stayed on as attorney general as well he might. He did not have to go to Halifax, as he could farm out the office, conducting his judicial business through a deputy while retaining as much of the salary as he could bargain for with that deputy.[14] In fact if not in legal theory, the judgeship belonged to him and he was free to take out of it whatever profits he could, consistent with parliamentary statutes. The situation is best illustrated by a letter which Sewall received from Thomas Hutchinson during 1771. Sir Francis Bernard, the former governor of Massachusetts, had written from London informing Hutchinson that the British government, hoping to make the attorney general independent of the General Court, had decided to bestow a permanent salary of £150 on that office. Bernard suggested the result might have to be some complicated office juggling to satisfy Sewall.

> In the first place Mr. Sewall can't hold the Attorney General's place and the place of Judge of the Admiralty also—It was proposed to give Mr. Sewall £300—which I said would satisfy him for quitting his Judge's Place, but that was not agreeable to the nature of the Establishment and it was not tho't [proper?] to make an addition to it in the way of a pension. This was the plan first proposed but it would not go down at the Treasury. Mr. [John] Robinson the Commissioner [of the American customs] is desirous of the place at Halifax. Lt. Gov. [William] Franklin is also very desirous of it. As they both spoke to me on the Subject I have brought them together that they should not act in opposition to each other. Mr. Robinson is willing to exchange with Mr. Sewall, place for place, and says he can prevail at the Treasury to have it allowed. Mr. Franklin is willing upon his being appointed to engage to pay Mr. Sewall 200£ a year in addition to his Salary as Attorney General and to get the stipulation approved of by [First Lord of the Admiralty] Lord Sandwich. . . . Lord Hillsborough [Secretary of State for America] has no objection to either [plan], those Offices not being in his department. It will remain with Mr. Sewall to signify whether each of those Offers or either and which of them will be agreeable to him.[15]

---

14. See Mary Beth Norton, "A Recently Discovered Thomas Hutchinson Letter," 82 *Proc. Mass. Hist. Soc'y* 105-06 (1970). Sewall did go to Halifax in 1769 when pressures in Boston made his absence expedient. Hiller B. Zoebel, *supra* note 9, at 131.

15. Letter From Governor Thomas Hutchinson to Attorney General Jonathan Sewall, 16 September 1771, reprinted in Mary Beth Norton, *supra* note 14, at 108.

Thus Sewall, on being offered a permanent salary as attorney general is being told that he should surrender his judgeship. To persuade him to do so, candidates for the Halifax post have been found who will sweeten the prospect by making up part of his loss. John Robinson, who had fled the Boston mob and would prefer to live in the safer town of Halifax, offers to switch jobs. Sewall can have his Boston-based position as a commissioner of the customs paying £500 a year[16] if Robinson gets the judgeship. Governor Franklin was experiencing financial difficulties at the time[17] and so anxious to find new income that he would pay Sewall one third of the salary he expects to receive if Sewall resigns.

Neither proposal bore fruit for Sewall retained both offices. He did not relinquish the attorney generalship until 1775 when as a Tory he could no longer function in it. He remained on as judge of the admiralty for over twenty years, never living in Nova Scotia, but collecting the salary—perhaps as a pension or reward for his loyalty to the Crown.[18]

Surely this private-privilege attitude toward public office affected performances and diminished usefulness. First-rate lawyers might be appointed but when they farmed out their duties they must have had to settle on lesser figures who would be satisfied with the diminished salary. At the very least the sense of public obligation, traditional in the English judicial system, was lacking. The consequences may have been minimal with some other farmed-out law offices which were understood to be sinecures[19] but an active admiralty judge at Halifax might have made a contribution toward enforcement of the acts of trade,[20]

---

16. Joseph R. Frese, "Some Observations on the American Board of Customs Commissioners," 81 *Proc. Mass. Hist. Soc'y* 3, 4 n. 5 (1969).

17. See Catherine Fennelly, "William Franklin of New Jersey," 6 *Will. & Mary Q.* 371-73 (1949).

18. Mary Beth Norton, supra note 14, at 106.

19. For example, the provost marshalship of South Carolina. See Richard Maxwell Brown, *The South Carolina Regulators* 68-73 (1963).

20. "The Acts were a coherent body of legislation, enacted between 1660 and the Revolution, which regulated the flow of colonial trade, laid duties on some aspects of it, and established a system of enforcement. The basic regulatory provisions were: that vessels engaged in the plantation trade had to be English or colonial

the navigation acts,[21] and the customs laws—the most important and frustrating challenge faced by British authority in North America after 1763. Considering all the problems encountered by those who had the responsibility for making these laws work, it surely did not help to have the admiralty judge in Halifax devoting his time to a different office at Boston.

The problems of enforcement were so vast it may be doubted whether an active and energetic Judge Sewall would have made a difference. One difficulty was the laws themselves. They were so detailed that a reading could raise more questions than answers, at least for minor officials caught between hostile American merchants and unsympathetic superiors in London. For example, consider the customs laws:

> A strict observance of the laws was almost impossible. Despite instructions and rate books, few men were qualified to understand all the ramifications of the acts. Who was to judge the subtle flavors of the wines imported, or to know accurately the hundreds of different classes of cloths and other goods brought in? The written guides given to local officials were veritable miracles of elaboration, but special exceptions and provisions changed from day to day and the legal niceties involved were exasperating and bewildering. . . .
>
> The laws were not only involved and forever changing but the statutes if literally interpreted occasionally operated to defeat their original purpose. Under the regulations made in 5 George II, c. 22 the exportation of hats from one colony to another was forbidden under severe penalty. [John] Swift [collector at Philadelphia] was of the opinion that he would "as soon eat fire as sign a cocket for Hatts," yet what was he to do when a consignment came directly from Manchester to Philadelphia for merchants in New Jersey or Delaware? A shipment of hats came from Bermuda with a certificate from the collector and comptroller there that they were legally imported. Should the shipment be seized? Both Swift and the commissioners were of the opinion that such action would be contrary to the purpose of the act which was designed to promote the English hat industry. Further, were goods sub-

---

built, owned, or manned; that certain enumerated goods produced in the colonies could be shipped only to England or to another colony; and that most European goods could be shipped to the colonies only from English ports," 2 *Legal Papers* . . . supra note 4, at 98.

21. See generally Oliver M. Dickerson, *The Navigation Acts and the American Revolution* (1951).

ject to duty if they had been shipped before the imposition of a duty but not landed until after it was in effect? . . . When the Crown attorney general and the Board of Customs disagreed on all these points, what was the collector to do? To enforce the law according to its letter left him open to civil action by outraged merchants; non-enforcement might lead to dismissal by the Board of Trade.[22]

Even if the customs laws had been clear and uncomplicated the task of a revenue agent in North America would not have been easy. The first lesson any customs official learned when arriving in Massachusetts was that the common-law courts were more against him than for him. In fact, if it had not been for the common-law courts, their procedures and their powers, the customs laws might have been enforced. One point is certain: they were of little help. The attorney general could not be counted on to prosecute violators. He had no funds, no staff and above all no incentive to investigate breaches of the imperial trade laws. If he prosecuted, he had to take time from his private practice—his chief livelihood—and if he won he received little for his effort. The customs officials, the governor and the Crown divided all forfeitures three ways, leaving nothing for the attorney general. According to the ethics of eighteenth-century public service he had every reason to let them hire their own lawyers.[23]

Another stumbling block was the grand jury. To bring violations of the customs statutes before a common-law court, an indictment had to be obtained and that was an almost impossible task. To avoid the grand jury, the commissioners of the customs in 1768 tried to persuade the Massachusetts Attorney General to proceed by information. They selected what they must have thought was a perfect test case. John Hancock had ejected from the steerage of his brigantine, *Lydia,* a tidesman who had been assigned to supervise the discharge of his cargo. The man could

---

22. Alfred S. Martin, "The King's Customs: Philadelphia, 1763-1774," 5 *Will & Mary Q.* 201, 203-04 (1948).

23. Hiller B. Zobel, supra note 9, at 105-106. Lawyers were not the only ones. In 1763, to improve enforcement of the trade laws, Parliament provided that captains of men-of-war making a seizure received a share of the proceeds. The consequence, Governer Bernard pointed out, was that collectors and governors ceased calling on the navy for aid. Benjamin Woods Labaree, *The Boston Tea Party* 54 (paperback edition, 1968).

inspect on topside, Hancock insisted, but not below deck.[24] The controlling statute gave customs officers a right "freely to go and remain on Board until the Vessel is discharged of her Lading." Sewall refused to file an information, doubting its propriety in such a case despite the unavailability of an indictment. He ruled the words "on Board" in the statute meant "on the Deck" only. Customs officials who went into "the hold" without a warrant were acting unlawfully.[25] It was a common lawyer's opinion, justified by the common-law rules of criminal construction. It may be doubted if an admiralty court following civil law would have been so narrow.[26] The commissioners of the customs asked London to overrule Sewall's opinion and order him to proceed by way of information. When their request was rejected the last hope was gone that American common-law courts could be used to enforce the revenue and trade acts.

For all practical purposes the only tribunal available to the customs officers was the unpopular vice-admiralty court—unpopular because it sat without a jury and followed the rules of civil rather than common law. The very fact it had no jury and its judges were appointed and paid by the Crown should have made it an effective and sympathetic forum for law enforcement. Yet it never lived up to official expectations. One problem was that after the Townshend Acts were passed, Colonial lawyers tended to boycott the vice-admiralty courts and customs officials could not always find a competent attorney to prosecute their cases. In some colonies there was no advocate general and in others only young, inexperienced lawyers took the job.[27] Massachusetts was an exception for Jonathan Sewall and later Robert Auchmuty were capable lawyers; yet even with them at hand the vice-ad-

24. 2 *Legal Papers* . . . supra note 4, at 174, and Hiller B. Zobel, supra note 9, at 72.

25. Oliver M. Dickerson, supra note 13, at 503-04.

26. The Boston vice-admiralty court, for example, ruled that "landing" is not essential to constitute importation. Bringing prohibited goods into port, showing a fraudulent intent, though without landing or breaking bulk, is sufficient to work a forfeiture of ship and cargo. Bishop v. Brig Freemason, *Quincy Reports* 387 (1763).

27. Carl Ubbelohde, *The Vice-Admirality Courts and the American Revolution* 159-61 (1960).

miralty court did not function as its planners had hoped. It might supplement the common-law jurisdiction and it might be free of the common-law jury but it was not free of the common law itself.

The vice-admiralty courts had been designed to do a special job. When the colonial common-law and admiralty courts proved faulty instruments for enforcing the imperial revenue and regulatory statutes, London had created these courts. It had modelled them on the High Court of Admiralty and on its jurisdiction. As a result, they inherited admiralty's relationship to common law and after the Revolution of 1688 that relationship was an inferior one. Common-law prerogative writs held the upper hand in England and in Massachusetts the common-law courts stood in the same constitutional position as those in the mother country. For example, when an advocate general, seeking to collect revenue on smuggled molasses, had potential witnesses jailed by the vice-admiralty to force their testimony, the Superior Court of Judicature intervened with writs of habeas corpus.[28]

More menacing to the customs service was the King's Bench power to stay vice-admiralty proceedings by writ of prohibition. Even the Tory judges of Massachusetts Bay were willing to issue such writs when they felt the vice-admiralty court overstepped its prerogatives and was treading on common-law jurisdiction.[29] This was a constitutional tradition made sacred to English lawyers by the Revolution of 1688 and a Tory was as ready as anyone else to uphold the common law's supremacy. However, there can be differences in the use of the writ of prohibition: differences in kind as well as in degree. In the province of Massachusetts where the high-court judges were Tories, the writ of prohibition was not employed indiscriminately to harass the vice-admiralty jurisdiction. The Whigs needed control of the superior court for it to have been a Whig weapon. Only in Rhode Island, thanks to its charter and politics, did the Whigs have that advantage. Legitimate proceedings in which the vice-admiralty court had cog-

---

28. Letter from William Bollan to the Duke of Newcastle, 12 April 1766, in 59 *Proc. Mass. Hist. Soc'y* 415, 418 (1926).

29. Scollay v. Dunn, *Quincy Reports* 74 (1763); 2 *Legal Papers* . . . , supra note 4, at 68.

nizance could be and sometimes were stayed by partisan judges in Rhode Island.[30] It was court against court; one Colonial and common law, the other imperial and civil law. Such a rivalry would strike today's lawyer as odd or chaotic yet an educated eighteenth-century layman would have seen it as both historically logical and constitutionally necessary. Any superior-court judge who stayed proceedings valid under parliament's revenue statutes could appeal to English constitutional traditions and few would question his principles. The appeal might be a sham, the application of principles might be partisan, but the argument was nonetheless effective as it had the ring of constitutional familiarity. A Whig judge in Rhode Island who chose to side with a merchant against the enforcement of the trade and customs acts could employ law to evade law and as a result, the collectors of import duties seeking to seize contraband or to libel carriers of illegal goods, could not always depend on the court that had been especially designed to give them a forum and validate their actions.

In colonies other than Rhode Island where the Tories controlled the upper bench, the Whigs had other, less direct judicial weapons with which to hamper the effectiveness of revenue officials and the vice-admiralty courts. They might not be able to play court against court but they were able to call upon two related common-law institutions: the grand jury and the traverse jury, both of which the Whigs could usually dominate in Massachusetts.

The grand jury had obvious uses although a Tory attorney general could nullify most of them by simply not prosecuting a Whig-inspired indictment. Perhaps the most unique instance when it played a role was the suit over John Hancock's ship, *Liberty*. The seizure of the *Liberty* by the navy for violation of the revenue laws had precipitated one of Boston's most memorable riots (i.e. it was the cause of British troops being sent to Massachusetts). Although the ship was successfully condemned in an *in rem* proceeding conducted at vice-admiralty,[31] the commissioners of the customs had not been satisfied. Perhaps they were still

30. Carl Ubbelohde, *supra* note 27, at 168-70.
31. 2 *Legal Papers . . .*, *supra* note 4, at 174-76 & 185-86.

annoyed at Hancock for defeating them in the *Lydia* action or the failure of the local government to prosecute the rioters who had put them in fear of their lives. In any event, if they decided to risk a legal test of strength, John Hancock was a logical target. He had led the opposition to the commissioners ever since they landed at Boston, "both with his political attacks and with the example of his own violation [of the law]. If the law could be applied strictly to him others would fall into line."[32]

The procedure which they selected was harsh and surely to a Whig seemed to be high Toryism at its most arbitrary extreme. They brought an *in personam* proceeding against Hancock, based on evidence supplied by one of their own tidesmen. Their authority was the American Act of 1764 which permitted informations to be filed on the criminal side of vice-admiralty against persons "assisting or otherwise concerned" in landing goods without the payment of duties. This time there was no difficulty persuading Jonathan Sewall to draft the information. Now he was acting in his capacity as advocate general in admiralty rather than as attorney general and by naming himself the "informer" he became entitled to one third of the judgment. The other two thirds went to the Crown and to the governor of Massachusetts Bay.[33]

From a Whig point of view the proceeding against Hancock was outrageous and it soon became the most celebrated trial in America. Not only had Hancock already lost the *Liberty* in the earlier vice-admiralty case but now he was being prosecuted without an indictment before a court which sat without a jury. Tories might justify it on the grounds that no jury could be found to convict violators of the acts of trade[34] but to Whigs constitutional liberty was giving way to arbitrary government. Not only did Sewall and the unpopular governor, Francis Bernard, stand to benefit personally as prosecutors but it was easy for the Whig press to argue that they were determined to ruin Hancock while enriching themselves. They had asked for the legal maximum penalty, an enormous total of £54,000, and the

32. Ibid, at 186.
33. For the information see, Appendix I, *Quincy Reports* 457-58 (1865).
34. 2 *Legal Papers* . . . , supra note 4, at 188.

court set bail at £3,000.[35] It is small wonder that the defense attorney, John Adams, tried to turn the trial into a stage for constitutional propaganda by asserting that the customs duty Hancock sought to evade was void because it was authorized by a statute which he had consented to neither by his own vote nor by the vote of his representative.[36]

Much as the Hancock prosecution contributed to the development of John Adams' constitutional thought, it is just as noteworthy for its outcome. The vice-admiralty court, borrowing its procedure from the English High Court of Admiralty, employed the whole range of civil law: interrogatories, irregular sessions, secret examination of witnesses and direct participation of the judge.[37] Yet important as this forum was to Great Britain, the civil-law procedure was not as clearly established as we might expect. John Adams seems to have tried to exploit this fact when he sought to impeach the testimony of Joseph Maysel, a key witness for the Crown. By questioning another witness he attempted

---

35. Carl Ubbelohde, supra note 27, at 119-26.

36. Appendix I, *Quincy Reports* 459-61 (1865). Adams also contended that penalties recovered in Admirality deprived his client of the right to trial by jury. This was a defect all the more grievous as comparable offenses in England were tried by jury in the Exchequer. It should be noted that Adams's argument did not question the constitutionality of the statute, but (like the argument of James Otis against the writs of assistance) contended that such a statute must be construed in the narrowest possible manner, and, if so construed, would not apply to Hancock. When the argument was circulated, however, the constitutional argument could not be missed. It was circulated not in its original form, but in the instructions of the Boston town meeting to its representatives. May 1769, on the right to trial by jury. These instructions, drafted by Adams, came almost verbatim from his argument in Hancock's case. Ibid. See also, 2 *Legal Papers* . . . , supra note 4, at 191-92.

37. Ibid, at 188. Indeed, the dislike of the civil law, shared by most American Whig lawyers, is reflected in Adams' objection to what he called "a painfull Drudgery. There were few days through the whole Winter, when I was not summoned to attend the Court of Admiralty. It seemed as if the Officers of the Crown were determined to examine the whole Town as Witnesses. Almost every day a fresh Witness was to be examined upon Interrogatories. They interrogated many of his [*Hancock's*] near Relations and most intimate Friends and threatened to summons his amiable and venerable Aunt, . . . I was thoroughly weary and disgusted with the Court, the Officers of the Crown, the Cause, and even with the tyrannical Bell that dongled me out of my House every Morning." Ibid, at 182.

to show that Maysel was a fugitive from justice, guilty of a "heinous crime." If that fact were established as true, under Massachusetts common law Maysel would be incompetent to testify.[38]

> The Crown opposed the line of questioning, pointing to the common-law rules that only a witness' general character for truth was admissible as oral testimony, and that a written record of conviction was necessary to establish a specific crime. Adams argued that the civil law, which he said would permit his evidence, should be followed, since this was a Court of Admiralty.

The admiralty judge ruled against Adams, holding that not only was the evidence inadmissible by civil law but that common law controlled as this was a statutory proceeding.[39] Maysel therefore could not be impeached unless Adams produced a written record of his conviction, something Adams may not have been able to do. Maysel was competent to testify and conceivably his evidence might have been enough to justify Hancock's conviction. It was at this point that the Whigs displayed their resourcefulness and the admiralty procedure with its long delays came to their aid. Before Maysel's evidence could be taken down, the Suffolk county grand jury indicted him for perjury and he fled the province.[40] The case against Hancock was then dropped. It is not certain just why Sewall felt he could not proceed but a good reason seems to be the failure of evidence, especially the departure of Maysel.[41] If so, the Whigs had engineered a splendid little coup, demonstrating that when necessary they had one technique that could be used to frustrate Tory judicial proceedings.

Of more lasting significance than the outcome of the trial was its propaganda value to the Whigs. The commissioners of the customs not only failed to convict Hancock but they gave their opponents a perfect case for attacking both them and the vice-

38. See Rex v. Pourkfdorff, *Quincy Reports* 104 (1764). For a discussion see William E. Nelson, *The Americanization of the Common Law During the Revolutionary Era: A Study of Legal Change in Massachusetts, 1760-1830* 59 (unpublished doctoral dissertation, Harvard University, 1971).

39. 2 *Legal Papers* . . . , supra note 4, at 183. For the interlocutory decree see, Appendix I, *Quincy Reports* 461-62 (1865).

40. 2 *Legal Papers* . . . , supra note 4, at 183-84.

41. Ibid, at 184.

admiralty jurisdiction. Newspaper accounts may have been biased but so was their audience and they hit their mark. Before long the commissioners of the customs had become obnoxious in the eyes of many Americans. "Their effectiveness was permanently damaged and they served until the Revolution in an atmosphere of constant hostility." Even more telling was the effect on the vice-admiralty court. No more actions of this sort would be brought in the future and even its civil business declined. Previous to the Hancock prosecution, many litigants (e.g. seamen suing for wages) had preferred the vice-admiralty to the common law for both convenience and speed. Now lawyers sought to avoid it. "The jurisdiction was more and more invoked only in enforcement of the Acts of Trade, and ordinary civil maritime cases were tried in the common-law courts."[42]

The criminal grand jury was a Whig defensive weapon useful in several ways (as Hancock's case showed) for preventing prosecutions but otherwise of limited utility. More potent by far and of greater antiquity in the battle against British customs laws was the civil traverse jury. "Hampering activities of the customs officials by suits at common law," the historian of vice-admiralty has written, "had long been a defensive weapon at the disposal of aggrieved merchants."[43] In the hands of the Whigs it became an offensive weapon. Common-law judgments were used not only to harass but to drive customs agents out of both Charles Town, South Carolina and Albany, New York.[44] Even naval officers who seized vessels for violating the trade or navigation statutes, faced the prospect of being sued for large sums and having both their assets and their careers tied up for years in litigation. "Captain John Brown, the commander of His Majesty's Ship *Hawke*, was under indictment in a New York common-law court for three years before he was convicted and presented with a damage judgment of more than £4,000 for a seizure he had made. . . . At least part of the time he was not allowed to leave the province, and he had to turn the command of his vessel over to his lieutenant."[45]

---

42. Ibid.
43. Carl Ubbelohde, supra note 27, at 166.
44. Ibid, at 166-67.
45. Ibid, at 165-66.

These legal games sometimes developed into an art. The naval captains had special cause for concern in the Delaware River, where shippers had devised a scheme which threatened to defeat the Royal Navy. George Talbot, commanding the man-of-war *Lively*, explained the procedure: When we Board . . . [the merchant vessels], the Master with every one on board, take to their boat and go away then the Vessel is to be left by us, and an Action is brought on for Damages." If the crew of the man-of-war stopped the exodus, "a Writ . . . [was] issued for confining them [the merchantmen] on board their own Vessel." In either case a suit at common law took place which automatically spelled conviction of the captains. Talbot claimed that "When an Action is laid, Justice is out of the question. We are sure it will be against us, no one will be our Bail, not a Lawyer in the Province that has a Salary from the Crown, and any we employ will seem to Act for us, but Secretly Act against us."[46]

Failure of bail was depressing enough. The hostility of the bar was even more menacing. Worst of all was the certainty of "conviction." It might be thought that Talbot was exaggerating a bit, giving a typical layman's view of the law: a trap in which the innocent are ensnared; a maze through which only the unjust can find their way. But what he says was not an exaggeration. Eighteenth-century courts were not twentieth-century courts because eighteenth-century juries were not twentieth-century juries. The court could instruct them on the law but there was no one to instruct them that they had to listen. It was not the stubborn refusal of Whig jurors to follow the law laid down by Tory judges but the law itself that made the jury a potential weapon for the Whigs or for any eighteenth-century political majority.

There are three simple and related points that have sometimes been misunderstood: (1) a political majority could control Massachusetts juries; (2) juries were the judges of the law as well as of fact; and (3) courts had little power to control and no power to overrule jury verdicts.

The Whigs could control the civil traverse juries because they controlled the town meetings. As one contemporary Bostonian wrote to the English radical John Wilkes, "By a Law of this Province, the Jurors are return'd by the Selectmen, after the

46. Ibid, at 167-68.

choice has been made by the Town."⁴⁷ True, the Whigs would
have to control every town meeting in the country, not an easy
task as Boston's dislike of customs officials was not shared with
the same intensity by the inland farm communities of Suffolk
County. Yet there was enough unity of purpose for William Mo-
lineux to boast that the Whigs "would always be sure of Eleven
jury men in Twelve."⁴⁸ While one Tory or neutral might give a
customs defendant some hope of getting a hung jury, the fact
was unlikely to deter his opponents.⁴⁹ As the Richardson-murder
conviction was to demonstrate, eleven men were sometimes all
that the Whigs needed.

Secondly, control of the jury meant everything in Massachusetts at that time. Perhaps straining contemporary English law to
suit their own predilections, lawyers interpreted *Bushell's Case* as
holding "that the jury should always decide the law as well as the
fact."⁵⁰ John Adams spoke for most, including many Tories
when he wrote:

---

47. 3 *Legal Papers* . . . , supra note 4, at 17.
48. Hiller B. Zobel, supra note 9, at 169.
49. After 1765, a tory juror would probably have to come from a town outside
Boston. The chances of getting one probably diminished as time went on, as suggested by Chief Justice Hutchinson's charge to the jury at the March, 1769, term of
the Suffolk Superior Court. He confessed to *"some Reason* to fear" that town meetings were sending jurors perfectly willing to convict certain types of criminals,
yet willing to "connive at and pass over in Silence and entirely smother other
Crimes of an alarming Nature." He had to be referring to riots and political
crimes, and said that some Suffolk county towns had a history of returning jurors
interested in prospective litigation. Chief Justice Hutchinson's Charge to the
Grand Jury, *Quincy Reports* 306, 312-13 (1769) . Happily for a customs-official defendant, if a tory was returned, the whig-plaintiff could not remove him by challenge as no challenges were allowed in civil cases. While we cannot guess what the
chances were that a tory could be on a Suffolk jury, it must be stressed that even
the certainty of one or more militant-tory jurors would not have deterred a
political plaintiff from using the courts to harass crown officials. Although he
might know he would not win damages, a hung jury would serve his political objective: of striking back at the customs official; putting him to personal expense
in both money and time; warning him to be more cautious in the future; and
gaining the esteem of the Boston mob by publicly demonstrating the plaintiff's
whiggery.
50. 1 *Legal Papers* . . . , supra note 4, at 214. For *Bushell's Case* see 124 *Eng. Rep.*
1006 (C.P. 1670) .

Everything that is said by the Court to the jury, is uniformly styled in our books a direction. So the Court give a charge to the grand jury to present a particular offence, &c. But the question is whether the jury are bound, in point of conscience or of law, to observe that direction and find according to it? Are they subject to any penalty, or fine or imprisonment if they find contrary to that direction? No man will say that they are.

And again:

Therefore the jury have a power of deciding an issue upon a general verdict. And if they have, is it not an absurdity to suppose that the law would oblige them to find a verdict according to the direction of the Court, against their own opinion, judgment and conscience? It has already been admitted to be most advisable for the jury to find a special verdict, where they are in doubt of the law. But this is not often the case; a thousand cases occur in which the jury would have no doubt of the law, to one in which they should be at a loss. The general rules of law and common regulations of society, under which ordinary transactions arrange themselves, are well enough known to ordinary jurors. The great principles of the Constitution are intimately known; they are sensibly felt by every Briton; it is scarcely extravagant to say they are drawn in and imbibed with the nurse's milk and first air.[51]

---

51. It is interesting to consider that a few years earlier Adams had written that law required training and professional study: "A man whose Youth and Spirits and Strength, have been spent in Husbandry, Merchandize, Politicks, nay in Science or Literature will never master so immense and involved a science." Hiller B. Zobel, supra note 9, at 9. Thomas Hutchinson, who felt juries should follow the instructions of judges, wrote on the other hand: "I never presumed to call myself a Lawyer. The most I could pretend to was when I heard the Law laid on both sides to judge which was right." Ibid, at 10. Of course, each man's attitude toward the independence of the jury was shaped by current politics. John Adams, in his diary, made clear that he thought of the jury as part of the Whig struggle against arbitrary government:

"As the Constitution requires, that, the popular Branch of the Legislature, should have an absolute Check so as to put a peremptory Negative upon every Act of the Government, it requires that the common People should have as compleat a Controul, as decisive a Negative, in every Judgment of a Court of Judicature. No Wonder then that the same restless Ambition, of aspiring Minds, which is endeavouring to lessen or destroy the Power of the People in Legislation, should attempt to lessen or destroy it, in the Execution of Lawes. The Rights of Juries and of Elections, were never attacked singly in all the English History. The same Passions which have disliked one have detested the other, and both have always been exploded, mutilated or undermined together."

Quoted in 1 *Legal Papers* . . . , supra note 4, at 229.

Now, should the melancholy case arise that the Judges should give their opinion to the jury against one of these fundamental principles, is a juror obliged to give his verdict generally, according to this direction, or even to find the fact specially, and submit the law to the Court? Every man, of any feeling or conscience, will answer no. It is not only his right, but his duty, in that case, to find the verdict according to his own best understanding, judgment, and conscience, though in direct opposition to the direction of the Court.[52]

William E. Nelson, who has conducted more research into this period of Massachusetts judicial history than any other scholar, sums up the theory as follows: "In each case, a jury is free, if justice requires, to adhere to rules and customs formulated in the past; if, on the other hand, justice requires departure from those rules, the jury is free so to depart."[53] So, too, when politics required the jury was free to depart and did quite as often as not.

It should be noted that even had juries been required to follow court instructions it is doubtful they could have done so in some of the more controversial litigations—they might not have known what the instructions were. When instructions were given[54] they were rendered seriatim and since all cases were tried before at least three judges and usually more, "jurors were often left with final power to determine which judge's interpretation of the law was correct."[55] Even if all the members of the court agreed as to the law and rendered only one charge the jurors might still be confused. The judges were not the only ones to explain the law to them. All throughout the prerevolutionary period advocates in Massachusetts jury trials were permitted to argue law as well as fact. Lawyers in their summations spent as much time quoting from law books and expounding rules or principles as they did clarifying their evidence or attacking the testimony from the other side. If their rules or principles were Whiggish, a Boston jury might well conclude that they better knew law than did the Tory judges and would take "instructions" from them. Advocates were free to score political points as they

---

52. These two quotations are reprinted in *Quincy Reports*, 566-67 (1865).
53. William E. Nelson, supra note 38, at 68.
54. As judges shared the theory that jurors knew the law, they often did not bother to instruct them. Ibid, at 61-62.
55. Ibid, at 63.

were permitted to say just about anything they pleased. "Custom house officers," John Adams argued in one case for the plaintiff "[are] vested with very important power and if deviated from may become fire brands in the hands of Fools." In this instance the jury returned a verdict for Adams' client of £2700 on goods worth £1041.[56] Certainly significant is the practical result: jurors more than judges or lawyers made the law of prerevolutionary Massachusetts. In political cases Whig juries made Whig law.

Erving v. Cradock is a case in point. The plaintiff, John Erving, was a member of the governor's council and the defendant, George Cradock, was temporary collector of the port of Boston. Here is a Tory's view of that litigation explained by Governor Francis Bernard to the Lords of Trade.

> Mr. *Cradock* . . . as Collector, seized a Vessel of Mr. *Erving's* charged with contraband trade & libelled her in the Court of Admiralty. Mr. *Erving* appeared personally in Court & prayed leave to compound [*i.e.*, to settle[57]] which being agreed to by the Governor & Collector as well as the King's Advocate, was allowed by the Court at one half of the value, which upon appraisement was ascertained at above £500 sterling. The sum Mr. *Erving* paid into Court; & it was equally divided between the King, the Governor & the Collector. . . . And now Mr. *Erving* has brought his action against Mr. *Cradock* for damages accrued to him by means of this seizure.[58]

In other words, after compounding the seizure in open admiralty court and paying the compromise sum, Councilor Erving turned to the common-law courts to recoup his loss and perhaps to punish Collector Cradock for his official zeal. The writ was trespass[59] and as Bernard put it, "The pretence for this action is, that the seizure was illegal and a trespass, and that the payment of Mr.

---

56. Hiller B. Zobel, supra note 9, at 223. In one case, however, John Adams was not permitted to argue law, though it may be significant that the trial at bar concerned slander and Adams was stopped from saying that the words in question were not actionable. See *Quincy Reports* 564 (1865); 1 *Legal Papers* . . . , supra note 4, at 142 & 149.

57. For a discussion and definition of "compounding" see, Hiller B. Zobel, supra note 9, at 15.

58. Letter From Governor Francis Bernard to the Lords of Trade, 6 August 1761, Appendix II, *Quincy Reports* 553-54 n. 2 (1865).

59. Erving v. Cradock, *Quincy Reports* 553 (1761).

Erving was not voluntary, but extorted by violence and *duress."*[60] The governor, who had already received his one-third share of the settlement, was alarmed. He asserted the common-law suit was a plot to destroy both the admiralty jurisdiction and the customs service. True it was a personal action, "But," he warned the Lords of Trade,

> it is generally understood that Mr. *Erving's* is only a leading action to a great many others; and that if he meets with success, every one that has had goods condemned, or been allowed to compound for them at their own request, will bring actions against the Officer who seized them. Your Lordships will perceive that these actions have an immediate tendency to destroy the Court of Admiralty and with it the Custom house, which cannot subsist without that Court.[61]

As far as Bernard was concerned, the suspicion of a conspiracy was confirmed by the conduct of counsel and judges when the case was first tried in the Inferior Court of Common Pleas before a Suffolk county jury. There, if we can believe the governor and it seems reasonable to do so, "the chief subject of the harangues of the council for the plaintiff (and some of the Judges too) were on the expediency of discouraging a Court immediately subject to the King and independant of the Province and which determined property without a jury; and on a necessity of putting a stop to the practices of the Custom house officers, for that the people would no longer bear having their trade kept under restrictions, which their neighbours (meaning Rhode Island) were entirely free from."[62] Two of the judges,[63] according to Governor Bernard, "directed the jury to find a verdict for the plaintiff, and give him for damages every farthing he was out of pocket; and said they must put a stop to these proceedings of the Custom house officers; if they did not there would be tumults and bloodshed; for the people would bear with them no long-

---

60. Letter From Governor Francis Bernard to former Governor Thomas Pownall, 28 August 1761, Appendix II, *Quincy Reports* 555 n. 2 (1865).

61. Letter From Governor Francis Bernard to the Lords of Trade, 6 August 1761, ibid, at 555 n. 2.

62. Ibid.

63. The Inferior Court of Common Pleas consisted of four Judges, any three to be a quorum.

er."[64] Thus *Erving v. Cradock* contained three elements that were to become common in Massachusetts trials over the next decade and a half: (1) Whig political theory was offered to the jury as controlling law; (2) the jury was invited to use civil tort damages as a criminal-law-type sanction to punish a revenue-agent defendant for enforcing an unpopular statute; and (3) the vice-admiralty jurisdiction was put on trial. The vice admiralty was "convicted" and in a real sense so was Collector Cradock. The jury returned a verdict "near £600 sterling damages,"[65] about £100 above the sum for which Erving had compounded.

Cradock appealed to the Superior Court of Judicature, which meant a trial *de novo* with each party allowed to enter further pleas and new evidence. More importantly it meant trial before judges more of the Tory persuasion. Even had they been partisan they did not have to bring in politics as had the inferior-court judges. They could and they did instruct the jury according to the law and the law was clear: whether Cradock had been guilty of a trespass (a fact not proved the court pointed out), he was purged of that trespass by the composition confirmed in the vice-admiralty court, the decrees of which were of equal force with a judgment at common law.[66] Chief Justice Thomas Hutchinson was emphatic. There was no doubt, he charged, "that the decree of the Court of Admiralty, where it had jurisdiction, could not be traversed and annulled in a court of common law."[67] Notwithstanding the jury found for the plaintiff, voting him damages of £740 lawful Massachusetts money or £555 sterling.[68]

Cradock was now in a serious position. He had been performing his duty and the upper court had ruled he was not liable, but the jury held otherwise and he faced the prospect for paying far more than his share of the "compounding" or of going to jail. The court could not enter judgment for him no matter how

---

64. Letter From Governor Francis Bernard to Former Governor Thomas Pownall, 28 August 1761, Appendix 11, *Quincy Reports* 555-56 n. 2 (1865).

65. Ibid.

66. Letter From Governor Francis Bernard to the Lords of Trade, 2 August 1761, ibid, at 556 n. 4.

67. Quoting Hutchinson's *History*, ibid, at 557 n. 4.

68. Erving v. Cradock, *Quincy Reports*, 553, 555-56 (1761).

strong the judges thought his case to be.[69] He might move for a new trial[70] a motion which could have been granted by an inferior court and not without precedent in the Superior Court of Judicature.[71] But after studying all the available records, Nelson concludes "that a motion for a new trial could not be granted on the ground that a verdict was against the law solely because the jury had disregarded the court's instructions."[72] In Massachusetts the jury's verdict was truly final. All that Collector Cradock could do was take an appeal outside the province to the King in Council while trusting that the governor would somehow delay execution of judgment or keep him out of jail until orders came from London.

Cradock took his appeal and Erving withdrew, acknowledging in superior court that the second judgment had been satisfied.[73] It is hardly surprising that he did so. In a similar situation John Hancock did the same. One of his ships had been seized and condemned at the Boston admiralty court for importing more goods than had been entered in the report of the customs house at the Scottish port where they had been loaded. Hancock sued the officers of customs for the value of the ship and cargo. Again Chief Justice Hutchinson gave the jury clear instructions that an admiralty decree could not be traversed at common law and again the jury ignored him. When the customsmen appealed to the King in Council Hancock, like Erving, withdrew. Thomas Hutchinson believed Hancock did not dare pursue the appeal because trial in London would have exposed his smuggling operations and hurt his reputation.[74] This explanation is doubtful. Hancock did not defend the appeal because he knew he had no more chance of winning before the King in Council than the customs officials had had of defending themselves before a Boston jury. Besides, if his purpose was to harass the revenue service, he had

---

69. 1 *Legal Papers* . . . , supra note 4, at 215.

70. Angier v. Jackson, *Quincy Reports* 84 (1763).

71. See John Adams's "Note," in 1 *Legal Papers* . . . , supra note 4, at 218.

72. William E. Nelson, supra note 38, at 66.

73. Erving v. Cradock, *Quincy Reports* 553, 556 (1761).

74. Thomas Hutchinson, *The History of the Province of Massachusetts-Bay* 161-62 (1828).

done well enough. As these were personal actions the defendants had been put to expense out of their own pockets as well as to a good deal of trouble, being forced to take time from their duties to consult with their lawyers and attend the trials. A civil suit in Massachusetts could be a very real annoyance as the plaintiff had the option of attaching all of the defendant's property. Just to lose in superior court even without paying the judgment, could be costly. A few actions of this type and Hancock and his fellow merchants could expect the customsmen to proceed more cautiously in the future—even if appeal to London meant certain reversal. If the appeal were defended and the facts of harassment brought officially to the notice of the British government, the Crown might be obliged to indemnify the customs officers. Without an appeal the Whigs could hope the revenue men would be left to bear the costs themselves.

There is one further case to consider, for it sheds light on the question whether Whig litigants really sought to win money damages or were as interested in using the traverse jury to harass the revenue service. It is the case of James Otis against John Robinson, an especially unpopular customs commissioner, and it was the *cause celebre* of the day.[75] Otis and Robinson staged a cane-swinging brawl in a Tory coffee house and Otis, having received the worse of it, sued Robinson alleging damages in the amount of £3000. The traverse jury in the Inferior Court of Common Pleas, brought in a plaintiff's verdict setting damages at "the astounding amount of £2000 (higher than any contemporary tort award) and in terms of twentieth century purchasing power an exceptionally substantial recovery."[76] Not satisfied, Otis appealed to the Superior Court of Judicature. He must have thought there was a good chance that a second jury would vote him an even higher sum. So, too, did Robinson, for through his attorney he confessed his liability and gave Otis the apology that he had demanded. Otis thereupon remitted all but £112, 10 shillings, and 8 pence, an amount covering the costs, the medical bills, and his attorney fees.[77] The revealing fact is that Otis

---

75. See John C. Miller, *Sam Adams: Pioneer in Propaganda* 219 (1936).
76. Hiller B. Zobel, supra note 5, at 197.
77. Ibid.

could have easily gotten more money and not run the risk of an appeal to the King in Council. His lawyer, John Adams, could have asked the jury for damages in the amount of £299, and there seems to have been no rule to stop him from informing the jurors that such a sum was one pound less than the statutory amount required for an appeal to London. The jury verdict would have been final (save for Robinson's useless right to appeal to a superior-court jury) and Otis would have been richer. Adams pressed for an unrealistic verdict instead and the unpopular revenue agent was forced to humble himself before the Whigs. It cannot be doubted that Adams could have persuaded the jury to bring in the lesser amount. "From the best account I can get of the trial," Hutchinsoin wrote, "had Mr. Otis assaulted Mr. Robinson, in the same manner after receiving the like insult and abuse, the jury would not have given him a shilling."[78]

"They now begin to talk," Governor Bernard wrote of the Whig merchants, "of bringing more actions against Custom house officers who have made seizures and have had them condemned or compounded in Court for them. A Custom house officer has no chance with a jury, let his cause be what it will. And it will depend upon the vigorous measures that shall be taken at home for the defence of the officers, whether there be any Custom house here at all."[79]

Bernard does not say what the British government should do but surely he knew when he wrote in 1761 that London was not ready to interfere with Massachusetts juries. That day would not come until 1774. Perhaps he thought the vice-admiralty court could be given exclusive jurisdiction over personal actions involving customs officials. This solution too would have been a drastic innovation. The best he could really hope for was the power to suspend execution of judgment until appeals could be heard by the King in Council, for speedier and less expensive methods of appeals, and finally for a fund from which to reimburse government-employed defendants forced to pay damages resulting from politically-inspired-jury verdicts. As usual the ministry did

---

78. Ibid.

79. Letter From Governor Francis Bernard to the Lords of Trade, 2 August 1761, Appendix 11, *Quincy Reports* 556-57 n. 4 (1865).

nothing, leaving the "custom house officials" with little choice but to consider their own interests and to proceed with greater caution when enforcing the trade laws.

For the Whigs these jury verdicts were defensive harassment, for royal officials they were another symptom of conspiracy, but for customsmen they posed a personal dilemma. If they did not do their duty they might lose their source of livelihood and perhaps face official censure. If they did their duty they might end up facing debtor prison. It was truly a dilemma, as it was a problem for which even the best legal advice could offer no safe solution. Nowhere was this fact better demonstrated than in Boston during the Stamp-Act crisis, when Benjamin Hallowell was comptroller of the port and William Scheaffe was collector. As the time drew near when documents would have to be stamped, both men were in a quandry. The stamp agent, Andrew Oliver, had not only resigned his office but when they approached him for stamps he replied that he had no commission to distribute stamps and would not distribute them if he had. They then turned to the crown attorneys for advice and one of the issues which they raised has been summarized by Edmund S. and Helen M. Morgan (who read the original letters but do not furnish us with clarifying quotations):

> Suppose they should refuse to grant clearances on the ground that they had no stamped paper. To grant clearances was their job, and no one else could do it. If they refused would they not be liable to suits for damages from every individual who applied for a clearance and was refused? On the other hand, suppose they granted a clearance on unstamped paper, and suppose further that the ship proceeding under this clearance were seized by the British Navy and condemned for proceeding under improper clearance papers. Would they not be liable in such a case to a suit for the value of the ship? Whatever they did were they not thus liable to innumerable suits? And were not the New England merchants notoriously quick to sue customs officers whenever they could?[80]

These are apparently the questions that Hallowell and Sheaffe put to Edmund Trowbridge, then the attorney general of the

---

80. Edmund S. Morgan & Helen M. Morgan, *The Stamp Act Crisis: Prologue to Revolution* 135 (1953).

province, and to Robert Auchmuty, the advocate general of the admiralty court. From one or both they received an answer which the Morgans characterized as "a reluctant opinion" and which they summarized as follows: "that the Comptroller and Collector would not be liable to damages if they cleared ships on unstamped paper, provided they certified that no stamped paper was available."[81] This opinion was truly bold for two Tory lawyers to have rendered. While it said nothing about the constitutionality of the Stamp Act, it did give the Whigs as much as they could have hoped for and was hardly calculated to please their superiors in London. Yet it satisfied neither the comptroller nor the collector who seem to have wanted more of a guarantee of immunity than mere legal advice.

> Sheaffe and Hallowell next pressed the Attorney and Advocate for more explicit instructions, about how the clearances should be drawn up, and whether bonds as well as clearances might be unstamped. The only result was that Trowbridge got cold feet and withdrew his former advice. On November 30 he wrote, "I do not look upon myself as the Proper Person by whose advise You (in an affair of such importance, and which seems to be at present a matter rather of prudence than of Law) are to govern yourselves and therefore must be excused advising you either to grant Cockets or Clearances upon unstamped Papers or to refuse to do it."[82]

It may be, as the Morgans suggested, the attorney general got "cold feet" but it is doubtful. Rather it seems he was being asked a question which no lawyer could have answered and on being pressed too far, he threw up his hands in disgust. Trowbridge was the most respected lawyer in Massachusetts Bay and it is true that he had a reputation to protect. As attorney general he was caught between the passions of the Whig population, some of whom were his private clients, and the governments (both in Boston and London) from whom he sought official favor. Had he been asked to rule on the constitutionality of the Stamp Act or to have given advice on the question whether it was legal to issue clearances without stamps, he might well have gotten "cold feet" and shied away from an answer. No matter what

---

81. Ibid, at 136.
82. Ibid.

he ruled he would have been damned on one side without winning marks from the other. But from what the Morgans say, it seems that he was not being asked for an opinion on either of these questions. It was not the constitutionality of the Stamp Act that troubled Comptroller Hallowell and Collector Sheaffe, but their own personal liability. They did not ask whether London would fine them or remove them from office for using unstamped paper but whether Boston merchants could and would successfully sue them if they refused to do so. They were asking Trowbridge an unanswerable question and the explanation lies with Massachusetts-Bay jurisprudence and especially with the rules of special pleading, not with a lawyer's cold feet.

As the verdict in *Erving v. Cradock* demonstrates, it was not difficult for a Massachusetts lawyer to frame a case that the court had to submit to a jury. There the superior court clearly did not have jurisdiction for the matter had been settled by a vice-admiralty court and the judgment of that court could not be traversed at common law. Yet the judges of the superior court had not only been unable to overturn the jury's verdict after it was rendered, they had not dismissed the action earlier. They did not do so because they could not do so and the reason they could not do so was that Cradock's case was not patently bad on the surface, probably because the writ of trespass drawn by his lawyer said nothing about the fact that the seizure (or trespass) had been compounded in admiralty. Had the writ set forth the admiralty decree the defendant, Cradock, might have demurred and the superior court would have dismissed the action. But if the writ omitted reference to the admiralty settlement, the defendant could not demur without confessing the allegation of trespass and judgment would have been entered against him.

Unable to demur the defendant's first alternative was to plead the general issue: answer "not guilty" to the charge of trespass. If he did so he would not be able to bring forward his defense of law until the jury was seated and then it was for the Whig jury, not the Tory court to render the verdict. A second alternative for Cradock was to plead specially, that is to raise the defense in his answer by citing the fact of the previous, binding, admiralty decree. If the plaintiff replied by admitting the decrees (and perhaps citing further special matter by way of avoidance) the court would have the legal issue before it and the judges could have dismissed the writ. No Whig lawyer would have done so (nor would he have demurred to the answer as to have done so would also have led to dismissal). He would have denied the fact alleged in the answer (i.e. the admiralty decree) and thus created an issue of fact that the court had to submit to jury. Once the jury was sworn and he began to offer evidence, the plaintiff's lawyer would no longer deny the admiralty decree. He would have gotten his argument before a jury despite the fact that it was bad at law and because it was a customs case he could expect the jury to ignore the law and find for his client.

It was these rules of special pleading that made it possible for a Whig lawyer to get any case before a jury and made it impossible for the attorney general to advise the comptroller and collector how to make themselves judgment proof. As long as Boston juries insisted on ignoring the law and voting their politics, no one could have advised them.

But what of the advice that Trowbridge did give them? The Morgans say at first he told the two men that they "would not be liable to damages if they cleared ships on unstamped paper, provided they certified that no stamped paper was available."[83] If Trowbridge did say this, he was going just about as far as any lawyer would have dared to go. Perhaps all he was saying was that if the officials did make the certification of unavailability, it was unlikely they would ever be sued.

It should be noted that Trowbridge was answering the second question that had been put to him by Hallowell and Sheaffe: whether the two officials would be liable for the value of a ship cleared on unstamped paper and later seized by the royal navy for sailing without proper clearance. Trowbridge's supposition had to be that if the unstamped clearance was accompanied by a certification that stamps were not available in Boston, the navy would not seize a ship sailing under such paper or if it did, the admiralty court would dismiss the seizure. There was a risk here,

83. Ibid.

for no one knew what orders might come from London but even if the supposition proved false and the ship was both seized and condemned, it was more than likely that the owner of the vessel would not sue Hallowell and Sheaffe; he would sue the captain of the naval ship. From a political point of view, to sue the captain might be more effective for it would cause the government greater annoyance, call to account a man who profited personally from the seizure, and perhaps tie up a naval vessel. From a legal point of view it would be preferable for the writ of trespass could be used and the only fact that the plaintiff would have to prove would be the seizure. Even a Tory judge would tell the jury that the burden was on the captain to justify his actions.

Trowbridge could reasonably render advice based on such suppositions. That was a lawyer's job. What he could not do was give Hallowell and Sheaffe a guarantee they would not be sued at all. Consider the first hypothetical question they put to him: what if they refused to grant clearance for a ship because the ship's papers were not stamped. On its face this is an easy case. Unstamped papers are illegal, the comptroller and collector were obeying the law when they refused to sign them, therefore they are not liable for loss resulting from a failure to grant clearance. But as Trowbridge well knew, the prospective plaintiff could avoid that legal defense. The writ would say nothing about stamps or the Stamp Act. All it would allege was that the defendants had harmed the plaintiff to his damage of such and such an amount. All that the shipowner needed to sue the officials was a proper writ. To draft a proper writ his lawyer's problem was to frame the harm in the disguise of an actionable wrong without acknowledging that the harm was related to stamps.

The Whig shipowner—whether he really wanted to collect money damages or was only doing his share to harass British custom officials—would have had to frame his allegation of liability within an action on the case. As the potential defendant, by refusing to issue clearance without stamps has in common-law definitions done nothing, he cannot be sued in trespass. It is an old maxim of English common law that "not doing is no trespass" unless there is a duty to act: a duty imposed by law, such as the duty of an innkeeper to protect the property of guests. An innkeeper could be sued in trespass by a guest where goods were stolen from the defendant's inn even though the defendant proved he did nothing to aid the thief. "Not doing" is no defense for the innkeeper as the law imposed on him a duty to act. Unless seeking consequential damages, the plaintiff in that action will sue in trespass as he need prove only the loss of his goods. If he sued in case the burden would be on him to prove that the innkeeper-defendant had been guilty of deceit or carelessness or negligence.

The problem that the action of case posed for the Whig lawyer representing the merchant in 1765 whose ship was denied clearance, is that the court in a writ of case would have to be framed in terms of nonfeasance. There were few good counts in nonfeasance then—at least compared to today—except for contract actions brought in assumpsit. For a cause to sound in tort it had to allege misfeasance or the defendant might demur. To avoid the risk that the port officials would demur and that the demurrer would be sustained by the court, the plaintiff might embellish his writ of case with a count of malice: charging that the defendant had failed to act (i.e. issue clearance papers) due to his malicious intent to cause harm to the plaintiff. It is extremely unlikely that the plaintiff's counsel would feel it necessary to clutter up his writ with counts requiring special proof because it was unlikely that the defendant would demur to a writ of case on the grounds that it failed to allege a misfeasance. Indeed, the plaintiff might have welcomed a demurrer. For the defendant to have demurred would have run the very strong risk that the court would have overruled the demurrer, ending the action then and there with a verdict for the plaintiff. Such was certainly true in Massachusetts Bay.

As Professor Nelson's studies show, Massachusetts Bay courts during the prerevolutionary period permitted relief by way of a common-law action for damages against a public official who had committed a wrong, even when that wrong was in the nature of nonfeasance.

> Such actions were frequently brought, for instance, against sheriffs for their misconduct or that of their deputies, for whom they were liable. Such suits generally alleged some misfeasance or neglect in per-

forming a duty relating to civil litigation, such as failing to serve a writ of attachment, failing to take bail of a defendant, failing to keep attached goods in possession pending trial, or failing to levy execution or to levy it properly. Suits could also be brought against constables for similar misfeasance or neglect, as well as against jailors who permitted prisoners to escape.[84]

Three allegations were essential in order for a plaintiff to establish a cause of action in these cases: "first, the loss of his recovery from a judgment; second, that the loss occurred as a result of the neglect or misfeasance of the sheriff or his deputy; and third, that the sheriff against whom he had brought suit was responsible for that neglect or misfeasance."[85] Another analogy, less strong but nonetheless valid authority, were numerous cases brought against towns for failure to support a plaintiff-pauper.[86] More to the point was an Essex County decision just five years before the Stamp Act which held a justice of the peace liable for official misconduct when he failed "to take a recognizance from a defendant who was to appear before him in the future."[87] "There was," Professor Nelson concludes, "little that one acting on behalf of the government could do without rendering himself liable to an action at law in the event that he wronged another."[88]

On one point there was no dispute, certainly not in the minds of crown officials. They were as liable in common-law actions as were Colonial officials. Considering the political attitudes of Boston juries, they may well have felt that the mere liability to answer the writ made judgment against them certain. Moreover, they undoubtedly suspected that damages were not the primary objective of some potential Whig litigants. The Whig shipowner-turned-plaintiff might be seeking nothing more than to establish with the "mob" his credentials as "a friend of liberty." Money certainly could be made by suing these two potential defendants[89] but better still was the opportunity to embarrass London. For the

---

84. William E. Nelson, supra note 38, at 11-12.

85. Ibid, n. 19.

86. Ibid, at 10-11.

87. Ibid, at 13.

88. Ibid, at 13-14. Here Nelson is referring to various statutory penalties as well as to common-law actions which might be brought against public officials.

89. At a time when the "common sort" could live comfortably in Boston on

Stamp Act itself could be put on trial and a Boston jury could be asked to rule on its constitutionality. The verdict might be meaningless at Westminster Hall but it would have marvelous propaganda value in the colonies.

Let us suppose the Stamp Act had not been repealed and the collector of the port of Boston refused to issue clearance papers permitting the ship of a merchant to sail from the harbor. The merchant brings our writ of case alleging that the collector has neglected to perform his duty, as a result of which the plaintiff's ship was not able to sail and that anticipated profits in a stated amount were thereby lost. Before he dare demur to the writ, the collector's lawyer would have to have absolute confidence not merely in the Tory leanings of a majority of the court but also that those judges would permit themselves to be guided by their political predelictions and dismiss the case. They would be hard pressed to do so, for the writ will allege only that the defendant neglected his duty to the plaintiff's loss, not why he neglected it. Nothing will be said about the Stamp Act or unstamped paper. On its face, the writ should go to further pleading and it is for the defendant to bring forth the defense that due to the action of the Boston mob, stamps were not available and without them clearance papers could not be issued.

But how does the defendant's lawyer, once he decides against the risk of filing a demurrer, establish these defenses? The most obvious answer is to plea specially, not a common practice in colonial Massachusetts.[90] In answer to the plaintiff's writ, the defendant would plead that it was not unlawful for him to pass

---

£40 a year, the comptroller had a salary of £70 and the collector of £100. Moreover, there was good money to be made on fees. During 1768-69 (a winter of nonimportation agreements) the substitute collector at Salem took in fees of £443 sterling during six months. The post had a salary of £40. Joseph R. Frese, supra note 16, at 4-5. See also, Hiller B. Zobel, supra note 9, at 66.

90. 1 *Legal Papers* . . . , supra note 4, at 28. But see 2 Thomas C. Amory, *Life of James Sullivan* 5 (1859). The purpose of special pleading was to narrow issues and it was one of the few ways then available to lawyers to exercise some control over admissible evidence. See William E. Nelson, supra note 38, at 50. Some references by historians to special pleading make little sense. For example, "Lawyers had long taken the lead in public affairs; the art of special pleading, refined in the courtroom, proved equally successful in the political arena." Arthur M. Schlesinger, *Prelude to Independence: The Newspaper War on Britain 1764-1776* 10 (1958).

clearance papers without afixing stamps to them and either (1) the plaintiff refused to purchase the stamps or (2) stamps were unavailable due to no fault of the defendant's.

In a nonpolitical case a plaintiff might well demur to this answer thus framing a legal issue for the court. In our action of the Boston merchant against the collector of the port, however, the plaintiff will not demur and the defendant's attorney knows it. Rather the plaintiff would plead over by denying generally the facts stated in the answer, thus bringing the pleadings to a close and moving for trial by jury. Once the jury is empanelled and arguments can be offered, all options are within the election of the plaintiff's attorney. He may either deny that his client refused to purchase stamps[91] or say stamps were unavailable,[92] thus creating issues of facts for the jury or he can argue that the collector neglected his duty when he refused to issue papers without stamps because the Stamp Act was unconstitutional and he was not bound to obey it. Quite likely, with a good Whig jury the defense might choose the latter argument adding to the discomfort of British officials. Today the argument that the collector neglected his duty when he obeyed the Stamp Act would create a question of law for the court, but not during 1765. A Suf-

---

91. It should be noted that such denials did not involve perjury. The burden of proof to sustain his answer is on the defendant, and the plaintiff's lawyer would be arguing or denying that the defendant sustained that burden. Besides, at that time neither the defendant nor the plaintiff were competent to testify and there might be no direct evidence on the question. To be certain, a writ might be drawn alleging a date when no other witnesses were present. If witnesses had been present on other occasions when the plaintiff requested unstamped clearance and they testified to that fact, the plaintiff's attorney might still argue that the defendant had the burden of proving there had been no change of mind. If witnesses were testifying to the plaintiff's intention at the exact time the clearance was passed, they probably would not be whigs but men easily discredited (*e.g.*, other customhouse employees) by an effective lawyer. Yet it does seem that perjury was a factor in customs litigations. Thomas Hutchinson stressed strongly in 1769, warning that witnesses who swore falsely in the vice admiralty were quality of an indictable crime even if they believed that court to be unconstitutional. Chief Justice Thomas Hutchinson's Charge to the Grand Jury, *Quincy Reports* 309-10 (1769). See also, James Kendall Hosmer, *The Life of Thomas Hutchinson, Royal Governor of the Province of Massachusetts Bay* 138 (1896).

92. Thus playing on whig suspicions that colonial officials had received the stamps and were hiding them until the controversy calmed down.

folk County jury could express popular dislike for the Stamp Act by returning a verdict of "guilty" and, in theory at least, would be holding that as a matter of law the Stamp Act was unconstitutional.

Because of the political implications of a holding on the issue of constitutionality, the defendant's lawyer (who quite possibly would be the solicitor general or another crown official) would not plead specially. Rather than answer the writ with a specific defense, he would plea the general issue, "not guilty." The legal questions and the evidence would not change; the trial would be much the same. But at least the Whigs would not have the satisfaction of having the constitutional issue exposed by the specific pleadings. It would be hidden by the general issue, depriving the trial of some propaganda value.

Remarkably, the same rules of pleadings would have led to opposite strategies in that second hypothetical case posed by Hallowell and Sheaffe: a ship cleared without stamped paper and then seized by the royal navy for sailing without proper documents. There the defendant could have turned the tables on the Whig-plaintiff by pleading specially. Again the action would be case, not trespass, for although the defendant had acted and did pass the clearance papers, the damages were consequential, not direct.[93] To be actionable, the plaintiff would have to allege some fault on the part of the defendant, perhaps carelessness: his neglect to fix stamps to his documents as a result of which the ship's papers were not in order, the ship was seized and condemned, to the loss of the plaintiff in such-and-such amount. The defendant cannot demur, as the writ is good on its face, and the court would enter judgment for the plaintiff. If he pleaded the general issue he could, at trial, establish all his defenses: the knowledge of the risk on the part of the plaintiff; the unavailability of stamps; the fact that there was no alternative to unstamped paper; his fear of mob violence; and the advice of the attorney general. But the merchant then could have put the Stamp Act on trial before a Whig jury with the inevitable result. Rather, the defendant would plea specially, denying that the loss

---

93. The plaintiff could sue in trespass the captain of the naval vessel.

was the consequence of his carelessness: that knowing stamps were unavailable the plaintiff had nonetheless demanded clearance and thus had assumed the risk of loss. Had the plaintiff demurred to this answer Chief Justice Hutchinson would have dismissed the writ on the grounds that the answer was a good plea in abatement. True there was a factual element here—whether the plaintiff by demanding clearance had intended to exonerate the defendant from liability for the consequences—and the plaintiff might argue that the question should go to the jury. Chances are Hutchinson would have disagreed. But what else could the plaintiff do except demur to the answer? If he filed a replication he would have to support his allegation of carelessness by specifying the fact that the defendant failed to use stamps. He would be saying that the Stamp Act was constitutional. No Whig seeking to embarrass the British government or to harass the customs officials would take that position. Even if his his only purpose was to collect damages he would not want to proceed before a Boston jury for he would be asking them to hold as a matter of law that parliament had authority to impose an internal tax on Massachusetts. True, the decision would be implicit under the general issue but it would not be on the record and a competent lawyer could persuade the jurors that it was not a serious consideration. It would be on record if the defendant pleaded specially and no Whig would want to touch it. This consideration may be another reason why Trowbridge advised Hallowell and Sheaffe that if they certified the unavailability of stamps they would not be sued.

Of course, none of these writs were ever filed. The Stamp Act was repealed and as ships that had sailed without stamps were never seized, the crisis passed away. But the idea was there and, as Hallowell and Sheaffe proved, customsmen were nervous. They felt harassed and had good reason to examine the law before they acted. For almost a century the grand and traverse juries of America had been reluctant to support their work with either indictments or convictions. That problem had been solved when Great Britain introduced the vice admiralty. In the 1760s the juries added a new dimension to London's political difficulties in America, showing that they could be offensive as well as defensive instruments for keeping British officialdom off balance. True, they were more irritating then fatal and their use against revenue officials was not likely to destroy either the empire or the customs service. Still, a lesson had been taught and as the constitutional controversy intensified and spread, the Whigs found there were many other ways that the legal institutions which they controlled could be used to protect friends and punish enemies.

CHAPTER 13

FUNDAMENTALS OF DISCIPLINARY PROCEEDINGS IN THE PUBLIC SERVICE*

RICARDO LEVENE h.

Professor of Criminal Law, University of Buenos Aires

ARTICLE 18 OF THE Argentine Constitution sets out the constitutional principles applicable in penal proceedings throughout the entire country, notwithstanding the power given the provinces to enact their own procedural codes. In effect, it adopts the principle of *nullum crimen nulla poena sine previa lege et indicio;* the prohibition against citizens being tried by special commission or by judges other than those in whom a cause would ordinarily be vested by law; or being compelled to testify against themselves or arrested without a warrant duly signed by a competent authority. Among other things it establishes the inviolability of the home and of correspondence and the right to a trial in defense of one's person and property.

These guarantees should be understood to extend to all types of proceedings, especially those of a criminal character and including administrative penal proceedings. The importance of extending such guarantees to this latter sphere is even greater when one considers the absence in administrative criminal law not only of codification but of legislation generally, and even of forms, foundations, and basic principles. Procedures in this field are characterized by anarchy and diversity, by contradictions between such principles as do exist, and by that arbitrariness and undue discretion which are the inevitable consequence of these other characteristics.

In their continual effort to perfect institutions, students of the

---

* Translated by Professor and Mrs. H. H. A. Cooper and E. M. Wise.

criminal law ought to give urgent and careful attention to the trial of disciplinary matters in the public service. The aim should be to establish a system which will ensure a speedy trial and respect for individual rights and guarantees, as well as effective repression, through the means of flexible and up-to-date rules which permit all proper possibilities for a legal defense.

In the public service, disciplinary power and the sanctions attached to it are conditioned on the legal relationship of employment (i.e. on the existence of a link between the administration and its agent). Since what is punished by means of sanctions is the nonfulfillment of duties,[1] it presupposes a public power to establish hierarchic relationships of a penal character, although of course this process differs from the ordinary criminal law.

Thus, this law of disciplinary proceedings pertains strictly to the realm of public administration (i.e. to entities of a public nature) for although private bodies may also impose disciplinary measures, often for vague deeds such as "misconduct," these disciplinary powers do not come within the purview of criminal law, which is public law.

It is also the case that in true administrative disciplinary law the *tipo legal* (or descriptive definition of the elements of the offense) is almost always absent. It is generally admitted that the proceedings are not governed by the principles of *nullum crimen nulla poena sine lege* or of *legale iudicium* (a view taken by both Villegas Basavilvaso and Sebastian Soler, although the latter acknowledges that this does not constitute a "desideratum").[2] This opinion is shared by Manzini[3] who also states, based on Forti and Vico, that true criminal proceedings may give rise to a suspension of the disciplinary process and that the criminal sentence may *ipso jure* constitute a disciplinary punishment.[4] Other authors, among them Villegas Basavilvaso, further assert that the principle of *ne bis in idem* is inapplicable when the deed is both a crime and a disciplinary offense.

---

1. Benjamin Villegas Basavilvaso, *Derecho Administrativo*, Vol. 1, Buenos Aires, 1949, p. 121.

2. Sebastian Soler, *Derecho Penal Argentino*, Vol. 1 Buenos Aires, 1945, p. 23.

3. Manzini, *Tratado de Derecho Penal*, Vol. 1, Buenos Aires, 1948, p. 134.

4. *Ibid.*, p. 132.

Faced with this situation which must be considered extremely unsatisfactory, we have to conclude that the principle of *ne bis in idem* is applicable when summary administrative proceedings are instituted a second time for the same deed or administrative fault.

In this regard, one Argentine court has indicated that an administrative fault which has already been punished cannot be the subject of a new hearing, not even on the basis of supposedly new facts, if these merely constitute an external manifestation of the same deed or fault that has already been punished.[5]

It is also our view that a hearing is an essential prerequisite for the imposition of a disciplinary sanction, whether it be dismissal, suspension, or fine. Such a hearing should be regarded as a guarantee given to the employee which enables him to put his case and to exercise his right of defense in whatever manner he deems appropriate (as was said by the High Court of Justice of Cordova on June 28, 1968).[6]

A legally sophisticated defense is not really necessary in this sort of disciplinary proceeding but if the defendant chooses to avail himself of such a defense, he should be allowed certain of the ordinary rights of defense.

He should be allowed, particularly, the right to offer evidence in rebuttal, etc., for as we have already shown, the constitutional right of defense at the trial stage, with all of its consequences *(ne bis in idem, etc.),* applies as much in the sphere of administrative penal proceedings as it does in the ordinary criminal law.

The Argentine Supreme Court for its part has declared that the right of defense at the trial stage is infringed by not admitting into the proceedings such rebuttal evidence as may be opportunely introduced.[7]

Likewise, in a case where the law is silent, the principles of the Penal Code (Article 4) should be applied. This is not a matter of free extension by analogy, but rather, primarily, a proper ap-

---

5. Camara Federal de Parana. April 29, 1969.

6. *Allende de Amestoy, Azucena v. Municipalidad de Cordova, Diario de Jurisprudencia Argentina,* November 27, 1968.

7. Argentine Supreme Court, Judgment T243, p. 500, and *Diario La Ley,* December 26, 1969.

plication of the terms of the last part of that Article—especially so since all that is constitutionally prohibited is the use of an accusation by analogy in order to punish otherwise unpunishable behavior.[8] In this way, we would obtain the benefit of being able to apply to disciplinary administrative proceedings, in cases where the law is silent, such basic penal and procedural principles as, for example, the statutory period of limitation on actions in criminal cases.

The rights of the interested party must be made effective by means of a mechanism for review, which should be established in every sphere, whether it be national, provincial, municipal, centralized or independent, since the public service must be internally organized on a vertical basis in order to carry out its executive functions. It must, moreover, take steps to guarantee the legality, justice and equity of its own conduct with respect to its subordinates. To this end, those members of the public service itself who are affected by its activities must be granted the right to challenge administratively the decisions it makes, as well as the right to be heard and judged by the higher courts.

The public service itself should be interested in maintaining control over all its departments, in submitting its acts to legal regulation and review in order to determine if they comply with law and in granting, where necessary under its own rules, effective remedies for the vindication of the legal order.

In light of the considerations previously mentioned and taking account of the principles reiterated at many Congresses on Procedural Law which are applicable to this subject, we would formulate the following rules which should govern the conduct of disciplinary proceedings:

1. The central, provincial and local governments should promulgate legislation for all their departments with respect to administrative penal proceedings. These proceedings should be characterized by speed, economy and certainty, and those officers charged with the exercise of this jurisdiction should be clearly indicated, appropriate respect being paid to the principle of the "natural judge."

---

8. Second Criminal Court of Tucuman, April 17, 1968, in *Diario La Ley*, October 25, 1968.

2. The central, provincial and local governments should issue regulations for all of their respective departments which will establish an appropriate mechanism for review.

3. In administrative penal proceedings, no one should be punished for a disciplinary violation unless he has had a proper trial based on a statute existing prior to the date of the alleged offense. No one should be considered guilty until a final judgment has been entered against him; nor may anyone be subjected to disciplinary administrative proceedings more than once for the same matter. In cases of doubt, the decision should be that which is most favorable to the accused.

4. In order for a disciplinary sanction to be imposed there must previously have been a hearing at which the accused was allowed to exercise his right of defense.

5. The accused may be assisted by counsel from the first moment of proceedings against him and may present himself voluntarily to the hearing officer in order to explain his position and to submit evidence. In every case, he must be summoned to testify in his own defense and allowed to make his rebuttal; he must be advised of the matters of which he is accused.

6. Evidence in rebuttal opportunely submitted by the accused or defense counsel must be admitted into the proceedings.

7. The evidence offered should be properly evaluated according to the usual critical standards.

8. Disciplinary administrative proceedings should be conducted in plain and simple language. Evidentiary facts which are used to support the conclusions on which a decision is based should be expressly set out in it and the law on which the determination is based should be cited.

9. In the absence of express legal provisions applicable to these disciplinary administrative proceedings, the appropriate Code of Criminal Procedure should be used to supplement any deficiency.

10. Unless there is an express prohibition in the law governing the case, the relevant principles of the General Part of the Criminal Code should apply to these proceedings.

CHAPTER 14

THE GERMAN CODE OF REGULATORY OFFENSES

TILMANN SCHNEIDER

Ruhr University, Bochum

INTRODUCTION

THIS PAPER WILL DISCUSS the 1968 German Code of Regulatory Offenses. A sufficient reason for offering a contribution on this topic is Professor Hall's own very extensive discussion of regulatory offenses—although it is true that he has considered these offenses mainly from the point of view of strict liability.[1] There is also a special reason for approaching this topic in terms of comparative criminal law. Comparative law is most useful when it manages to accomplish two practical purposes: when it provides material which will aid in the solution of concrete legal and particularly legislative problems; and when it supplies the knowledge of foreign law necessary to settle a case involving foreign law.[2] The first aim—the solution of concrete problems—presupposes certain conditions. The problem to be solved must be the same or at least similar in the countries under study. This in turn will be true only if the cultural development of those countries is sociologically, economically, and ideologically similar. Further, the specific problem must not have been resolved in a manner which strongly depends on the influence of historical accidents—something which often happens when an issue dates from the Middle Ages. Cultural development in the United States and Germany provides an almost perfect example of such

---

1. Hall, *Principles of Criminal Law* 324 et seq. (2d ed. 1960).

2. Jescheck, *Entwicklung, Aufgaben und Methoden der Strafrechtsvergleichung* 25 et seq, (1965); T. Schneider, *Der Fonds de Garantie Automobile* 15 et seq. (1967).

similarity (although Germany is nowadays usually a little bit behind the United States), and the problem we propose to consider
—the use of sanctions in enforcing official regulations—is basically a very modern problem,[3] especially in areas such as economics, environmental and consumer protection and traffic regulation. Even allowing for the strong impact which the historical
development of the law has had on the solution of most modern
problems, it is nonetheless possible to conclude that approaches
to the use of regulatory sanctions have been basically rationalistic
and ahistorical which is essential if comparative study is to serve
the first purpose we have mentioned. The use of comparative
law to solve concrete problems connected with the enforcement
of economic regulations has, in fact, been demonstrated by
Kadish.[4]

The second practical aim of comparative jurisprudence mentioned above is to help solve actual cases relating to foreign law.
In this connection, the importance of comparison corresponds to
the qualitative and quantitative importance of the particular
topics which are subjected to comparison.

In Germany, regulatory sanctions are contained in a whole host
of statutes embracing all branches of the law, particularly German administrative law. Administrative laws which embody regulatory sanctions include, for example, those governing building
construction[5] and environmental[6] and consumer protection.[7] In
the field of tax law, virtually every statute incorporates regulatory sanctions.[8] But the main relevance of the German Code of
Regulatory Offenses is in the two areas of economic regulation and
traffic regulation. The first area includes laws governing anti-

---

3. Starrs, "The Regulatory Offense in Historical Perspective," in *Essays in
Criminal Science* 235 (Mueller ed., 1961).

4. Kadish, "Some Observations on the Use of Criminal Sanctions in Enforcing
Economic Regulations," 30 *U. of Chi. L. Rev.* 423 (1963).

5. Bundesbaugesetz (Bundesgesetzblatt, subsequently referred to as BGBl, 1960,
Part, I, p. 341).

6. Gesetz ueber Vorsorgemassnahmen zur Luftreinhaltung (BGBl. 1965, Part. 1,
p. 413); Wasserhaushaltsgesetz (BGBl. 1957, Part. I, p. 1110).

7. See Arzneimittelgesetz (BGBl. 1961, Part. I, p. 533); Handelsklassengesetz
(BGBl. 1951, Part, I, p. 970).

8. See Reichsabgabenordnung (Reichsgesetzblatt 1931, Part. I, p. 161) and excise
tax laws.

trust,[9] foreign trade,[10] bank loans,[11] shop closing hours,[12] retail trade[13] and all the rules which implement market regulations of the EEC.[14] The importance of the second area—traffic regulation—is best illustrated by the fact that there are over twice as many prosecutions for traffic violations as for violations of the ordinary criminal law.

HISTORY OF THE CODE

Essentially, the regulatory offense has been known for centuries.[15] In Germany, the Prussian Landrecht of 1794 drew a distinction between "real" criminal law and regulatory offenses (also called administrative or police offenses). For the latter, concrete damage was not essential, whereas actual harm was a necessary element of the criminal offense. This distinction did not work out well in practice and it does not appear in the German Penal Code of 1871; the liberal state, in full flower at the time did not have much need of regulation. Shortly afterwards, however, criminal and regulatory offenses again began to be distinguished. Numerous drafts for a new penal code urged their separation. But, in fact, the current Code of Regulatory Offenses derives from another source. During the early forties a special kind of regulatory offense had been created as part of legislation imposing controls on the economy. After World War II this development continued and resulted in the introduction in 1952 of a first Code of Regulatory Offenses which included sanctions for all the regulatory offenses contained in various separate laws. Using this Code as a starting point, the legislature continued to separate criminal and regulatory sanctions and to expand the scope of the latter. This rapid extension of regulatory sanctions and the intention to extend them even further to other areas, made it necessary that the Code be extensively rewritten; and the

9. Gesetz gegen Wettbewerbsbeschraenkungen (BGBl. 1966, Part. I, p. 37).

10. Aussenwirtschaftsgesetz (BGBl. 1961, Part. I, p. 481).

11. Gesetz ueber das Kreditwesen (BGBl. 1961, Part. I, p. 881).

12. Gesetz ueber des Ladenschluss (BGBl. 1956, Part. I, p. 875).

13. Gesetz ueber die Berufsausuebung im Einzelhandel (BGBl, 1957, Part. I, p. 1121).

14. European Market Organization for Agricultural Products.

15. For the Anglo-American law, see Starrs, supra, note 3.

new Code of Regulatory Offenses was finally brought into force in 1968.[16]

BASIC PRINCIPLES OF THE REGULATORY OFFENSE

From a theoretical point of view,[17] the crucial problem in connection with regulatory sanctions is the matter of distinguishing them from civil and especially from criminal sanctions. Since the Code of Regulatory Offenses does not define particular violations in detail, the obvious solution of this problem is simply in terms of the character of the sanction itself and indeed §1 of the Code uses the character of the sanction to distinguish regulatory offenses from other violations of law. If the legislature prescribes a certain distinctive sanction for certain prohibited behavior, that behavior will be considered to constitute a regulatory offense. The distinctive sanction attached to regulatory offenses is called *Geldbusse* (literally "monetary repentance"), which will be translated herein as "penalty." It is opposed to the *Geldstrafe* (literally "monetary punishment"), the criminal fine imposed for criminal offenses by the Penal Code or by some collateral law. It should be noted that the Code of Regulatory Offenses does not include deprivation of liberty as a first-order sanction. Nonetheless, the complex problem of distinguishing between regulatory and criminal offenses continues to exist for the legislature and is presented to the courts in the form of constitutional questions.

The problem of the distinction between regulatory and criminal offenses has long been a subject of controversy. At one time, the central question was whether there really is any essential distinction between them at all. There once was a strong tendency to answer by saying that the difference is only quantitative.[18] Later, most authors came to acknowledge that there is a distinction. One approach was to separate the two kinds of offenses according to the legal interests protected.[19] Criminal offenses are characterized by direct injury or danger to particularized legal interests,

---

16. BGBl. 1968, Part. I, p. 481.

17. For the empirical perspective, see the concluding section of this paper.

18. See Welzel, "Der Verbotsirrtum im Nebenstrafrecht," *Juristenzeitung* 1956, p. 238 et seq.

19. This started with Feuerbach, *Lehrbuch des peinlichen Rechts* §22 et seq.

while regulatory offenses are minor violations of the external order of the community and are only indirectly related to specific protected legal interests. Another approach, opposed to this external one, relies on a rather more material criterion for the distinction between criminal and regulatory offenses. According to this theory, the criminal law is based on a preexisting socioethical order whereby behavior is regarded as wrongful even without legal proscription. The regulatory offense, by contrast, would not be regarded as ethically wrong per se but only becomes so because of legislative decision.[20] Obviously, this distinction is simply the *mala in se-mala prohibita* distinction familiar in Anglo-American law[21] and naturally the objections which have been raised against this theory in Germany are the same ones which are familiar in the United States. The basic objection is that a distinction in these terms solves nothing but only shifts the problem to the equally difficult task of saying what does and does not constitute part of the preexisting socioethical order. Now, the majority of writers agree that for most of the offenses contained in these two groups—or at most for the hard core of each—a distinction is nevertheless possible on the basis of general criteria drawn particularly from the hierarchy of values embodied in the West German Constitution.

If a given case does not clearly fall within the one group or the other, its proper classification must be left to the legislature. This is especially true with respect to borderline cases where evaluative criteria are constantly changing. It makes no difference that there may be historically, over the long term, a change in the criteria by which even supposedly hard core cases are evaluated.[22] For the present time this evaluation is contained in the Constitution.[23]

The Code has been constructed on this premise. Although there is a significant difference between regulatory and criminal

---

20. This theory has been developed by M. E. Mayer, *Rechtsnormen und Kulturnormen*, p. 16 et seq. (1903).

21. See Hall, supra, note 1, p. 337 et seq.

22. See Hall, supra, note 1, p. 340 et seq.

23. German Federal Constitutional Court, *Entscheidungen des Bundesverfassungsgerichts* (BVerfG) 22, p. 78 et seq., *Neue Juristische Wochenschrift* (NJW) 1967, p. 1219; BVerfG 27, p. 18 et seq., NJW 1969, p. 1619 et seq.

law, the former is considered to be part of the criminal law, as that term is used in the Constitution. Constitutional provisions reaffirming traditional principles of criminal law are regarded as referring to all sanctioned behavior historically part of the criminal law,[24] including regulatory offenses. Thus constitutional safeguards with respect to both substantive criminal law and criminal procedure serve to protect the perpetrator of a regulatory offense. Articles 92, 97 and 101 of the Federal Constitution set out the accused's right to due process of law before an impartial and independent judge. Article 103, para. 1, provides for the right to a judicial hearing and Article 103, para. 2, adopts the principle of *nullum crimen nulla poena sine lege,* i.e. the principle that conduct may not be subjected to sanction unless it has been expressly declared to be wrong by law prior to the pertinent act. This principle also prohibits the imposition of sanctions by virtue of judge-made law or by means of analogy. Another safeguard, especially interesting from the point of view of Anglo-American law, concerns the requirement of what German law calls "guilt," which is more or less the equivalent of *mens rea.*[25] The German Federal Constitutional Court has declared that every sanction involving penal elements must be based on *mens rea* and has applied this requirement *expressis verbis* to regulatory offenses.[26] Penal or quasi-penal sanctions imposed without guilt violate the *Rechtsstaatsprinzip* (literally "principle of the legal state") and also Article 2, para. 1, of the Constitution which guarantees the free development and freedom of action of the individual person. These statements by the court have put an end to debate concerning the requirement of guilt except for the academic argument which relates to the problem of presumptions of guilt, which has not been resolved in this context.[27] On the other hand, the Constitution is taken to permit the prosecution of regulatory offenses when initiated in the first instance by the relevant administrative agency rather than by the public prosecu-

24. Federal Constitutional Court, loc. cit., note 23.

25. BVerfG 20, p. 333, NJW 1967, p. 195 et seq., Kadish and Paulsen, *Criminal Law and its Process* 100 (1969).

26. BVerfG 9, p. 167, NJW 1959, p. 519.

27. See supra notes 25 and 26.

tor, provided the offender is accorded the right to object to this procedure and to be tried in the courts.[28]

With regard to the sanction itself, we have mentioned that the Code distinguishes between the criminal fine and a penalty. The penalty, unlike the criminal fine, is not entered as part of one's criminal record. In the case of an uncollectable penalty, there is no substituted punishment as there is in the Penal Code, but a kind of ethically neutral deprivation of liberty. The most significant change contained in the new Code with respect to the basic orientation of the law of sanctions is that the character of the regulatory sanction is now very different from that of the penal sanction. It is sufficient to say that German penal law, deeply rooted in German idealistic philosophy, finds the justification for punishment in the traditional concepts of retribution and penitence. Historically, however, more rationalistic aims have been incorporated in the criminal law and through amendments, the Penal Code has become a mixture of different penal theories. Although there is a definite tendency towards a more rationalistic conception of criminal law, even the new General Part of the Penal Code which will become effective in October 1973[29] still adheres essentially to a mitigated form of retributive sanction. This position is usually justified not only in terms of the assumption of free will on the part of the normal perpetrator, but also by the idea that criminal behavior deserves moral reprobation. For the vast area of regulatory offenses, this latter concept has been abandoned. The regulatory sanction does not imply a moral judgment; it is ethically neutral.[30] While the practical impact of this delineation is not wholly obvious because the average person does not much care about the ethical significance, the label, attached to the payment he has to make, it does represent an important step in the development of the law of sanctions as a whole. The penalty is still repressive but it serves the rationalistic purpose of making sure that a specific order is obeyed, of guarding

---

28. BVerfG supra, note 23.

29. BGBl. 1969, Part. I, p. 717.

30. See The Explanatory Preamble to the Draft Code, p. 27, Bundestagsdrucksache V/1269.

against even slight infringements of more important legal interests and of depriving the offender of an illegally obtained profit.

CONTENTS OF THE CODE

This paper can only deal, of course, with the leading issues raised by the Code's 112 sections ("paragraphs" in German legal usage).

The Code is divided into two main parts. The first part contains general provisions with regard to substantive law—more specifically, a set of basic doctrines similar to the General Part of the Penal Code. We find here provisions dealing with the territorial application of the Code (§4), general prerequisites for imposition of the regulatory sanction (§5 et seq.), the penalty itself (§13 et seq.), the concurrence of offenses (§15 et seq.), confiscation (§18 et seq.), corporate liability (§26), the statute of limitations (§27 et seq.) and finally a few definitions of particular offenses (§31 et seq.). Particular offenses are normally defined in special administrative or economic laws apart from the Code, both because of their vast number and because of the necessity to continually adjust them to keep abreast of rapid social and economic change.

The second part of the Code deals with procedure in regulatory cases beginning with the power of prosecution (§35 et seq.) and going on to general procedural provisions (§46 et seq.), preliminary decisions (§65 et seq.), objections to such decisions and trial (§67 et seq.), appeals (§79 et seq.), the independence of regulatory and criminal proceedings (§81 et seq.), the finality of judgments and post-conviction remedies (§84 et seq.), collateral sanctions (§87 et seq.), execution of decisions (§89 et seq.) and costs and expenses (§105 et seq.). In the following discussion of the main issues posed by the Code, we shall largely follow the order of the Code itself.

Substantive Law

"Mixed Offenses"

The so-called mixed offenses are those which lie close to the borderline between regulatory and criminal law. According to the Code, the evaluation of a particular offense as regulatory or criminal is a matter for the legislature and does not depend on the material substance of the offense.

There are two kinds of mixed offenses. With regard to so-called "real" mixed offenses the law provides only in a very general way for the classification of particular offenses as regulatory or criminal. This approach is questionable because the discretionary power which it vests in the authorities may violate the principle of *nullum crimen sine lege*. Moreover, the precise criteria according to which an offense is classified will not be known to the perpetrator in advance and this means his behavior may be deemed criminal because of circumstances of which he is unaware. This result is objectionable in terms of the guilt-oriented philosophy of German criminal law. The legislature, therefore, has avoided the creation of any new "real" mixed offenses and they are not dealt with in the Code. The older "real" mixed offenses (e.g. §3 of the Code of Economic Offenses[31]) carry their own criteria for classification.

The "real" mixed offense has to be distinguished from the so-called "fictitious" mixed offense. These are cases involving two different offenses; the basic offense is a regulatory violation while in its aggravated form it may also constitute a criminal offense. For example, in connection with the law regulating advertisements for drugs,[32] the basic (regulatory) offense is made out by a showing of negligent conduct while the aggravated (criminal) offense requires that the same behavior on the part of the accused must have been intentional. To these offenses the objections described above do not really apply and there is no need to make particular provision for these cases in the Code.

Federal Legislative Power

Section 2 of the Code establishes federal legislative power with respect to general rules governing regulatory offenses, including those offenses which have been promulgated by state laws. This is important because most of these offenses are indeed created by state legislation. This federal power has been affirmed by the

---

31. Wirtschaftsstrafgesetz (BGBl. 1954, Part. I, p. 175).
32. Heilmittelwerbegesetz (BGBl. 1965, Part I, p. 604).

Federal Constitutional Court[33] as a part of the power to enact penal law conferred by Article 74 (5) of the Constitution, notwithstanding the differences between regulatory and criminal offenses.

Applicability of Provisions of the Penal Code

Since regulatory law is part of the larger field of criminal law, the rules and doctrines of the Penal Code might have been made generally applicable to regulatory offenses. The Code of Regulatory Offenses adopts the method of self-contained rules and doctrines, resolving problems without cross-references to the Penal Code, despite the fact that the rules contained in the two codes are partially identical. In the course of developing regulatory offenses, doctrines different from those of the Penal Code and stemming from the special needs of regulatory law came to be included in special administrative legislation. The comprehensive revision of the Penal Code, in progress at the time, brought to light new ideas about the law of sanctions which had not yet been finally incorporated into the Penal Code when the Code of Regulatory Offenses was enacted. As a result it was necessary in the new Code to set out rules and doctrines explicitly in order both to refine and coordinate the various statements contained in specific administrative laws and to make use of ideas which had been developed in the course of the penal code revision.

The Uniform Perpetrator Concept

Where several persons participate in criminal activity, German criminal law distinguishes between co-principals and the so-called mediate principal. The latter includes what in American law would be considered, on the one hand, cases of crime committed through an innocent agent and, on the other, cases of accessoryship before and during the fact. Accessoryship after the fact is not regarded in German law as a form of complicity in the true sense of the term. These distinctions which are not unlike those drawn by the Common Law, have led to a host of difficulties in particular cases and have inspired a lengthy and acrimonious controversy which is still raging.

---

33. Loc. cit. supra, note 23.

To avoid this sort of controversy, §9 of the Code of Regulatory Offenses abolished these distinctions and declared that all persons concerned in the commission of an offense are principals. This uniform perpetrator concept is in line with the tendency of American law.[34] In Germany this innovation sparked a new round of controversy. It was questioned whether the new solution is, on the whole, any better than the traditional one.[35] The General Part of the new German Penal Code[36] has not followed the approach of the Code of Regulatory Offenses because the uniform perpetrator concept has not been considered an appropriate one with respect to criminal offenses. According to the Code, it is not essential to formally categorize the several participants in an offense. Instead there is supposed to be an assessment, for sentencing purposes, of the contribution of each participant which will take into account the actual extent of his participation.

Unification of the Law of Regulatory Offenses

A number of important substantive issues are dealt with in the Code of Regulatory Offenses, mainly in an effort to unify disparate rules scattered among various administrative statutes.

This is particularly true with respect to the principal regulatory sanction, the penalty. If one compares the criteria for sentencing contained in the Penal Code with those contained in the Code of Regulatory Offenses (§13 et seq.), one sees a shift in the basic premises of the two codes.[37] While in criminal law the chief emphasis is on ascertaining the perpetrator's guilt, the Code of Regulatory Offenses mainly stresses the violation itself, i.e. the external aspects of the alleged perpetrator's conduct. At the same time, the relative unimportance of regulatory offenses is reflected by the sanction imposable for them, which ranges from five to one thousand DM. In purchasing power this is the Ger-

34. See Model Penal Code Tent. Draft No. 1 (1953), App., Statutory Treatment of Complicity, 40-41.

35. Particularly Cramer, "Die Beteiligung an einer Zuwiderhandlung nach §9 OWiG," NJW 1969, p. 1929 et seq.; Dreher, "Plaedoyer fuer den Einheitstaeter im Ordnungswidrigkeitenrecht," NJW 1970, p. 217.

36. Zweites Gesetz zur Reform des Strafrechts, BGBl. 1969, Part. 1, p. 717.

37. See our discussion of the "Basic Principles of the Regulatory Offense," *supra*.

man equivalent of $2.50 to $500. However, the Code permits special laws to exceed this maximum limit, mainly in the field of economic regulation. The German antitrust law, for example, provides for a maximum penalty of 300,000 DM (about $150,000).

In §13 (2), the Code settles a delicate issue. It provides that the overall economic position of the offender must be taken into consideration, but that it is to have no bearing on the amount of the penalty imposed in cases involving minor offenses. Consequently, the millionaire and the impecunious student must pay the same penalty for a relatively insignificant traffic violation. This is to enable the sanction to be imposed swiftly and efficiently—a result which is thought to be particularly desirable in connection with common traffic infractions which have accordingly been defined along with their corresponding penalties in a somewhat categorical manner. The situation is one in which the principle of material justice must yield to the demands of practicality. Under §13 (4) a penalty may exceed the maximum amount specified if that is necessary to deprive the offender of an illegally acquired profit. This provision is directed at certain economic offenses and is of great importance in this field.

Provisions of law concerning confiscation also required unification because they had previously been inserted sporadically and with variations in content, in different administrative statutes. Confiscation is, for the most part, a collateral consequence, i.e. it is imposed in addition to a penalty. Predominantly a measure of safety, it aims at the protection of society and of the legal order. But where the confiscated object belongs to the offender himself, it assumes the character of a sanction. Here the legislature was able to use the provisions developed in connection with the revision of the Penal Code. For purposes of §18 et seq., the principle of commensurate reaction is especially important, although it also has a bearing on the entire regulatory process and, for that matter, on the whole area of public law. This principle embodies the notion that the public reaction to particular conduct should not be disproportionate to the offense. Where several different sanctions are available, the State must choose the one that will achieve its objectives in the least onerous manner.

Other significant provisions in the Code deal with regulatory offenses committed by corporations.[38] Section 19 of the Code covers liability for the conduct of another, particularly of a corporation; §33 imposes sanctions for violations of the obligation to exercise control and is aimed at violations on the part of the managerial agents of a corporation; §26 contains rules for the imposition of corporate liability. These provisions mainly concern violations of economic regulations. As a consequence of industrialization and the concomitant development of the corporate form in the economic system, such regulations had become more and more numerous in particular regulatory statutes prior to enactment of the Code. The German Penal Code of 1871 took almost no notice of crimes committed by corporations. Despite a great number of amendments to the Code since that time, this situation has not greatly changed. Such abstention from the imposition of corporate criminal liability was probably a consequence not only of the systemic problems which would otherwise be posed but was also based on ideological considerations. At least in the field of regulatory law, an effort has now been made to resolve these problems. The whole notion of legal prescriptions directed at legal entities as opposed to natural persons represents a new departure for the German law of sanctions. The imposition of sanctions on corporations which has long been traditional in Anglo-American law is practically blasphemous in German doctrine as a result of the requirement of guilt. Such sanctions have become possible in Germany only by construing them as collateral consequences of the sanctions imposed on natural persons. This solution has, however, led to practical difficulties in specific cases.

It very often happens that the obligations created by a regulation are imposed only on certain persons, e.g. only the person who owes a tax has the obligation to pay it, only the person who imports or exports goods incurs duties under the foreign trade laws, etc. But in modern industrial society the division of labor not

---

38. See generally for regulatory offenses by corporations, H. Demuth and T. Schneider, "Die besondere Bedeutung des Gesetzes ueber Ordnungswidrigkeiten fuer Betrieb und Unternehmen," *Betriebs-Berater* 1970, p. 642 et seq.

infrequently results in a split between activity and liability. For corporations this split is an absolute economic necessity. Ordinarily, if one who is not personally liable acts for another and violates a regulation directed to that other person, he would not be subjected to the sanction provided for a breach of the regulation. But §10 is aimed at filling the gap this creates with respect to the activities of high-ranking managerial agents and of agents who are authorized to discharge, on their own responsibility, a duty imposed on the owner of a business, where they act within the scope of their employment and on behalf of the business or its owner. Section 10 explicitly refers to the factual position of the agent; it does not matter whether the authorization to act is legally valid or not. Section 33 deals with the relatively disputed problem which arises in ascertaining the liability of the owner or high managerial agent of a business for regulatory as well as criminal violations of duties imposed on the owner or the corporation where the violations occur in the course of operating the business and where it was possible to prevent them. The actual scope of this provision is somewhat limited because it mostly involves cases in which a duty of performance is imposed. We may conclude that the doctrine of omissions in the German law of sanctions generally leads to holding that the addressee of a legal duty is responsible for violations committed by another person.

As to corporate liability which is set out in §26, it would be presumptuous for a German lawyer to speak at any length about the general background and purposes of a phenomenon which has been so well explored during the course of its comparatively long history in Anglo-American law. In Germany, corporate liability presents a constitutional problem because of the previously mentioned principle of guilt. But the Federal Constitutional Court has held it sufficient if the requirement of guilt is satisfied with respect to the agent, for whose guilt the corporation may be consequently liable.[39] Moreover, corporate liability presents theoretical problems. This sort of vicarious liability on the part of a corporation based on the guilt of the agent is possible

---

39. Loc. cit., supra, note 25.

in the German system only because the regulatory sanction is not taken to imply moral disapproval. According to German doctrine, a corporation itself cannot act, so there is a lack of conduct which is a basic prerequisite for the imposition of sanctions. Although this problem could be circumvented in the same way the problem of guilt has been circumvented, the legislature believed that it was forced to construe the sanction imposed on a corporation as collateral to the principal sanction imposed on the agent. Thus the Code remains within the confines of traditional legal doctrine which does permit collateral measures to be imposed although they do not comply with the prerequisites required with respect to principal sanctions—as is the case, for instance, with confiscation of a person's property. It is quite obvious that this solution does not reflect the real conditions and purposes of corporate liability. The practical operation of this provision is clearly impaired by its somewhat contrived character.

The explanatory preamble to the draft Code[40] states that the purpose of §26 is to guarantee that the economic activities of corporations and natural persons shall be treated equally. Although this guarantee represents a progressive step, it has not recognized that corporations may have to be treated even more severely than natural persons because of their greater impact on all sectors of social life.

According to §26, corporations are liable both for regulatory and for criminal offenses committed by their agents but the only sanctions available for use against a corporation are those contained in the regulatory arsenal, namely, the penalty. But the offenses for which corporate liability is specified in §26 extend only to those committed by high-ranking managerial agents, which roughly speaking means members of the board of directors. Other agents, even those with considerable authority in the corporation, are not included. It would have been preferable here to follow the American example by which corporate liability may arise out of the activity of practically any corporate agent but is kept within reasonable confines by other criteria.[41]

---

40. Loc. cit., supra, note 30.
41. See Sec. 20.20, 2c of the New York Penal Law.

Of course §26 does restrict the liability of the corporation by insisting that the agent must have acted within the scope of his employment and on behalf of the corporation. The agent's offense must also be in breach of a duty imposed on the corporation or be intended for the profit of the corporation.

The aforementioned notion of corporate liability as a collateral sanction is vitiated, to some extent, by §26 (4). This provision provides for an independent sanction against the corporation in certain areas. Although this provision does not require that corporate liability be predicated on the actual imposition of sanctions against a natural person, it retains the other prerequisites of §26. Such independent liability of the corporation arises where the agent cannot be prosecuted for reasons of fact, as opposed to reasons of law. Thus independent liability will arise where the individual agent has not been caught, or the judge forebears imposing a sanction on him, or the prosecutor in his discretion decides not to prosecute. This independent proceeding may not be maintained, however, where the agent cannot be prosecuted because of legal obstacles such as the expiration of the statutory period of limitation. This is another effect of the legislature's interpretation of corporate liability as a collateral sanction which considerably impairs its operation. Still another significant gap in the law is created by the fact that §26 does not cover the *GmbH und Co KG.* The result is what some authors call a "penalty-oasis." The *GmbH und Co KG,* which is the most popular of the new economic entities, is an unlimited company with a limited liability company *(GmbH)* as a partner. The manager of the *GmbH* is not, strictly speaking, an agent of the *GmbH und Co KG,* although he regularly dominates both companies.

The penalty specified in §26 involves a maximum of 100,000 DM (about $50,000). It is possible, however, under §13 (4), to impose a sanction in excess of this maximum if it is necessary to do so in order to confiscate an illegal profit acquired by the corporation.

Procedure

In describing the procedural sections of the Code, it seems preferable to adopt the arrangement of the Code itself, which generally follows the successive stages of a regulatory prosecution from its initiation to the execution of the sanction.

The procedural part of the Code follows the same general lines as the German Code of Criminal Procedure. There are necessary differences derived from the different nature of the substantive law involved since the Code of Regulatory Offenses deals with violations of relatively minor importance which lack the stigma incurred in the criminal law. Naturally it will not be possible to describe the German law of criminal procedure in detail and to compare it with American law. However, given the similarity of procedural problems in both countries and the presentation of the different stages of the prosecution in their actual order, it is hoped that the reader will not find it too difficult to understand the following comments.

Power of the Administrative Agency to Prosecute and Sanction

According to §35, it is the administrative agency which is primarily authorized to prosecute and to impose sanctions for regulatory offenses. The public prosecutor and the courts have this power only if it is expressly conferred by law. The police have only investigatory functions although these may be quite important. However, the prosecutor who is investigating a criminal case must do so in all respects. If his criminal investigation reveals that a regulatory offense has been committed, he is also authorized to prosecute the regulatory offense (§40). On the other hand, the administrative agency must submit a case to the prosecutor whenever there is evidence of a criminal offense having been committed (§41). The prosecutor may take over a case whenever there is a connection between a criminal offense being prosecuted by him and a regulatory offense being handled by the administrative agency (§42).

General Procedural Rules

The procedural part of the Code is not a complete codification of the law governing regulatory proceedings. Therefore, §46 (1) states that provisions contained in the Code of Criminal Procedure shall be taken to apply, in an analogous manner, to regulatory proceedings. Since the Code of Criminal Procedure is an intricate piece of codification, it is often difficult to say precisely how its provisions should apply to such proceedings. It may be helpful to begin with those rules of criminal procedure that are not applicable. The Code itself, in §46 (3), explicitly mentions certain rules which do not apply in regulatory proceedings. It specifically excludes certain encroachments on personal liberty which may be justified in criminal investigations but which have no place in connection with relatively unimportant regulatory offenses. Detention for the purpose of inquiring into a defendant's mental state is absolutely prohibited. Nor do the provisions of the Code of Criminal Procedure relating to arrest apply in regulatory proceedings. Only preliminary detention without a warrant limited to the identification of the suspect is possible under certain conditions. One such situation is where the offense has been committed in the presence of the officer (§54). The seizure of mail and telegrams in the course of a regulatory investigation is excluded. Bodily examination of the suspect is restricted mainly to blood tests, which are of great importance in the field of traffic offenses. Only a judge is ordinarily authorized to order a blood test although it may be ordered by the prosecution where there is danger in delay. In cases of a traffic offense, however, a blood test may be ordered by police officers who are specially authorized to do so.

The regulatory process is controlled by certain doctrines or maxims of procedure. The most significant of these maxims will be discussed below.

In this respect the most characteristic trait of a regulatory prosecution is the discretion allowed to the administrative agency and the prosecutor (§47 (1)). This wide discretion, which is not generally characteristic of German criminal procedure, is comparable to the discretion conferred on prosecutors in American law. In ordinary German criminal procedure, the discretionary power of the prosecutor is minimal. Discretion in this context refers not only to the initiation but also to the mode of prosecution. For instance, the investigation of regulatory offenses is not circumscribed by the strict rules applicable in criminal prosecutions. Such a difference is justified if one considers the relative unimportance of regulatory offenses. This distinction also allows the prosecuting agency a certain flexibility in dealing with mass violations. During the trial stage, discretion to dismiss the charges is vested in the judge but he requires the consent of the prosecutor to do so (§75 (2)), unless pursuant to §75 the prosecutor does not take part in the trial. A special problem has arisen in cases of dismissal as result of the ancillary question of who is to bear the expenses of prosecution. In practice, trial judges very often try to condition dismissal of the charges on the defendant's waiver of any claim to recoup his costs. This is an instance of minor plea bargaining, which is clearly illegal under German law.

The maxim or doctrine of simplification of procedure is another characteristic of regulatory prosecutions and is opposed to the guiding principle of German criminal procedure which, through a rigorous network of rules designed to safeguard the defendant, generally excludes summary proceedings. Regulatory procedure, given the nature of the offenses involved, constitutes a prototypical case of summary process. The principal point to be mentioned in this connection is that if neither prosecution nor offender object, the court may decide a regulatory case without holding an open or "main" trial (§72). If a main trial is held, the offender is not, in principle, obliged to be present although the judge may order a personal appearance should he deem it necessary (§73 (2)). The prosecution need not be present at the main trial either (§75 (1)). In general, a judge is not overly restricted in the gathering of evidence. These matters are all regulated differently in criminal procedure.

Preliminary Procedure

The preliminary procedure begins with the initiation of an investigation and ends with a penalty order or with dismissal of the charges. Investigations are initiated by the appropriate administrative agency (§35). Their knowledge of a putative regulatory offense may derive from the police, their own activities, a private person or the prosecutor. Investigations are handled by the agency itself or by the police acting on its behalf.

In investigating regulatory offenses, the police largely have the same powers and duties that they have in criminal investigations (§53), although it is necessary to keep in mind the particular restrictions on regulatory investigations mentioned above.

The offender has a right to be heard prior to issuance of the penalty order. But he need not be heard orally. The requirement of a hearing, set out in §55, is quite regularly satisfied by sending the offender a form which is supposed to be filled out.

There is no doubt that the offender has a right to counsel at all stages of the process. This right is specified in §137 of the Code of Criminal Procedure and is made applicable by virtue of the aforementioned provision of §46 of the Code of Regulatory Offenses. In criminal cases an accused must be informed of his right to counsel prior to his first interrogation by the judge, prosecutor or police (§§136 (1), 163a (3) and (4), Code of Criminal Procedure). But the duty to inform an accused of his right to counsel does not obtain at the regulatory level (§55 (2)). It is acknowledged, however, that in complicated regulatory cases the offender does have to be informed of his right to counsel. One should note that in both criminal and regulatory cases if the rights of an accused person are infringed during the course of investigation, German procedure does not, as a general matter, impose an exclusionary rule which would prevent the use of tainted evidence. In these instances, the offender is instead restricted to a remedy directed at the illegal measure itself. An exception is the rule excluding coerced confessions, set out in §136a of the Code of Criminal Procedure, which is applicable in regulatory proceedings.

If the administrative agency concludes that the offense has been sufficiently proved, a penalty order is issued. The penalty order must comply with certain formal requirements set out in §66; it must contain a legal and factual description of the offense, a statement of the available evidence and a notice with regard to the offender's right to object to the order. A penalty order will be void only if it is seriously deficient; a serious deficiency exists, for example, if the order is issued by an agency which is completely without power or authority to do so. All other deficiencies become relevant only if the offender objects to the order.

In addition to the ordinary regulatory procedure which culminates, upon proof of an offense, in the issuance of a penalty order, §56 et seq. provide for a kind of ticket system called *Verwarnungsverfahren* or "reprimand procedure." The administrative agency and the police are granted authority to administer a reprimand. By such a procedure the Code provides for an even swifter and more summary proceeding in cases of petty regulatory offenses, particularly minor traffic violations. This procedure is limited by the maximum amount of the reprimand, which is 20 DM (about $10). With this procedure, a sanction of this size tends to be typical for minor offenses. The reprimand will be valid only if the offender is informed of his right to object to it but nonetheless consents to this procedure and pays the amount of the reprimand immediately or shortly thereafter. If he does not consent and pay, the ordinary regulatory procedure will be initiated. If the offender consents to paying the reprimand, he is protected by the fact that further prosecution for the regulatory offense will be barred even though it turns out that issuance of the reprimand was legally invalid; for example, because the offense is too serious to be a subject of this kind of sanction. His payment does not act as a bar to prosecution of the act as a criminal offense.

Where the prosecutor is authorized to prosecute a regulatory offense, he must cooperate fully with the administrative agency that would otherwise have power to prosecute it. In such cases, the adminstrative agency is in the position and has the same investigatory powers that the police do in regulatory cases.

Objections to Penalty Orders

The offender may object to the penalty order and must do so within one week either in writing or by putting his objection on record at the administrative agency which issued the order (§67). When an objection is filed, the agency submits the case to the prosecutor for his consideration (§69). Jurisdiction over further proceedings lies in the magistrate's court in whose district the administrative agency has its seat. If the objection is untimely or in improper form, it will be rejected as inadmissible.

Main Trial

The main trial which is held upon an admissible objection generally follows the rules of the Code of Criminal Procedure (§71). There are, however, quite a few pecularities of procedure contained in the Code of Regulatory Offenses. Where the court considers a main trial unnecessary, it may render its decision in a written summary proceeding, provided that neither the prosecution nor the offender object (§72 (1)). Prior to rendering such a decision, the court must inform them of the possibility of a written summary proceeding and of their right to demand a main trial. Unless a main trial is held, the court may not overrule a penalty order to the offender's detriment (§72 (2)). This provision is thought to promote swifter and more summary nonoral proceedings.

The offender is not obliged to be present at the main trial of a regulatory offense (§73 (1)), whereas in criminal proceedings the opposite principle prevails. The judge is authorized to order the personal appearance of the offender if he thinks it appropriate. If the offender does not then appear or offer a valid excuse for his nonappearance, the judge may either take steps to enforce his order or simply overrule the offender's objection to the agency's penalty order (§74).

The prosecutor's participation is discretionary. But unless he is present at the main trial, a prosecutor may not object to dismissal of the charges by the judge. If the court thinks the prosecutor's appearance is necessary, he is notified (§75). The court may also allow the administrative agency an opportunity to take part in the main trial (§76).

Review

The sole procedure for review of regulatory proceedings is the so-called appeal at law. This is a review of the case for legal error. Unlike review in most criminal cases, questions of fact cannot be appealed. An appeal may be taken from a judgment rendered either after summary written proceedings or after a main trial involving oral proceedings. The Code enumerates the grounds for appeal in §79.

The principal grounds on which an appeal may be taken are that the penalty amounts to more than 200 DM (about $100), the offender's objection to the penalty order was overruled, or judgment was rendered without a main trial pursuant to §72 despite the offender's objection to this mode of proceeding. The developing case law equates this latter situation with the one in which the notice required by §72 is not given. Where a main trial has been held, the appeal at law may be permitted upon motion for one of two reasons: (1) a review of the judgment will contribute to the development of the law, or (2) review is necessary to assure uniform application of the law (§80). Although there is a general tendency in all branches of the German law of procedure to limit the availability of appeal by criteria such as these, it is nevertheless very difficult to state precisely what these criteria entail.[42]

The appellate court will consider a case without a further main trial where the judgment under review has itself been rendered after a main trial. It lies within the discretion of the appellate court to hear the case by means of oral proceedings. In cases where a judgment is reversed on appeal, the appellate court may either render judgment itself or remand the case to the magistrate's court.

Relationship of Regulatory and Criminal Offenses

The court is authorized to consider a case in terms of criminal as well as of regulatory law, even where the offender was only charged with a regulatory offense. The court may find the offender guilty of a criminal offense only if he has been previously advised of that possibility and afforded the opportunity to defend himself properly. In that event, the case will be governed by rules of criminal procedure (§81).

---

42. See H. Demuth and T. Schneider, "Die Zulassung der Rechtsbeschwerde nach §80 OWiG," NJW 1970, p. 1999 et seq.

Conversely, in criminal proceedings, a court will consider every case in terms both of regulatory and criminal offenses committed by the accused (§82).

These provisions reflect legislative consideration of the desirability of flexible interaction between regulatory and criminal charges so as to avoid conflicting decisions on the same facts, to promote economy of procedure, and to protect the offender himself.

Finality and Post-Conviction Remedies

Finality of judgment is disadvantageous to the accused in the sense that it precludes him from pursuing additional remedies but advantageous in the sense that it protects him from further prosecution. This is true both in regulatory and criminal proceedings.

Where a case has been fully litigated in the regulatory process and the judgment of a court rendered whether with or without an oral hearing, new regulatory or criminal charges concerning the case are excluded (§84). On the other hand, the finality of the penalty order of an administrative agency is limited and will only exclude further regulatory charges. New criminal charges concerning the same case are permitted. A finding of guilt with respect to these new criminal charges supersedes the penalty order (§86).

The sole means by which a final regulatory decision may be challenged is the so-called "resumption" or reopening of proceedings, which is governed in principle by the provisions of the Code of Criminal Procedure. Since it is an exception to the principle of finality, resumption is allowed only in a limited number of situations. It is primarily permitted where new facts or proofs are produced which were not available to the court at the original trial (§359 of the Code of Criminal Procedure). With respect to regulatory decisions, the grounds on which resumption is permitted have been further restricted, so far as the offender is concerned, in cases where the amount of the penalty is minor, but have been partly expanded for the prosecutor who may seek resumption of proceedings if criminal charges of a serious nature are subsequently found to be warranted (§85).

Execution of Orders and Judgments

Once a regulatory decision becomes final, it may be carried into execution. The execution of a penalty order is determined by the laws governing execution of administrative orders (§90). Judgments are executed according to the rules for the execution of criminal decisions set out in the Code of Criminal Procedure (§91). If a penalty is not paid, the court may order detention of the offender as a means of forcing him to pay his debt (unless he declares himself bankrupt). Detention for failure to pay a penalty may not exceed six months and may not be ordered a second time with respect to the same amount (§96). Juvenile courts may impose particular obligations on juvenile offenders in lieu of collecting a penalty (§98).

Costs and Expenses

The Code provides for payment of the costs and expenses of the administrative as well as the judicial phase of regulatory proceedings. In §46, it incorporates by reference the provisions of the Code of Criminal Procedure with respect to the costs and expenses of court proceedings. With respect to costs and expenses in the administrative phase (ending with issuance of a penalty order), the Code deals with the matter at greater length but comes up with a system very similar to that of the Code of Criminal Procedure.

AN EVALUATION OF THE CODE

The craftsmanship of the Code is excellent. Criticism of the Code has been directed more to points of detail and rarely to its craftsmanship as a whole. The points criticized mainly concern its adoption of the uniform perpetrator concept and its rules concerning corporate regulatory liability. The technique of frequent cross-reference to the Code of Criminal Procedure is entirely apt because of the similarity of regulatory and criminal procedure. The general exclusion from the Code of provisions regarding specific offenses is practically inevitable because of the vast number of such offenses and the need for rapid adaptation of the sanctions imposed on specific behavior to changing social and economic conditions.

Rather more criticism has been directed to the basic premises of the Code. Several authors deny, even *de lege lata,* that there is any qualitative difference between regulatory and criminal offenses and regard the characterization of regulatory offenses in the Code as a mere label which cannot change the essence of the offense.[43] They further contend that the regulatory penalty embodies all the purposes of the criminal fine. However, as shown above, it is possible and justifiable to distinguish between regulatory and criminal offenses and there is a difference between the penalty and the criminal fine. Another objection which has been raised, specifically with regard to traffic violations, is that the real aim of the Code is to cut all penalties to the same pattern and have them administered uniformly by administrative agencies which are under the thumb of the government.[44] It is contended that the whole Code is nothing more than an attempt to evade constitutional safeguards prescribed for criminal offenses and, particularly, the right to be punished only upon proper judicial proceedings. Nevertheless, the uniformity of sanctions in cases of large-scale violations is a legitimate legislative purpose which aims at assuring, within certain limits, not only formal equality of treatment for all offenders, but also the reasonably practical operation of the administrative system. The sort of computerized process that is becoming necessary in dealing with such offenses as traffic violations will only be possible with a uniform and schematized system of sanctions.

Another significant point which seems to me to be crucial has not received much consideration. This is the queston of whether there is a material distinction between the set of offenses for which regulatory sanctions are provided and the set of offenses subject to the criminal process. Economic offenses such as antitrust violations and environmental and many consumer protection offenses are classified as regulatory. On the other hand, insignificant offenses such as petty larceny and petty fraud are con-

---

43. See Tiedemann, "Literaturbericht, Nebenstrafrecht einschliesslich Ordnungswidrigkeitenrecht," *Zeitschrift fuer die gesamte Strafrechtswissenschaft* 1971, p. 800 et seq.

44. Mattes, "Die Problematic der Umwandlung der Verkehrsuebertretungen in Ordnungswidrigkeiten," *Zeitschrift fuer die gesamte Strafrechtswissenschaft* 1970, p. 25 et seq.

tained in the Penal Code. In form, this is not a problem that pertains to the Code of Regulatory Offenses itself because particular substantive offenses do not generally appear in the Code. But it is not possible to ignore this problem in discussion of the Code, even though it is true that apart from traffic violations, the decision concerning imposition of sanctions on particular varieties of undesirable behavior was taken by the legislature before the Code was enacted. It is well known, particularly in the United States, that those offenses which are characterized as regulatory are generally committed by white-collar offenders, while crimes such as petty larceny and petty fraud are typically committed by members of the lower social strata. This is, however, only one reason for the line between regulatory and criminal offenses being drawn where it is. There are certainly other reasons, such as the fact that the wrongfulness of economic violations is not yet rooted deeply enough in public consciousness. At this point, it may be sufficient to say that the classification of behavior as regulatory or criminal is ultimately determined by ideological criteria and not by rational or empirically proven considerations. This holds as well for what is often said about the preventive efficacy of sanctions whether in the field of regulatory or criminal offenses. Shifting numerous minor traffic violations from the criminal to the regulatory field does seem to represent unquestionable progress since retaining these offenses in the criminal law can only taint the concept of criminality, as do victimless crimes in general.

The Code's efficacy cannot be evaluated without drawing certain distinctions. It is essential for this purpose to distinguish the various goals of the Code on the one hand and different types of regulatory offenses on the other. In connection with mass violations of traffic regulations, the Code aimed at reducing the courts' caseloads and in this respect the Code has been successful.[45] It has also been successful in unifying and schematizing the sanctions in this area. This has been done by drawing up penalty schedules which are obligatory for the administrative

---

45. Gerhard Winters, "Erfahrungen mit dem Bussgeldverfahren aus der Sicht des Verkehrstrichters," Kraftfahrt und Verkehrsrecht 1969, p. 342; Arbeitskreis 6 des 10. Deutschen Verkehrsgerichtstags, loc. cit., 1972, p. 46.

agencies and which actually have provided guidelines for the courts although they are not strictly binding on the judges.

It is difficult to determine whether the regulatory penalty has a sufficiently deterrent effect. This is part of the broader problem of how far deprivation of liberty is necessary in order to prevent undesirable behavior and to what extent general deterrence is possible. It may suffice to simply mention a few empirical inquiries in connection with traffic offenses in Germany which suggest that prison sentences have no greater deterrent effect than mere monetary loss.[46]

Outside the area of traffic offenses, there are practically no empirical studies owing to the difficulties involved in uncovering the facts of offenses such as economic violations. Also, the effect of the decriminalization of certain areas rarely shows up in empirical studies. Apart from the fact that the deterrent effect of prison sentences is doubtful, a financial loss may be sufficient for general prevention in cases involving economic offenses if the amount is such as to have a real influence on an individual's economic calculations. What comes practically to a test case of this thesis is now being conducted in Germany in connection with penalty orders issued against the producers of synthetic fibres. The penalties imposed on several companies for antitrust violations have been close to 50 million DM ($25 million in purchasing power). In these cases the antitrust agency invoked the provision of §13 (4) of the Code which allows skimming off an illegally acquired profit. If there are further cases of this sort and if the penalties considerably exceed the gain to the offenders, we shall soon see whether penalties of this type are sufficient to effectively prevent violations of those interests which the law is designed to protect. This is a clear case because in the area of economic activity behavior is generally rationalistic. One might derive from such considerations about the potential preventive effect of regulatory sanctions, a new set of criteria for distinguishing between regulatory and criminal offenses. But at present there is no definitive answer to these questions.

---

46. G. Kaiser, *Verkehrsdelinquenz und Generalpraevention,* p. 400 et seq., (1970), citing a study by the Department of Justice of Baden-Wuerttemberg from 1964.

PART V

THE CONTRIBUTION
OF JEROME HALL

CHAPTER 15

A SYNTHETIC CRIMINAL LAW THEORY: JEROME HALL'S CONTRIBUTION TO THE AMERICAN CRIMINAL LAW SYSTEM*

G. O. W. MUELLER

Professor of Law, New York University

IT WAS JOHN HENRY WIGMORE who outlined the steps of scholarly proceeding in criminal law.[1] The steps according to Wigmore are:

1. The analytic process: "tracing the logical implications of general principles as revealed in specific cases," i.e. the case-study process.[2]
2. The historic process.[3]
3. The legislative process.[4]
4. The synthetic process, i.e. "the process of building up individual rules and principles into a consistent system—of being able to trace every rule backwards and upwards to its more and more general expressions and of harmonizing these. . . ."[5]

Common-law scholars, trained in case-analysis only, are naturally accustomed to the analytic method.[6] The synthetic process of

---

* Reprinted with permission of the publishers from G. O. W. Mueller, *Crime, Law and the Scholars*, London, Heinemann Educational Books Ltd., and Seattle, The University of Washington Press, 1969, pp. 209-214 and 290-292.

1. Wigmore, "Nova Methodus Discendae Docendaeque Jurisprudentiae," 30 *Harv. L. Rev.* 812 (1917).

2. Ibid. at 822.

3. Ibid. at 823.

4. Ibid., loc. cit.: a very disputable inclusion at this point.

5. Ibid. at 824.

6. For that matter, all the casebooks published after 1939 and before 1949 were analytically sound, some more so than others, but none was successful in synthesis: Harno's second edition (Albert J. Harno, *Cases and Materials on Criminal Law and Procedure*, 1939); Michael and Wechsler's (J. Michael and H. Wechsler, *Criminal Law and its Administration*, 1940); Hall and Glueck's second edition (L. Hall and

thought is often dismissed . . . with the epithet of "speculative jurisprudence!" But its time must come, if our law is ever to be soundly reconstructed; and legal education must provide for this in its methods.[7]

The writers and teachers who were active during these last thirty years may all have felt a desire to reach general conclusions and resolutions. While many worked at it, none succeeded until 1947, though Burdick came close to the goal. Only an insider could realize what was going on among criminal-law teachers at that time. For an outsider the situation appeared as dismal in 1944 as it had been in 1924 or in 1904. Thus, when a distinguished Argentinian criminal-law scholar visited the U.S.A. in 1944, he gave a blunt—and quite appropriate—lecture:

> A theory of penal law that does not succeed in building a system can neither aim at the dignity of a science, nor at the modest dignity of a university discipline.[8]
>
> I must express a certain measure of surprise, caused by the fact that in a country like the United States, of democratic feelings so deeply rooted, the University chair, with very few exceptions, should neither have exceeded the mere empiricism of the "case system," nor have noticed the theoretical importance of a solid structure of the general part of criminal law on the basis of a consciously applied method. . . . [I]f the chair aspires to the truly constructive disinterested and scientific function that guides and does not serve empiricism, there is no other method except the compilation of a system.[9]

But Jerome Hall, as early as 1941, by recalling the tradition of Hale, Blackstone, Livingston and Bishop, had recognized that "important progress in criminal law in its purely professional aspect, is inseparable from philosophic insight and scholar-

---

Sheldon Glueck, *Cases and Materials on Criminal Law*, 1940) ; Robinson's (J. J. Robinson, *Cases on Criminal Law and Procedure*, 1941) —an unusually good analytical book, but unsuccessful in the market; Waite's second edition (J. B. Waite, *Cases on Criminal Law and Procedure*, 1947) ; and Dession's (George H. Dession, *Criminal Law, Administration and Public Order*, 1948) .

7. Wigmore, *supra* n. 1, at 824.

8. Soler, "The Political Importance of Methodology in Criminal Law," 34 *J. Crim. L. and Crim.* 366, 367 (1944) .

9. Ibid. at 369.

ship."[10] Hall meant to put "philosophic insight and scholarship" to use in creating a "science of criminal law" which would accord with the best recognitions of sociology and stand firmly grounded in ethics. In 1947, the first blueprint of the science was before us: *General Principles of Criminal Law*.[11] The best evidence of the significance of this work is the fact that this was the first and, generally, has remained the only American criminal law treatise which is deemed worthy of citation in continental textbooks.

Case analysis of a mass of data reveals certain problems which faithfully recur and which on the whole have been accorded equal treatment. Thus, if infants and mentally diseased persons are excused from liability, while "normal" adults are not, the question naturally arises: what do infants and mentally diseased persons have in common that is not present in "normal" persons? Positively stated: there is something necessary for each crime found in all normal people, but not found in infants and mentally diseased persons. Using this type of analysis for assembling the raw materials of a structure, Hall could then proceed to synthesize them, and the outline of a certain structure of criminal law appeared. The structure incorporated components of three distinct varieties. One of these components, consisting of "the rules," or definitions of the various crimes, would correspond to the "special part" of a continental penal code. But whereas the "general parts" of continental codes contain only one further variety of propositions (an undifferentiated one, frequently intermingled with extraneous, e.g. procedural, propositions), Hall

---

10. Jerome Hall, "Prolegomena to a Science of Criminal Law," 89 *U. Pa. L. Rev.* 549 (1941), subsequently ch. 1 in *General Principles of Criminal Law* (1947, 2nd ed. 1960).

11. "The vast majority of reviews recognized the complete novelty of Hall's approach and acclaimed the book. The general opinion of the profession can best be gleaned by consulting several reviews of the second edition, particularly those of Gooderson, [1962] *Cambr. L. J.* 118, Lord Chorley, 25 *Mod. L. Rev.* 604 (1960), and Sir John Barry, 4 *Sid. L. Rev.* 28, 31 (1962), who called it "the most valuable synthesis, the most consistently erudite, constructive and civilized dissertation upon the philosophy and theory of criminal law it has been this reviewer's good fortune to read."

finds that "general propositions" are of two varieties, which he calls principles and doctrines. But at this point we should let Hall speak for himself, by quoting from a convenient summary recently published:

> By doctrines I mean such notions as those concerning mistake of fact and law, necessity, coercion, infancy, insanity, intoxication, solicitation, attempt and conspiracy. In order to have the substantive criminal law fully defined one needs to unite the special part with the doctrines. Having done so, and not until one has done that, one derives a complete definition of each crime. In sum, each crime has distinctive characteristics stated in the specific part, and general aspects stated in the doctrines.
>
> Principles are broader generalizations than doctrines. There you ascend to a higher level of abstraction and, viewing the fusion of the specific part and the doctrines, you ask: what are the common ideas which run through this whole field of criminal law? The answer, I suggest, is that there are seven fundamental ideas, i.e. principles, which permeate and unify this branch of law. They are (1) legality, (2) harm, (3) act (effort), (4) *mens rea,* (5) the concurrence of the *mens rea* with the act to form the conduct, (6) causation, that is, a causal relationship between the conduct and the harm, and (7) the punitive nature of the sanction. These are the seven basic principles which comprise the foundation of the criminal law. . . .
>
> The European scheme . . . fails to distinguish doctrines from principles. But doctrines differ from principles in very important ways. For example, the doctrine that an insane person does not commit a crime because he lacks the necessary capacity is surely a different kind of generalization from the requirement that there must be a *mens rea* in every crime, that there must be a harm, and so on. The specification of insanity as a qualification of the special part goes to the definition of a crime; it is essential to the correct legal definition of the specific crimes. But principles are much broader notions which may also be viewed as standing outside the positive law of crimes, serving as descriptive propositions of a criminal science. . . .
>
> If some insight into the formal side, the architecture, of the criminal law has been given, it need only be added that this has practical importance for the lawyer because he cannot be familiar with every crime in the whole catalogue. He may never have had any occasion in law school or elsewhere to study the crime of counterfeiting or treason or many other crimes. But if one understands the principles of criminal law, one has the tools to work with and to analyze any crime. If he

has this equipment he can ask, what is the relevant mental state in this crime, what is the harm, what conduct is required, what about the concurrence of the mental side with the conduct, and so on. The principles permit and require one to ask the correct questions about each crime. And, of course, so far as the relevance of this for constructing a science of criminal law is concerned, one has only to look at any book of physics to realize that most of the progress in the physical sciences is due to the formal side of those sciences. The laws of physics are organized into a system so that a mathematical physicist, for example, never goes into a laboratory. He works equations on paper and then the experimental physicist takes the theorist's conclusion and tests it in the laboratory. We shall never attain any such rigorous organization of criminal law, but that objective is nonetheless important.[12]

Hall's treatise was followed by a casebook[13] which soon gained acclaim as one of the most widely adopted teaching tools. But, for a while, Hall's colleagues remained aloof. To be sure, Hall's new theory—the first successful American synthesis of criminal law—was acclaimed, but there was no immediate rush to follow the lead. In 1953, six years after the *Principles,* the first casebook was published which followed Hall's suggestion of a synthesis of criminal law—Professor Snyder's *An Introduction to Criminal Justice* (1953). Professor Morrow wrote about the book:

> Professor Snyder has chosen, happily, in the opinion of this reviewer, to arrange his material so that general concepts affecting all criminal conduct will be studied thoroughly before any specific crimes are considered. This arrangement, consistent with that of European criminal codes and the more carefully planned codifications in this country, now seems well on its way to general acceptance.[14]

Thereafter, the idea became accepted that there is advantage in a theoretically sound approach, and that the theoretical approach should be given a try. Several scholars fell in line, though

---

12. Hall, "The Three Fundamental Aspects of Criminal Law," in *Essays in Criminal Science* 159, 160, 162-163 (ed. G. Mueller, 1961). This chapter is based on an article previously published at 8 *J. Crim. L.* 1 (Tokyo, 1957).

13. Jerome Hall, *Cases and Readings on Criminal Law and Procedure* (1949), Supplement (1963); now Hall and Mueller, *Cases and Readings on Criminal Law and Procedure* (2nd ed. 1965).

14. Morrow, Book Review, 6 *J. Legal Ed.* 132, 133 (1953).

none with as radical and thorough a switch to synthetic jurisprudence as Hall had proved feasible and necessary. By way of example, while Professor Perkins' casebook of 1952[15] still followed the more established line, in 1957 he switched to a theoretically well-formed organization,[16] as did Hall and Glueck in their second edition (1958),[17] and, to some extent, Paulsen and Kadish in their entirely new book.[18] But Harno, in his fourth edition, retained the traditional approach[19] and two other recent casebooks departed radically from either model.[20]

In the textbook market, too, the new theoretical orientation of American criminal-law scholarship became noticeable. For the first time in history, there are now two student texts which one can recommend to the students without whispering: Wingersky's *Clark and Marshall on Crimes* (6th rev. ed. 1958), and, particularly Perkins' *Criminal Law* (1957), the condensation of many years of sound and organized thinking.

Hall himself "did not stop at positing his theory, but he constantly endeavored to explain the concepts in terms of which the theory is stated. Thus, at various places, he had dealt with each of the principles: legality,[21] harm,[22] conduct,[23] *mens rea*,[24] con-

---

15. But, as may be recalled, it was this edition to which Roscoe Pound wrote the introduction in which he demanded that students should be given a "sound fundamental grasp of law principles." Pound, Introduction to Rollin M. Perkins, *Cases and Materials on Criminal Law and Procedure* XIV (1952).

16. Rollin M. Perkins, *Cases and Materials on Criminal Law and Procedure* (2nd ed. 1958).

17. Jerome Hall and Sheldon Glueck, *Cases on Criminal Law and Its Enforcement* (2nd ed. 1958).

18. Monrad C. Paulsen and S. H. Kadish, *The Criminal Law and Its Processes* (1962), combining the functional and the theoretical approach.

19. Albert J. Harno, *Cases and Materials on Criminal Law and Procedure* (4th ed. 1957).

20. Fred E. Inbau and Claude R. Sowle, *Cases and Comments on Criminal Justice* (1960), a good book, especially for those wishing to stress procedure more than substance, which has been inordinately slighted; Donnelly, Goldstein and Schwartz (1952).

21. Jerome Hall, *General Principles of Criminal Law* ch. 2 (1947, 2nd ed. 1960).

22. Ibid. at chs. 3 and 4, especially in terms of completed and inchoate harm, though the concept as such was briefly explained in Hall, *Cases and Readings on Criminal Law and Procedure* 45-46 (1949).

23. Hall, op. cit. *supra* n 21, *passim*, especially chs. 7-9.

currence,[25] causation,[26] and punishment.[27] In 1958 he published a series of new and old studies in the volume *Studies in Jurisprudence and Criminal Theory*."[28] In 1960 there appeared the completely revised and much enlarged second edition of the *General Principles.*

While Hall's is, thus, the first American theory of criminal law —and has consequently become the most important individual stimulus for future development—it is not likely to be the final theory. Many questions remain unanswered, and friendly divisions of opinion on the scope of Hall's seven principles will continue to exist, for instance, whether *mens rea* is to be included within the concept of causation, to what extent *mens rea* absorbs other aspects of the mental process, by which principles such doctrines as accessoryship or attempt are to be explained, etc. I should think that Professor Hall himself would wish lively discussions to ensue and to continue on such problems, in the hope of reaching the ultimate perfection of American criminal-law theory. At this moment it is of relatively little significance on what specific issues there exists a split of opinion among the theoreticians, for all such differences pale in the face of the fact that American criminal-law thinkers are faced and concerned with a theory, and that this theory is being debated, criticized and improved. That is the big news for America, a common-law nation hitherto hostile to theory.[29] Even if Hall should turn out to be wrong in every particular—and that does not seem very likely —history has already proved him right in general: The evolution-

---

24. Ibid. at chs. 5-6, 10-14; Hall, "Ignorance and Mistake in Criminal Law," 33 *Ind. L. J.* 1 (1957); Hall, "Ignorantia Legis," 28 *Rev. Int'l De Droit Pénal* 293 (1955).

25. Jerome Hall, *Cases and Readings on Criminal Law and Procedure* 70-73 (1949).

26. *Studies in Jurisprudence and Criminal Theory* ch. 10 (1958).

27. Hall, op. cit. *supra* n. 21, at ch. 15.

28. See Mueller, "Criminal Theory: An Appraisal of Jerome Hall's *Studies in Jurisprudence and Criminal Theory*," 34 *Ind. L. J.* 206 (1959).

29. That a similar development may well be taking place in England is attested to by the fact that Professor Glanville Williams, the most astute British criminal-law scholar since Bentham and Stephen, has now published the second edition of his *Criminal Law—The General Part* (2nd ed. 1961).

ary process of law in every civilized nation demonstrates that the road of law leads from case-law via theoretical scholarship to perfected codes, with various intermediate steps, frequently in the nature of casuistic codifications. Moreover, Hall stands corroborated by our own sages who, decades ago, felt the workings of this evolutionary process and framed their demands for an accelerated process of maturation by demanding a theory of law.

In view of the development toward a theory of crime and of criminal law it will become increasingly difficult for all but the country-schoolmaster counterpart of the American criminal-law teacher to persist in a purely casuistic and functional approach toward his subject.[30] At one time it was virtually the credo of criminal-law teachers—as of lawyers generally—that "general principles do not decide concrete cases." That time, I humbly suggest, is gone forever. A throng may still condemn criminal-law theory with the epithet "conceptualism," which has become a rather derogatory term with the functionalists and so-called realists. For a long time all conceptualism has been regarded as an unnecessary or even false feat of intellectual acrobatics. But conceptualism may be true or false. A concept which accurately portrays life itself is no more false or useless than a photograph which accurately portrays the object on what the camera was focused. Just as a photograph may be helpful to mind and memory, a concept may be equally or more so. False are only those concepts which mock or ignore the nature which they ought to portray.

> While we have long known that the number of principles and doctrines of our criminal law which are necessary for deciding concrete cases is considerably smaller than the number of appellate cases on record, it has only been in the middle of the twentieth century that we have begun to make an effort at culling them from the mass of the court reports. What we have found and learned is most encouraging, especially in light of the data which the natural scientists could make

---

30. The English, so it seems, have come to the same conclusion. Six years after Hall published his *General Principles*, Glanville Williams came out with his superb analytical treatise *Criminal Law—The General Part* (2nd ed. 1961), which, as Lord Chorley suggested, "provides in a number of ways an even clearer elucidation and is certainly a worthy rival to the American volume." Book Review, 25 *Mod. L. Rev.* 604 (1962).

available to us. On the whole, our courts have reached just conclusions, though more on hunch than by actual insight. Here we can pinpoint the task which confronts us in the late twentieth century. We must stop working with hunches—we must turn to systematic search. Yes, ours is an old and established system of law. On the whole we have done pretty well over the centuries in operating on hunches. But now is the time, now we have the means, to turn to scientifically sound operations. What in the past we merely felt, should now be expressed—ready for use by all. Hunches have led to only superficially adequate solutions. Scientific work calls for analysis and search in depth, for systematic exploration to find and express all that is knowable. We criminalists have an exciting voyage of discovery before us. We know less of crime today than Columbus knew of the surface of the earth in 1492: Only the contours and crude intrinsic qualities are as yet apparent to us.

The novelty of the mid-twentieth century and of Hall's *General Principles* is simply that of insight and systematization. But not just in criminal law, not just in public law, not just in law, but everywhere, we can see the change which takes place on the American scene: the transmutation of our mode of life from the do-it-yourself, happy-go-lucky, hit-or-miss attitude in public life and technology to one of thorough scientific and planned advance to ever greater and more certain achievements. But in criminal law, as elsewhere, we can always plan only on and with the factor of life itself, never without or against it. That is what we know today.[31]

---

31. This and the preceding two paragraphs are the concluding paragraphs of a major study constituting the writer's attempt to present a synthetic theory of criminal law, along the lines suggested by Hall. Mueller, "The Public Law of Wrongs—Its Concepts in the World of Reality," 10 *J. Pub. L.* 203 (1961).

CHAPTER 16

JEROME HALL AND LATIN AMERICAN LEGAL PHILOSOPHERS: AN OVERALL PERSPECTIVE

PEDRO R. DAVID

Professor of Sociology, University of Buenos Aires
Professor of Sociology, University of New Mexico

THERE ARE THREE PROMINENT Latin American scholars with whose work it seems pertinent to compare Hall's pioneer studies in the philosophy and the sociology of law: Miguel Reale of Sao Paulo (Brazil), Miguel Herrera Figueroa of Buenos Aires (Argentina) and Luis Recasens Siches of Mexico City (Mexico). In different ways, the Latin American scholars just mentioned have tried, contemporaneously with Hall, to construct integrative or tridimensional perspectives of the law.

HALL AND REALE

In 1960, on the occasion of the third National Congress of Philosophy which took place at Sao Paulo, Brazil, I compared in some detail the Integrative Jurisprudence of Hall and the Tri-dimensional Philosophy of Reale.[1]

I mentioned at the time that both for Hall and Reale, norm, value and fact, are not considered separate entities but are rather fused in a unified whole. For Hall, the moment of synthesis co-incides with the coalescence in human conduct of norms, facts and values. For Reale, these are three aspects of the same entity: a dialectical process not of negation and resolution as in the Hegelian perspective but a process of implication and polarity. This integration of fact, norm and value results in according a central place to the factual sciences of law. Hall calls for a hu-manistic legal sociology or an empirical science of law while

---

1. Pedro R. David, "Perspectivas de dos filosofias del Derecho Intergrativas Hall y Reale," *Anais do III Congreso Nacional de Filosofia,* São Paulo, Brasil, 1960.

Reale talks about legal history, sociology of law, legal psychology and legal ethnology.

Hall sees in his humanistic legal sociology an integration of the presently fragmented spectrum of the social sciences. He contends that the anthropology of law, political science and, of course, the sociology of law may actually constitute or be reconstructed to constitute a single social discipline.[2]

Both Hall and Reale have denounced the unilateralism of legal positivism, specifically its Kelsenian formulation, without ignoring its basic contributions.

Thus Reale says: "We take a contrary position to Kelsen's logical normativism . . . Kelsen will never accept our perspective, since for him, the jurist as such, there is only theory of science of law, in its logical normative validity, and this does not imply, except in a secondary way, analysis of social or axiological criteria to account for the distinctiveness of legal norms."

Hall[3] has insisted that Kelsen's methodological purity is contradicted in Kelsen's own work due to his insistence on seeing facts in the structure of the *Grundnorm*, his references to minimum efficacy as a condition of the validity of legal norms and in his allusion to physical coercion as a necessary ingredient of legal norms.

Both Reale and Hall stand against reduction of the concept of law to fact. Hall has argued very convincingly against Scandinavian and American Legal Realism. Reale has demonstrated that Duguit's social solidarity is not only a fact but a concept with axiological connotations and claims that Duguit has confused the notions of "is" and "ought."

As to the area covered by the empirical science of law, Hall asserts that legal sociology is a comprehensive subject with humanistic concerns. He has shown what this implies in his classic *Theft, Law and Society,* which is indeed one of the outstanding contributions of the present century to the whole field of the sociology of law. For Reale, the empirical sciences of law are not parallel to the normative ones; rather facts, values and norms are

---

2. Jerome Hall, *Comparative Law and Social Theory,* Baton Rouge, Louisiana State University Press, 1963, pp. 111-112.

3. *Ibid.,* pp. 55-57.

aspects of the same reality of the total phenomena of the law. In his theory, the actualization of legal values in the social order cannot be disregarded in studying the empirical conditions of law. The philosophical foundations of the integrative perspective of Hall or the tridimensionalism of Reale allow for the emergence of a new theoretical model of the social sciences which transcends the once prevalent dichotomy between "real" and "cultural" sciences. The two can be integrated to constitute a humanistic social science.[4]

Hall and Reale are both very much concerned with history as an essential element of the empirical science of law. For Reale, causal explanations are insufficient because society itself is established historically and, in consequence, its laws are beyond mere causal explanation, although sociologists are nonetheless prone to view social facts as things. The synthesis achieved by Reale and Hall does not end at the theoretical level. Each suggests ways to achieve harmony between the legal and the social order. A cultural legal history, Hall suggests, would deal not only with legal concepts but also with relevant social problems, values, contexts and functions. He later adds that "since existing institutions have grown from past ones, our knowledge of them is a correlative affair" and he concludes "that although events can be fully understood only if their general patterns are also considered, such general knowledge may supplement, but it cannot displace, historical knowledge."[5]

The relationship between law and meaningful political science is also very significant for Hall. Since societies are legal organizations, political science should be legally oriented. While the State's law must be studied, it is law as a distinctive form of conduct which is the core of political data. Political science as well as political theory which emphasize the ethical, practical side of politics, should be as precise as possible and this can be achieved only by including legal norms in the data of politics and by elucidating their meaning in research.

Hall observes that theories centering on social action would be

---

4. *Ibid.*, p. 42.
5. *Ibid.*, p. 32.

much more precise if, following the precedent set by pioneers such as Durkheim and Weber, legal scholarship were consulted.

Hall remarks that "values are of paramount importance in understanding of the rule of the law from Plato's statement to twentieth century dictatorships," and, "this has been the focal point in the quest for equality, security and justice; and all of this is incomprehensible unless the ethical significance of the rule of law is understood."[6]

LUIS RECASENS SICHES

Luis Recasens Siches, a distinguished legal scholar at the Universidad Autonoma de Mexico, has systematically expressed views which are also directed toward the integration of norms, facts and values in law. However, Recasens asserts that "those dimensions are not three juxtaposed objects, but three essential aspects interrelated in reciprocal and indissoluble ways. . . ."[7] Later he adds: "it is evident that, in order to pass judgments on a historically given law, or in order to construct juridical ideals, there are needed not only mere valuational ingredients, but they ought to be integrated with the realities with which those ideas are going to be implemented. On the materials given by historical experience, juridical axiology projects its value judgments. . . ."[8]

This position leads Recasens, like Hall and Reale, to criticize Kelsen. Recasens says: "Let's see how, to start with, the separation, of Kelsenian inspiration, between the normative region and the region of real objects, fails in its basis. The base of the system is the so-called fundamental norm or constitution in a logical-formal perspective, which in itself does not stand as a juridical precept . . . that is to say that the validity of law (*vigencia*) requires a minimum of facticity." For Recasens, however, law is not conduct but is rather norm seen from an integrative perspective. Where for Jerome Hall the legal sanction is not an essential characteristic of legal norms in relation to social norms, for Recasens, legal norms are characterized by what he calls the phe-

6. *Ibid.*, pp. 120-121.
7. Luis Recasens Siches, *Tratado General de Filosofia del Derecho*, Mexico, Porrua, 1959, pp. 160-161.
8. *Ibid.*, pp. 390-391.

nomenon of "inexorable coaction." Any showing that legal norms are obeyed in most cases without the coactivity of force would not imply, according to Recasens, a legitimate objection to his theory since he does not assert that the use of force is necessary to bring legal norms into existence. It is an essential element of the legal norms in the sense that if they are not voluntarily obeyed, the use of force becomes imperative. Apart from the moral duty to obey a legal norm, there is a legal duty to do so simply because the legal norm is a norm of inexorable imposition, of inexorable coactivity. Inexorable imposition is then an essential characteristic of law.

In this respect, Hall's views are contrary to Recasens'. Hall has said:[9]

> Sociological analysis of the norms deals with two questions and terminates, first, in locating many of the State's laws in a wider field that includes the substantively similar norms of various subgroups. If "sovereignty" is treated either as formal or as a degree of power and the State's sanctions include measures other than physical force, the laws of the State are not substantively different from those of various subgroups. The principal issue in this regard concerns the alleged "inexorable imposition" of the State's sanctions, which is sometimes expressed as the State's monopoly of "legitimate force." But it is doubtful that the sanctions-processes of all other associations (for example, the Mafia, the family, and various other legal groups) are substantively different. It may be tenable and even helpful in social research to employ a set of criteria to distinguish the State's laws substantively from those of various subgroups. Such criteria might be the rank of the laws in the hierarchy of authority, the inclusiveness of the State's interests, the relatively organized arrangement of its laws, the formality of its procedure, the idea or claim of inexorability, as contrasted with the theoretical privilege of withdrawing from other associations, and the lack or lesser degree of the other characteristics, noted above. But this would be misleading unless the above-indicated facts concerning the problematical issues were also described.

MIGUEL HERRERA FIGUEROA'S INTEGRATIVISM

Miguel Herrera Figueroa, Rector of the John F. Kennedy University at Buenos Aires, Argentina, and formerly Professor of

9. Jerome Hall, *op. cit.,* p. 91.

Jurisprudence at the University of Tucuman, Argentina, should be included without hesitation among the Latin American legal scholars devoted to the advancement of integrative perspectives of the law. In his writings the traditional boundaries of the various social sciences—psychology, sociology, political science and social psychology—are redefined in order to facilitate a systematically constructed synthesis. Legal sociology is redefined as being in fact *"ius-psycho-sociology"* and is seen as a comprehensive discipline which transcends the dichotomies so very prevalent in the social sciences between the individual and society, subjectivism and objectivism and between the cultural and the real sciences. The many books and articles written by Herrera Figueroa are of special significance for the integrative approach.

In his *Sociology of Law,* Herrera Figueroa calls for a return to axiology and for closer attention to the phenomena of social action and social structure as seen from an historical perspective. History for Herrera Figueroa is a basic and intrinsic quality of human conduct and in the social sciences, as in human conduct, there is always an historical dimension. Justice is anchored in conduct and so are the other values linked with it: order, security, power, solidarity, cooperation, fraternity, peace, prudence and concord.

Herrera Figueroa stresses the importance of freeing sociology from various regional ontologies, each comprising a specific area of human conduct, e.g. sociology of law, economic sociology, political sociology, sociology of communications and so forth. Integration of the social sciences follows from the integration of facts, norms and values in human conduct. The factual level is concerned with the organismic and characteriological aspects of personality. The axiological level corresponds to its spiritual side; and the normative level to its cognitive side, to our knowledge of man and society.

Language and communication are basic ingredients of legal sociology. Culture without history, asserts Herrera Figueroa, is devoid of meaning. Consciousness and historical facts are both dimensions of social life. Culture is nothing but the historical dimension of mankind. Our past survives in our lives. Historical truth is not a rigid and static entity but something always fluid, alive, vital and dynamic.[10]

Law, then, is history and, in the sociology of the law, history appears in all its polychromatic forms.[11]

The work of Herrera Figueroa reveals among other influences, that of phenomenology and existentialism, especially the influence of Heidegger, Husserl, Marcel, Buber, Jaspers, Zuviri, May, and Gordon Allport; these appear in a dialectical perspective that rejects any compromise with the material or with the spiritual.

A theory of values which is deeply rooted in existentialist perspectives must, according to Herrera Figueroa, be cautious about aspiring to the construction of formalized systems since existence precludes any rigidity or essentialism. "Nothing could make values exist outside freedom." And freedom *is* human existence. As the main dimensions of human life, the *Mitsein* and *Dasein* are basic in Herrera Figueroa's thinking.

Like Jerome Hall, Herrera Figueroa has written extensively on criminology. His criminology, or criminal sociology, is carefully related to its axiological bases. Herrera Figueroa calls for a criminal law with existential connotations and is strongly opposed to the logical, rational unilateralism of certain schools such as the *Escuela Penal Tecnico-Juridica*.

CONCLUDING REMARKS

It is no exaggeration to say that, in this century, Jerome Hall and the late Dean Pound have been by far the North American legal scholars most well known in Latin America. Most of Hall's books on criminal law, criminology, jurisprudence and legal sociology have been translated into Spanish and Portuguese.

In 1960, on a Ford Foundation grant, I accompanied Professor Hall on a four months' lecture tour in various Latin American countries, among them Mexico, Colombia, Peru, Bolivia, Argentina, Chile, Uruguay and Brazil. Memorable round tables on jurisprudence, criminology and legal sociology were held at dif-

10. Miguel Herrera Figueroa, *Sociologia del Derecho*, Buenos Aires, Depalma, 1970, pp. 129.

11. *Ibid.*, p. 138.

ferent Latin American universities. These were attended by the most distinguished scholars of the area in the fields of criminology, criminal law, jurisprudence and the sociology of law. Without meaning to slight many others present, I can recall the participation of Professor E. Garcia Maynez and L. Recasens Siches (Mexico); Miguel Reale, Irineu Strenger, R. Cirell Czerna, Roberto Lyra, Paulo Dourado De Gousmao and the late L. Washington Vita (Brazil), Professor Miguel Herrera Figueroa, Enrique R. Aftalion, Werner Goldsmichdt, Alfredo Povina, Ernesto E. Borga, Jose Miguens, Alfredo Ves Losada, Francisco Andres Mulet, Sebastian Soler and the late Professors Ambrosio Gioja and Miguel Figueroa Roman (Argentina); Professor Cayetano Betancur (Colombia); Professor Jorge Millas (Chile); Professor Garcia Montufar, Abdon Valdez and Luis Barandarian (Peru); Professor Juan Llambias De Acevedo (Uruguay); and Professor H. Cajias (Bolivia).

More than ten years have passed since our tour and the integrative perspective of the law continues to receive increasing and widespread adherence in Latin America. Although for purposes of this article, I have restricted my comments to only three prominent scholars of the area, there is now a growing number of promising young people who share Hall's principal concern for a unified perspective of reason and reality in the law. This is indeed a very encouraging development at a time when technological, social and cultural change are making Latin American legal systems, where not obsolete, at least resistant to demands for social progress, innovation and social justice. It is, perhaps, the best tribute that history could render to the ideas of my distinguished teacher and friend, Professor Jerome Hall.

BIBLIOGRAPHY

Cirell Czerna, Renato: A dialectica de implicacao e polaridade no criticismo ontognoseologico, *Revista Brasileira de Filosofia,* Vol. IX, 1961.

————: Notas sobre o problema de certeza no direito, *Revista Brasileira de Filosofia,* Vol. VII, 1957.

David, Pedro R.: El Integrativismo, las Ciencias Sociales, VIII Interamerican Congress of Philosophy—Brazilia, 1972.

————: Bosquejo de la jusfilosofia integrativa de Jerome Hall, *La Ley,* Buenos Aires, Argentina, 16 January 1961.

————: Perspectivas de dos filosofias del derecho integrativas Hall y Reale, *Anais do III Congreso Nacional de Filosofia,* Sao Paulo, novembro de 1959, pp. 257-263.

————: *Sociologia criminal juvenil,* Buenos Aires, Depalma, 1968.

————: *Instituciones juridicos sociales,* Buenos Aires, Omeba, 1962.

————: *Conducta, Integrativismo y Sociologia del Derecho,* Buenos Aires, De Zavalia, 1970.

Hall, Jerome: *Comparative Law and Social Theory,* Baton Rouge, Louisiana State University Press, 1963.

————: Reason and Reality in Jurisprudence, *Buffalo Law Review,* Vol. 7, p. 351, 1958, Spanish translation by Pedro David, *sub. nom. Razon y realidad en el derecho,* Depalma, Buenos Aires, 1959.

————: *Studies in Jurisprudence and Criminal Theory,* New York, Oceana, 1958.

————: *Theft, Law and Society,* Indianapolis, Bobbs-Merrill, 1957.

————: *General Principles of Criminal Law,* Indianapolis, Bobbs-Merrill, 1947.

————: *Living Law of Democratic Society,* Indianapolis, Bobbs-Merrill, 1949.

Herrera Figueroa, Miguel: Delito formal, *Enciclopedia juridica,* t. VI, Buenos Aires, Omeba, 1957.

————: Jurista, *Enciclopedia juridica,* t. XV, Buenos Aires, Omeba, 1962.

————: Miguel Reale, filosofo y jurista, *Revista da Faculdade do Direito,* Sao Paulo, ano I, 1955.

————: *Psicologia y criminologia,* Buenos Aires, Omeba, 1967, and *Sociologia del derecho,* Buenos Aires, Depalma, 1968.

————: *Justicia y Sentido,* Tucuman, Edit. Richardet, 1948.

Reale, Miguel: Estructura E Fundamento Da Ordem Juridica, VIII Interamerican Congress of Philosophy—Brazilia, 1972.

————: *Pluralismo e Libertade,* Sao Paulo, Edicoes Saraiva, 1963.

————: *O Direito Como Experiencia,* Sao Paulo, Edicoes Saraiva, 1970.

————: Aspectos de teoria tridimensional do direito, *Revista dos Tribunais Ltda.,* Sao Paulo.

————: *Filosofia do direito,* Vol. I, t. I & II, Sao Paulo, Edicoes Saraiva, 1953.

————: *Horizontes do direito e da historia,* Sao Paulo, Edicoes Saravia, 1956.

Recasens Siches, Luis: Imperativo y norma en el derecho, *Estudios de Derecho,* Vol. XX, No. 60, Facultad de Derecho y Ciencias Politicas de la Universidad de Antioquia.

————: *Sociologia,* Porrua, Mexico, 1958, c. XXXI.

————: *Tratado de filosofia del derecho,* Mexico, Porrua, 1959.

————: La Naturaleza Del Pensamiento Juridico, VIII Interamerican Congress of Philosophy—Brazilia, 1972.

Irineu Strenger: Contribucao de Miguel Reale a teoria do direito e do estado, *Revista Brasileira de Filosofia.*

————: Contribucao a-um a Teoria geral dos Modelos Juridicos, VIII Inter-american Congress of Philosophy—Brazilia, 1972.

Veiga, Glaucio: Sobre um livro de Miguel Reale, *Revista Brasileira de Filosofia,* Vol. VI, 1956.

Washington Vita, Luis: Miguel Reale, historiador de ideas, *Revista Brasileira de Filosofia,* Vol. IX, 1959.

CHAPTER 17

A BIBLIOGRAPHY OF THE WRITINGS OF JEROME HALL

BOOKS

Theft, Law and Society, Boston, Little, Brown & Co., 1935, xxxv, 360 pp.; 2d ed., Indianapolis, Bobbs-Merrill Co., 1952, xxv, 396 pp.; excerpts in D. R. Cressey and D. A. Ward (eds.), *Delinquency, Crime, and Social Process*, New York, Harper & Row, 1969, pp. 100-111; and in W. J. Chambliss (ed.), *Crime and the Legal Process*, New York, McGraw-Hill, 1969, pp. 32-51.

General Principles of Criminal Law, Indianapolis, Bobbs-Merrill Co., 1947, 618 pp.; 2d ed., 1960, x, 650 pp.; Spanish translation of Chapter 2 of 1st ed. in 54 *La Ley*, Buenos Aires, Summer 1949; German translation of Chapter 1 of 2nd ed. in 72 *Zeitschrift für die gesamte Strafrechtswissenschaft*, 385-412; excerpts in H. Morris (ed.), *Freedom and Responsibility*, Stanford University Press, 1961, pp. 214-218, 365-375, 425-436.

Cases and Readings on Criminal Law and Procedure (editor), Indianapolis, Bobbs-Merrill Co., 1949, xiv, 996 pp.; 2d ed. (with G. O. W. Mueller), 1965, iv, 1032 pp.; 3rd ed. (with G. O. W. Mueller and B. J. George), *forthcoming*.

Living Law of Democratic Society, Indianapolis, Bobbs-Merrill Co., 1949, 146 pp.; Korean translation, 1955; Portuguese translation, 1958; excerpts in T. Cowan (ed.), *The American Jurisprudence Reader*, New York, Oceana, 1956, pp. 42-52; and in B. F. Brown (ed.), *The Natural Law Reader*, New York, Oceana, 1960, pp. 214-225.

Studies in Jurisprudence and Criminal Theory, New York, Oceana Publications, 1958, 300 pp.

Comparative Law and Social Theory, Louisiana State University Press, 1963, vii, 167 pp.

Foundations of Jurisprudence, Indianapolis, Bobbs-Merrill Co., 1973, viii, 184 pp.

ESSAYS, ARTICLES AND REVIEWS
1930

Bar Examinations, *Dakota Law Review* 3:43-46, 1930.

Meeting of the Association of American Law Schools, *Dakota Law Review* 3:46-48, 1930.

Review: Derby, Cases on Criminal Law, 1930, *Dakota Law Review* 3:115-116, 1930.

Review: *Encyclopedia of the Social Sciences,* Vols. 1-2, 1930, *Illinois Law Review* 25:233-235, 1930.

Review: Frankfurter & Greene, *The Labor Injunction,* 1930, *Dakota Law Review* 3:116-118, 1930.

Review: *The Illinois Crime Survey, Dakota Law Review* 3:165-166, 1930.

1931

Social Science as an Aid to Administration of the Criminal Law, *Dakota Law Review* 3:285-298, 1931.

Review: Pound, *Criminal Justice in America,* 1930, *Dakota Law Review* 3:229-230, 1931.

1932

Has the State a Right to Trial by Jury in Criminal Cases? *American Bar Association Journal* 18:226-228, 1932.

Analysis of Criticism of the Grand Jury, *Journal of Criminal Law & Criminology* 22:692-704, 1932.

Law as a Social Discipline, *Temple Law Quarterly* 7:63-83, 1932; *Bar Briefs* 9 (1):92-106, Dec. 1932.

Review: Alexander and Staub, *The Criminal, the Judge and the Public,* 1931, *Illinois Law Review* 26:942-945, 1932.

Review: Borchard, *Convicting the Innocent,* 1932, *Dakota Law Review* 4:181-182, 1932.

Review: Burtt, *Legal Psychology,* 1931, *Illinois Law Review* 27: 463-465, 1932.

Review: Howard, *Criminal Justice in England,* 1931, *Dakota Law Review* 4:95-97, 1932.

1934

Federal Anti-Theft Legislation, *Law & Contemporary Problems* 1:424-434, 1934.

1935

Review: Harrison, *Police Administration in Boston,* 1934, *Columbia Law Review* 35:1328-1330, 1935.

1936

Legal and Social Aspects of Arrest Without a Warrant, *Harvard Law Review* 49:566-592, 1936.

Edward Livingston and His Louisiana Penal Code, *American Bar Association Journal* 22:191-196, 1936.

The Law of Arrest in Relation to Contemporary Social Problems, *University of Chicago Law Review* 3:345-375, 1936.

Criminology and a Modern Penal Code, *Journal of Criminal Law & Criminology* 27:1-16, 1936.

Review: Smith, *Prisons and a Changing Civilization,* 1934, *Georgia Law Journal* 24:1099, 1936.

Review: Underhill, *Criminal Evidence,* 1935, *Journal of Criminal Law & Criminology* 26:954-956, 1936.

1937

Nulla poena sine lege, *Yale Law Journal* 47:165-193, 1937.

Review: Vollmer, *Police and Modern Society,* 1936, *Brooklyn Law Review* 6:400-401, 1937.

1938

Committee on Survey of Crime, Criminal Law and Criminal Procedure, *Journal of Criminal Law & Criminology* 29:562-579, 1938.

1939

The Work of the Louisiana Supreme Court for the 1937-1938 Term: Criminal Law and Procedure, *Louisiana Law Review* 1: 371-386, 1939.

Recent Penal Legislation, *Louisiana Law Review* 1:541-549, 1939.

Review: Brown, *Lawyers and the Promotion of Justice,* 1938, *Louisiana Law Review* 1:862-866, 1939.

Review: Pound, *Formative Era of American Law,* 1938, *Harvard Law Review* 52:1191-1194, 1939.

1940

On Research in Law—A Challenge and a Proposal, *Louisiana Law Review* 2:479-480, 1940.

Criminal Attempt—A Study of Foundations of Criminal Liability, *Yale Law Journal* 49:789-840, 1940.

Review: Rusche and Kirchheimer, *Punishment and Social Structure,* 1939, *Journal of Criminal Law & Criminology* 30:971-973, 1940.

Review: Scott, *Law, The State and The International Community,* 1939, *Washington University Law Quarterly* 26:147-148, 1940.

1941

Crime as Social Reality, *The Annals of the American Academy of Political and Social Science* 217:1-11, September 1941; *Studies in Jurisprudence and Criminal Theory,* pp. 200-214.

Drunkenness as a Criminal Offense, *Journal of Criminal Law & Criminology* 32:297-309, 1941.

Prolegomena to a Science of Criminal Law, *University of Pennsylvania Law Review* 89:549-580, 1941.

Review: Hatcher, *Edward Livingston,* 1940, *Louisiana Law Review* 3:656-658, 1941.

Review: Fuller, *The Law in Quest of Itself,* 1940, *North Carona Law Review* 19:264-268, 1941.

Review: Rodell, *Woe Unto You, Lawyers!,* 1939, *Ethics* 51:359-360, 1941.

Review: Radin, *Law as Logic and Experience,* 1940, *Iowa Law Review* 26:915-918, 1941.

Review: Jackson, *The Machinery of Justice in England,* 1940, *Journal of Criminal Law and Criminology* 32:104, 1941.

Review: Radzinowicz and Turner, *Penal Reform in England,* 1940, *Journal of Criminal Law & Criminology* 32:105-106, 1941.

1942

The Youth Correction Authority Act: Progress or Menace?, *American Bar Association Journal* 28:317-321, 1942.

New Federal Criminal Rules: Objectives of Federal Criminal Procedural Revision, *Yale Law Journal* 51:719-782, 1942; in part in *Studies in Jurisprudence and Criminal Theory,* pp. 215-234; in part in A. Goldstein and J. Goldstein (eds.), *Crime, Law and Society,* New York, Free Press, 1971, pp. 231-237.

Proposal for Co-operative Research on the Bill of Rights, *Bill of Rights Review* 2:280-283, 1942.

A 2-2-2 Plan for College-Law Education, *Harvard Law Review* 56:245-269, 1942.

Review: Cairns, *The Theory of Legal Science,* 1941, *Virginia Law Review* 28:851-852, 1942.

Review: Boorstin, *The Mysterious Science of the Law,* 1941, *Lawyers Guild Review* 2 (4):44, 1942.

Review: Timashef, *An Introduction to the Sociology of Law,* 1942, *American Journal of Sociology* 47:765-767, 1942.

Review: Pound, McIlwain and Nichols, *Federalism as a Democratic Process,* 1942, *Journal of Criminal Law and Criminology* 33:170-171, 1942.

1943

Interrelations of Criminal Law and Torts, *Columbia Law Review* 43:753-779, 967-1001, 1943.

Materials on Criminal Law, Procedure and Administration of Germany and the Balkan States, 223 pp., mimeographed 1943.

Review: *Report to the Judicial Conference of the Committee on Punishment for Crime*, 1942, *Indiana Law Journal* 18:161-162, 1943.

Review: Maestro, *Voltaire and Beccaria as Reformers of the Criminal Law*, 1942, *Journal of Criminal Law and Criminology* 34:35, 1943.

Review: Pound, *Outlines of Lectures in Jurisprudence*, 1943, *Journal of Crminal Law and Criminology* 34:115-116, 1943.

1944

Review: Padover (ed.), *The Complete Jefferson*, 1943, *University of Pennsylvania Law Review* 92:339-342, 1944.

1945

Criminology in G. Gurnitch and W. E. Moore (eds.), *Twentieth Century Sociology*, New York, The Philosophical Library, 1945, pp. 342-365.

Intoxication and Criminal Responsibility, *Columbia Law Review* 45:677-718, 1945.

Toward a Liberal Legal Education, *Iowa Law Review* 30:394-407, 1945.

Review: Radzinowicz and Turner (eds.), *The Modern Approach to Criminal Law*, 1945, *Journal of Criminal Law & Criminology* 36:263-265, 1945.

1946

Indiana Law and Legislation, 1940-1945: Criminal Law and Procedure, *Indiana Law Journal* 21:391-405, 1946.

Review: Vanderbilt, *Studying Law*, 1945, *The Annals of the American Academy of Political and Social Science* 245:212-213, 1946.

1947

Integrative Jurisprudence, in P. L. Sayre (ed.), *Interpretations of Modern Legal Philosophies—Essays in Honor of Roscoe Pound*, New York, Oxford University Press, 1947, pp. 313-332; in *Studies in Jurisprudence and Criminal Theory*, pp. 25-47; translated into Spanish as Teoria Juridica Integralista, in *El Actual Pensamiento Juridico Norteamericano*, Buenos Aires, Editorial Losada, 1951, pp. 51-89.

1948

General Introduction to the seven volumes of *20th Century Legal Philosophy Series*, Cambridge, Mass., Harvard University Press, 1948, pp. vii-xii.

Report of the State Penal and Correctional Survey Commission, *Indiana Law Journal* 24:1-24, 1948.

1949

Concerning the Nature of Positive Law, *Yale Law Journal* 58: 545-566, 1949.

The Place and Uses of Jurisprudence: Introductory Remarks, *Journal of Legal Education* 1:475-481, 1949.

Pedagogical Discovery Via the Seminar, *Journal of Legal Education* 2:209-212, 1949.

Review: Dession, *Criminal Law Administration and Public Order*, 1948, *Yale Law Journal* 58:341-344, 1949.

Review: Radzinowicz, *A History of English Criminal Law*, 1948, *Texas Law Review* 27:735-736, 1949.

Review: Cairns, *Legal Philosophy From Plato to Hegel*, 1949, *The Annals* 264:152-153, 1949.

Review: Ross, *Towards a Realistic Jurisprudence*, 1946, *Harvard Law Review* 63:181-185, 1949.

1950

Law and Religion—A Commencement Address, *Christian Leader,* Boston, 132:343-348, 1950.

Review: Cohen, *Reason and Law,* 1949, *The Annals of the American Academy of Political and Social Science* 270:182, July, 1950.

Review: *Social Meaning of Legal Concepts—Criminal Guilt,* 1950, *Indiana Law Journal* 26:150-152, 1950.

1951

The Proposal to Prepare a Model Penal Code, *Journal of Legal Education* 4:91-94, 1951.

The Challenge of Jurisprudence: To Build a Science and Philosophy of Law, *American Bar Association Journal* 37:23-26, 85-87, 1951.

Administration of Criminal Justice in Connecticut—Proposals for a Long-Range Program, *Connecticut Bar Journal* 25:294-298, 1951.

An Open Letter Proposing a School of Cultural Legal Studies, *Journal of Legal Education* 4:181-184, 1951; *American Political Science Review* 45:1157-1159, 1951.

Review: Stone, *The Province and Function of Law: Law as Logic, Justice, and Social Control,* 1946, *Annals of the American Academy of Political and Social Science* 278:205-206, 1951.

1952

Science and Reform in Criminal Law, *University of Pennsylvania Law Review* 100:787-804, 1952; in *Studies in Jurisprudence and Criminal Theory,* pp. 235-252.

What Should Be the Relation of Morals to Law?, *Journal of Public Law* 1:259-322, 1952.

Codification of the Criminal Law, *American Bar Association Journal* 38:952-954, 1952.

Review: Durkheim, *Suicide—A Study in Sociology*, 1951, *Northwestern University Law Review* 47:553-554, 1952.

1953

Science and Reform in Criminal Law in P. Wiener (ed.), *Readings in Philosophy of Science*, New York, Scribner, 1953, pp. 297-310.

Police and Law in a Democratic Society, *Indiana Law Journal* 28: 133-177, 1953.

Some Basic Questions Regarding Legal Classification for Professional and Scientific Purposes, *Journal of Legal Education* 5:329-343, 1953; in *Studies in Jurisprudence and Criminal Theory*, pp. 143-157.

Psychiatry and the Law (with Karl Menninger). *Iowa Law Review* 38:687-704, 1953.

1954

Unification of Political and Legal Theory, *Political Science Quarterly* 69:15-28, 1954; in *Studies in Jurisprudence and Criminal Theory*, pp. 83-94.

Revision of Criminal Law—Objectives and Methods, *Nebraska Law Review* 33:383-426, 1954; in *Studies in Jurisprudence and Criminal Theory*, pp. 253-266.

1955

Ignorantia Legis, *Revue Internationale de Droit Pénal* 26:293-308, 1955.

The Scholarship of Professor George Dession, *Buffalo Law Review* 5:7-8, 1955.

Teaching Law by Case Method and Lecture, *Journal of the Society of Public Teachers of Law* 3:99-106, 1955.

Criminal Responsibility of Governments and Their Organs in International Law, *Law and Economics* 1:157-181, Tel Aviv, 1955.

1956

El progreso de la Teoria Juridica Nortamericana durante los ultimos cincuenta anos, *Revista del Colegio de Abogados del Distrito Federal* (Caracas) 20:157-173, 1956.

Psychiatry and Criminal Responsibility, *Yale Law Journal* 65: 761, 1956; in *Studies in Jurisprudence and Criminal Theory*, pp. 267-295.

Responsibility and Law: In Defense of the M'Naghten Rules, *American Bar Association Journal* 42:917-919, 984-989, 1956.

Plato's Legal Philosophy, *Indiana Law Journal* 31:171-206, 1956; in *Studies in Jurisprudence and Criminal Theory*, pp. 48-82.

Law and the Intellectuals, *Journal of Legal Education* 9:8-17, 1956.

American Tendencies in Legal Philosophy and the Definition of "Law," *Comparative Law Review of Japan* 3:1-15, Tokyo, 1956; in *Studies in Jurisprudence and Criminal Theory*, pp. 119-130.

1957

The Progress of American Jurisprudence (1906-56), in A. L. Harding (ed.), *The Administration of Justice in Retrospect,* Southern Methodist University Press, 1957, pp. 24-41; in *Studies in Jurisprudence and Criminal Theory*, pp. 131-142; excerpts in B. F. Brown (ed.), *The Natural Law Reader,* New York, Oceana, 1960, pp. 213-214.

International Criminal Law From the Perspective of American Law and the Science of Criminal Law, in Laun and Constantopoulos (eds.), *Aktuelle Probleme des Internationalen Rechts,* Berlin, Walter De Gruyter, 1957, pp. 82-91.

Professional Responsibility—International Aspects, *Seton Hall University Centennial Law Day: Addresses on Professional Responsibility,* Seton Hall University School of Law, May 5, 1956 (1957), pp. 95-101.

The Three Fundamental Aspects of Criminal Law, *Journal of Criminal Law* 8:1-8, Criminal Law Society of Japan, 1957; reprinted in G. O. W. Mueller (ed.), *Essays in Criminal Science,* London, Sweet & Maxwell, 1961, pp. 159-169.

Ignorance and Mistake in Criminal Law, *Indiana Law Journal* 33:1-44, 1957.

1958

Authority and the Law, in *Nomos I,* C. Friedrich (ed.), Harvard University Press, 1958, pp. 58-66; in *Studies in Jurisprudence and Criminal Theory,* pp. 95-102.

Mental Disease and Criminal Responsibility—M'Naughten versus Durham and the American Law Institute's Tentative Draft, *Indiana Law Journal* 33:212-225, 1958.

Reason and Reality in Jurisprudence, *Buffalo Law Review* 7:351-403, 1958; translated into Spanish as *Razon y Realidad en el Derecho,* Buenos Aires, Depalma, 1959.

The Present Position of Jurisprudence in the United States, *Virginia Law Review* 44:321-330, 1958.

Law Teacher's Tour Around the World, *North Dakota Law Review* 34:297-307, 1958.

Review: Radzinowicz, *A History of English Criminal Law and Its Administration From 1750,* Vols. 2-3, 1957, *Michigan Law Review* 56:480-482, 1958.

Review: Friedrich, *The Philosophy of Law in Historical Perspective,* 1958, *California Law Review* 46:858-859, 1958.

Review: Fellman, *The Defendant's Rights,* 1958, *American Political Science Review* 52:861-862, 1958.

1960

Jhering, Rudolf von, in *Encyclopaedia Britannica* 13:66, 1960.

Savigny, Friedrich Karl von, in *Encyclopaedia Britannica* 20:16, 1960.

1961

La position presente de la philosophie du Droit aux Etats-Unis, *Melanges en l'honneur de Paul Roubier,* Vol. 1, 1961, pp. 261-271.

Legal Sanctions, *Natural Law Forum* 6:119-126, 1961; in H. Lasswell and H. Cleveland (eds.), *The Ethic of Power,* New York, Harper, 1962, pp. 209-220.

A Latin American Lecture-Conference Tour, *Journal of Legal Education* 13:424-429, 1961.

Filosofia Juridica Integrativa, *Instituto de Filosofia del Derecho y Sociologia* II:25-40, La Plata, 1961.

1962

The Perspective of Integrative Jurisprudence in M. J. Sethma (ed.), *Contributions to Synthetic Jurisprudence,* Dobbs Ferry, N.Y., Oceana; Bombay, N. M. Tripathi, 1962, pp. 30-50.

Scientific and Humane Study of Criminal Law, *Boston University Law Review* 42:267-281, 1962.

The Psychiatrist and Crime: A Threat to Society, *National Observer,* August 20, 1962, p. 8.

1963

M'Naughten Rules and Proposed Alternatives, *American Bar Association Journal* 49:960-964, 1963; reprinted in R. D. Knuten (ed.), *Crime, Criminology and Contemporary Society,* Homewood, Ill., Dorsey Press, 1970, pp. 257-264.

Negligent Behavior Should Be Excluded from Penal Liability, *Columbia Law Review* 63:632-644, 1963.

Vers une philosophie integrative du droit, in *Melanges en l'honneur de Jean Dabin,* Vol. 1, Brussels, Émile Bruylant, 1963, pp. 101-125.

1964

Elements of Natural Law Philosophy, in S. Hook (ed.), *Law and Philosophy,* New York University Press, 1964, pp. 210-218.

From Legal Theory to Integrative Jurisprudence, *Cincinnati Law Review* 33:153-206, 1964.

Science, Common Sense, and Criminal Law Reform, *Iowa Law Review* 49:1044-1066, 1964.

1966

Comparative Law and Jurisprudence, *Buffalo Law Review* 16:61-66, 1966.

Philosophy and Legal Vocationalism: Theoretical Considerations and Practical Proposals, *Journal of Legal Education* 19:193-198, 1966.

Psychiatric Criminology: Is It a Valid Marriage? The Legal View, *Buffalo Law Review* 16:349-359, 1966.

Analytic Philosophy and Jurisprudence, *Ethics* 77:14-28, 1966.

1968

Psychiatric Criminology—The Legal View, in S. Halleck and Bromberg (eds.), *Psychiatric Aspects of Criminology,* Springfield, Charles Thomas, 1968, pp. 23-40.

Theft, Law and Society—1968, *American Bar Association Journal* 54:960-967, 1968.

The Relationship Between the Ontological and the Normative Elements Under Axiological Aspects, *Archiv fur Rechts—und Sozialphilosophie* N.R. 6:125-143, 1968.

Science and Morality of Criminal Law, *Arizona Law Review* 9:360-371, 1968.

1970

Methods of Sociological Research in Comparative Law, in J. Hazard and W. J. Wagner (eds.), *Legal Thought in the United States of America under Contemporary Pressures,* Brussels: Émile Bruylant, 1970, pp. 149-169.

Filosofia Analitica y Jurisprudencia, *Instituto de del Derecho y Sociologia* 1-23, La Plata, 1970.

1971

Justice in the 20th Century, *California Law Review* 59:752-768, 1971.

1972

The Purposes of a System for the Administration of Justice, in S. E. Grupp (ed.), *Theories of Punishment,* Bloomington, Indiana University Press, 1972.

1973

Perennial Problems of Criminal Law, *Hofstra Law Review* 1:15-31, 1973.

INDEX

Prepared by Edward J. Bander
New York University Law Library

A

Abraham, H. J., 14 n6
Adams, John, diary of, 221 n4 et seq.
Allington, T. B., 185 n143
American Psychiatric Association, sociopathic personality, term adopted by, 166
Amory, Thomas C., 243 n90
Ancel, Marc, 3-10
Andenaes, Johannes, 159 ns23, 24, 177 n113
Annesley, P. T., 165 n49, 166 ns59, 62
Anonymous v. Weiner, 209 n47
Application of President and Directors of Georgetown College, 205 n36
Arendt, H., n34
Arens, R., 163 n41
Argentina
  Constitution Article 18, 248
  constitutional guarantees as to penal proceedings, 248-252
  disciplinary proceedings in the public service, 248-252
  rules to govern, 251-252
  disciplinary sanction
  hearing, necessity of, 250
  review of, 251
Arieff, A. J., 164 n45
Auchmuty, Robert, 219
Auden, W. H., 182 n134

B

Ball, J. C., 178 n118
Barry, John, 285 n11
Bartholomew, G. W., 201 n47
Bassiouni, M. C., 193 n10
Beale, Joseph, 140 n43, 194 n13
Beaver, J. E., 163 n42
Beccaria, Cesare, 5, 90
  bibliographical information on, 25 n1
  crime, high rate of, 32

differs from youth, 29
equality before law, 30
intent, on, 33
judges, on, 28, 29
Marcuse, and, 25 et seq.
parasitism, on, 33, 34
reforms suggested by, 28
sentencing, on, 32
youth, and modern, 25-34
Bedau, H. A., 177 n117
Bediav, N., 129 n17
Belaev, N., 124 n2
Bemmelen (see Van Bemmelen)
Bennett, James V., 185 n142
Bentham, J., 5
Berger, P. L., 47 n36
Bernard, Francis, 215
Berner, A. F., 138 n34, 141 n47, 149 n78
Bishop v. Brig Freemason, 219 n26
Bishop, J., 125 n8, 284
Blackstone, W., 125 n8, 135 n30, 144 n63, 151 n80, 284
Bodenheimer, Edgar, 154 n3
Bolam v. Friern Hospital Mgt. Com., 194 n14
Bouzat, P., 124 n3, 130 n19, 132 n24
Bravery v. Bravery, 207 n44
Brennan, Ellen E., 214 n12
Bromberg, W., 175 n106
Brown v. U.S 141 n47
Brown, Richard M., 216 n19
Burdick, W. L., 284
Byrd, Sharon, 123

C

Calhoon, Robert M., 214 n11
Cannibalism, 131
Capital punishment, Code revision and, 85
Cardozo, B., 16, 22
Carrara, F., 5, 7

317